:
The source and summit
of leadership

The Source and Summit of Leadership

Fr Nathaniel Haslam, LC

In order to help people to reach their full, God-given potential, today's world needs leaders with a holistic understanding of the human person – one composed of body, mind and spirit with a need for meaning, healthy relationships and a transcendent purpose. Fr. Nathaniel Haslam makes a valuable contribution to this topic by providing clarity to the question of how to respect and nurture the dignity of the person, the necessary foundation for professional growth and truly successful leadership.
Fr. Charles Sikorsky, LC, JD, JCL, President, Divine Mercy University

The Source and Summit of Leadership delivers a comprehensive overview of Leadership styles, then elevates the reader with godly wisdom which allow us to fulfill our highest calling as a leader!
Bob Dill, President and CEO, Hisco

Fr Nathaniel does wonderful job of combining secular leadership theory with biblical principals. His book goes beyond empirical leadership science and seamlessly incorporates critical insights into the transcendental calling God has on our roles as leaders, and provides much wisdom about our true purpose and how to assert our leadership influence on what matters most....So regardless if you are a stay at home parent, a young professional or a seasoned leader, this book will help you grow as a successful leader pleasing to God.
Peter Freissle, Founder of His Way at Work and CEO of Polydeck Screen Corp.

The Source and Summit of Leadership is a vast journey through history, cultures, religious and secular wisdom. He speaks to the whole person, body and soul, not stopping short at merely proposing reflections but calling to action with a distinctly practical approach and challenging applications. The precious and expansive citations make you come away from this book as if you had read multiple volumes on leadership and virtue. I believe you will be enriched and challenged by this publication, as was I, to take to heart with renewed determination the investment of your unique leadership talents in service of others."
Fr Thomas Montanaro, LC Director of Global Leadership Development

This is a perfect book for anyone wanting to be a better leader themselves or to form other leaders. Christian based leadership is sorely needed in the world today and Fr. Nathaniel delivers a timely book. He provides a great Christian Leadership Model that is a framework for leadership. Highly recommended.
Jeff Garrett, Founder & Executive Coach, Ascent Performance Group

The most extraordinary leaders are the ones who have the courage to stand up and do the right thing in the face of overwhelming outside pressure and sometimes at great personal cost. Leadership is a practice that takes a lifetime to hone. *The Source and Summit of Leadership* contains principles to guide us through our practice.
Nina Vaca, Chairman and CEO, The Pinnacle Group

The Source and Summit of Leadership

Father Nathaniel Haslam, L.C.

First edition 2022
Copyright © 2022 Nathaniel Haslam, L.C.

All rights reserved. No part of this book may be reproduced, stored in a retrieval system, or transmitted in any form or by any means, electronic, mechanical, photocopying, recording, or otherwise, without the prior written permission of the author.

ISBN: 9798429200750

Graphic design by Alejandra Felix
Editor: Arantxa Hernández
T. Cover photography by Sachin C Nair / Pexels.

TABLE OF CONTENTS

FORWARD

INTRODUCTION

ACKNOWLEDGMENTS

PART I – The State of Leadership

    Chapter 1 - The Leadership Landscape   23
    Chapter 2 - The Dilemma of How to Lead   41

PART II – Valuable Insights on Leadership

    Chapter 3 - Insights from Great Leaders   53
    Chapter 4 - Different Worldviews   71
    Chapter 5 - A Judeo-Christian Understanding of Leadership   79

Part III – Towards a More Robust Leadership Model

    Chapter 6 - The Source and Summit of Leadership   97
    Chapter 7 - A Christian Leadership Model   109

PART IV – Leadership in Practice

    Chapter 8 - Holistic Virtue Development   131
    Chapter 9 - 4 Leadership Decision-making Principles   161
    Chapter 10 – Leadership in Different Sectors of Society   173

Chapter 11 – Your Call to Leadership   213

Appendix 1 – Christian Leadership Model   219

Appendix 2 - Recommended Leadership References   220

Appendix 3 – Leadership Growth Plan   223

FORWARD

Fr Nathaniel's book, *The Source and Summit of Leadership*, takes a comprehensive view of the factors impacting inspired leadership in a diverse yet complex and interrelated way. From macroeconomic and political systems, culture and the impact of social mores, the media, educational influences and the cacophony of voices of moral relativism expanded by the Information Age, he extensively details the impact of each on the concept of leadership. He spends significant time defining each diverse force, yet brings resolution to their dissonance. Fr Nathaniel's book offers a seamless and concise set of qualities that engender focused formation and guideposts for leadership inspired by Christian virtues, imbued with humility, self-awareness and a compelling and authentic will to succeed. It is a scholarly work that will inspire future leaders and role models with Godly principles to become "Good Shepherds" for their flock, no matter the societal venue or profession.

Dan D'Aniello
Co-Founder, The Carlyle Group

INTRODUCTION

Go to the heights! *The Alpinist*, a 2021 documentary, shows Canadian climber Marc-André Leclerc, making one of his death-defying climbs. Ice axes in hand, He climbs everything from sheer rock faces to vertical ice waterfalls. Marc was known for his daring free solo ascents of numerous mountains such as Torre Egger in Patagonia and the Emperor Face of Mount Robson. Though his risky summit attempts eventually led to his death at age 26, you cannot help but be awed by his drive to go to the heights. At his memorial service, his mother mentioned that 'some people think about doing bold things but never try. Marc-Andre went for it and did not hold back'.

This book is about going to the heights. It is about going all the way. It is seeking to climb to the source and summit of leadership. If you are reading this, you are curious—tantalized by the prospect of climbing the heights of leadership.

What is your purpose? What is the meaning of your life? What do you seek? What do you want? What is true happiness? How do we find it? What will be your legacy and contribution to society? These questions resonate in our hearts today as they did centuries and millennia ago with our predecessors. We each struggle to find clear answers to them; sometimes we run away from them since answering them implies facing hard personal realities, decisions and lifestyle changes.

Think of Tom in the United States. He is 21 and is graduating from a good college. He looks forward to his first job, finding the right one to marry and improving the world. At the same time, he worries if he will be accepted among peers at work. Tom is an ethical person who wants to positively influence those with whom he works, but he realizes moral convictions are not always appreciated. How would you lead in his situation? What behaviors and traits are most important for his leadership as he transitions to the corporate world?

Think of Annabel in Venezuela. Now 25, she seeks a life of meaning, purpose and impact on the history of the world. She has dreams and aspirations: to have a fulfilling job, a life-long relationship, raise a family and make an impact on the lives of others. At the same time, she faces the economic and societal challenges posed by a totalitarian regime which controls society with a tight fist. What do you do? Blame others for your situation? Make excuses why you cannot move forward and make a difference in life? How do you become a leader? In fact, what is leadership?

Think of Bruce who runs a Fortune 500 company. He is nationally recognized CEO who is also convinced of his Christian faith. He sees how large corporations often acquiesce to special interest groups which want to turn business into a platform for their ideologies. Bruce does not subscribe to this behavior. As a consequence, CEOs of other large companies pressure him to succumb, but he does not budge. What would you do in his shoes? Would you stand strong to the pressure to go against your ideals? Would you change your stance because you do not like being called names? Do you compromise your ideals the moment someone challenges your position?

Any path forward is hard. Whether you are in South America or another continent, you can easily see your life as conditioned and steered by forces outside your control. In a sense, you might think you are a victim of your upbringing or cultural surroundings. While recognizing the tendency to think this way, the reality is you are free to choose to lead yourself and then lead others. No matter your circumstances, You can be a leader. If you do not believe me, listen to Major Dick Winters who famously led Easy Company's 506th Parachute Infantry Division during World War II and was the main character featured in the HBO miniseries '*Band of Brothers*' (named after the book with the same title). "You came from the cities, backgrounds, and places that I came from. You had some of the same problems and situations…I will never be able to speak like Churchill or have the ambition of Patton, but I can have the quiet determination of Easy Company. I can be a leader; I can be loyal; I can be a good comrade… Surely I can do the same in my normal life."[1]

Where are the leaders? This question has echoed through centuries. Each age has its light and dark, its triumphs and challenges, its heroes and its villains. The 21st-century has been one of chaos and uncertainty. The destruction of the Twin Towers in 9/11, terrorist attacks in other countries, widespread unrest including racial tensions as well as the recent Coronavirus pandemic which brought the world to a standstill. The world has never been more united thanks to social media and the Internet, but it is so distant in many ways such as the divide between rich and poor as well as the availability of higher education and medical care. We see an exaltation of the global free market economy and democracy, yet also a desire and effort towards more totalitarian forms of politics that use violence to impose a minority's vision and desires. People look for leaders with strong convictions as a militant relativism quickly proclaims with authoritarian bombast that there is no truth.

Leadership is a hot topic. Being a leader is desirable. "A simple Google search of "leadership books" returns more than 84 million hits."[2] This is not a fringe subject, but rather something men and women seek to live. It is a perennial topic since leadership is part of human nature. We all influence and are influenced. Influence is the basic subject matter of leadership, yet "there are many ways to finish the sentence "Leadership is . . ." In fact, as author Ralph Stogdill pointed out in a review of leadership research, there are almost as many different definitions of leadership as there are people who have tried to define it. It is much like the words democracy,

---

[1] Winters, Dick, Beyond Band of Brothers, The Berkeley Publishing Group, New York, NY, 2006, viii.

[2] *Handbook for Teaching Leadership*, xi

love, and peace. Although each of us intuitively knows what we mean by such words, the words can have different meanings for different people.[3]

We often associate leadership with being great; with being a hero. When you look at the book, comic and movie franchises of the past 100 years, you see great leaders, heroes and heroines who help others. Superman. Batman. Captain America. The Avengers. Justice League. Bilbo and Frodo in *The Hobbit* and *The Lord of the Rings*. Wonder Woman. Harry Potter. The 'little guy' is chosen and called to do something special for humanity; he or she plays a role of leadership and is an instrument of salvation for others. When it comes to leaders "people are going to ask themselves two questions: first, does he know what he is doing? And second, can I trust him?...even if they answer the first question with a no, they'll forgive you if they answer the second question with a yes."[4] Trust is something we should give to those who consistently seek our best interests.

Where are the leaders? We fantasize and idealize leaders on the big screen, in comics and television, yet question where they are in life. We talk about leadership all the time. Listen to conversations on the street, at coffee shops, restaurants. Whether discussing international or local events, we regularly hear the themes of 'leadership' and 'leaders' What does this mean? "The future is taking shape now in our own beliefs and in the courage of our leaders. Ideas and leadership — not natural or social "forces" — are the prime movers in human affairs."[5] Men and women of all ages recognize the importance of leadership, but it means something different to each one based on age, experience and culture. For some, leadership is a series of traits. For others, it is to be in a recognized position of influence. For still others, it means the ability to help a group accomplish a shared goal. There is clearly a need to address the issue of leadership. Leaders in the different sectors of society should be beacons of light, hope and clarity but are often confused and easily swayed by the opinions of the masses and ideological fringes. Young leaders are often not mentored to have an transcendent vision of leadership. Leadership is reduced and corrupted to be the art of maneuvering and manipulating (people and circumstances) to get what one wants in life.

Where are the leaders? Books alone do not seem to do the job. Most leadership books and articles on the market make it readily apparent that it is easy to talk about leadership, but it is far different to actually become and live authenticity as a leader. Leadership is most often addressed in business schools and the business environment. Several other sectors of society (such as politics, education, the military and sports) have highlighted the importance of leadership and contributed to the literature and conversation over the past century. Is there is something missing? Are more books the solution? Should we give up hope on finding authentic

---

[3] Northouse, *Leadership*, Kindle version, 233

[4] Leman and Pentak, *The Way of the Shepherd*, 49

[5] George Roche III, *A World Without Heroes : The Modern Tragedy* (1987), p. 346

leaders? Is it a hopeless endeavor? To bring clarity, it helps to remember that leadership involves influence, leader traits (such as honestly, integrity and confidence) and transformation of the person.

Readers may find it humorous that I highlight that leadership books alone do not make you a leader and now I'm proposing you read mine. I will be the first one to acknowledge that this or any other book, by itself, will not make you a leader . It will require effort, mentorship, habit development, as well as dipping your toes into knowledge found in books and testimonies such as this one. The journey to become a leader is arduous, yet an exciting quest worth undertaking. The amazing thing about leadership is that anyone can develop influence and deploy it to help or hurt others. It's a great responsibility. As you may have heard from Peter Parker's dad in Spiderman: "with great power comes great responsibility."

This book is the fruit of over 20 years of training and experience. As a priest in the Congregation of the Legionaries of Christ, I have been blessed to partake in leadership development programs, books, mentorship from dozens of business, academic and non-profit leaders, and hundreds of one-on-on coaching . Additionally, my ministry has been focused on serving business and cultural leaders since my ordination 10 years ago. During this time, I have had the privilege to serve hundreds of influential men and women; I've helped each live their leadership with integrity and humility at the service of others.

This book is not meant to be an exhaustive treatise or handbook on leadership, but rather a synthesis of what you will find on the theme from perennial leadership wisdom as well as courses in education institutions and leadership training programs. My goal is to help you better understand the beauty, majesty and incredible mission of leadership. Whether you are a stay at home parent, young professional or experienced leader, leadership is something for you.

Does this book present secular (ie not referencing religion) concepts of leadership? Yes. Does this book also share insights and experiences about God and his vision of leadership? Yes. When you survey the lists of best selling leadership books, they fall into two camps: the purely Secular or the purely God-based.

The Secular include: *'The Seven Habits of Highly Effective People'*(Stephen Covey), *'Good to Great'* (Jim Collins), *'The Five Dysfunctions of a Team'* (Pat Lencioni), *'Extreme Ownership'* (Jocko Willink), *'The Effective Executive'* (Peter Drucker), *'Start with Why'* (Simon Sinek), *'The Leadership Challenge'* (Posner and Kouzes) and *'Dare to Lead'* (Brene Brown). In academic circles, a must read is *'Leadership: Theory and Practice'* (Northouse). Bestsellers such as these contain perennial human wisdom. You will be hard-pressed, however, to find references to God in these books. These and other such books ground their values, principles and moral axioms in 'agreed values' ,'human patrimony' ,'time-tested principles' and the often generically referenced 'Golden Rule'. They do not provide the ultimate foundations.

The Source and Summit of Leadership

God-based leadership bestsellers include: *'The 21 Irrefutable Laws of Leadership'* (John Maxwell), *'The Wounded Healer'* (Henri Nouwen) and *'The Mentor Leader'* (Tony Dungy). These books highlight God's presence in our lives and how it should inspire and guide our desire to lead. They do not go into great detail on many of the principles outlined in the secular leadership books mentioned above.

What you do not see in the mainstream leadership literature are books that effectively bridge the secular and the transcendent. Do we need the principles so often highlighted in secular leadership books? Absolutely. These are treasures of wisdom (often bolstered by research and studies in the humanistic sciences) which help us live in a civil society where men and women work together. Do we need God in our society and leadership? Absolutely. The human person is religious (transcendent and spiritual) by nature. We need to know the 'why' of life and the purpose of our leadership. This is beyond empirical science which only deals with material processes but cannot give us insights into our transcendent nature and purpose. In this book, I hope to unify the best of secular, human wisdom, and the insights from the Judeo-Christian tradition.

Why specifically the Judeo-Christian tradition? While other religious traditions can give us insights on leadership, Judaism and Christianity are in a unique position to contribute to the leadership conversation. They have been experts on the nature of mankind (our origin, meaning, purpose and finality) and human relations for thousands of years. These traditions place a special emphasis on harmonizing the human and divine. As I mentioned in my previous book, *'The Future of Leadership'*, the claim of Christianity is bold and audacious. It is either true and deserving of public celebration and promotion or blatantly false and worthy of condemnation. The Church proclaims Jesus Christ as the "source and summit" of human life. Jesus includes leadership. He stands at the center of history as the unique and pivotal revelation of true leadership. Can you be a good and effective leader without studying and following Jesus Christ? Yes, but you certainly cannot live or reach your full leadership potential without Jesus Christ. He, alone, makes this possible.

I encourage you to read this book not as an academic exercise but as a reflection on your own life. I wrote this book thinking of you, your mission and your purpose for being in this world. You are unique. You are loved. You matter more than you can imagine. As the former CEO of General Technologies once said, "most people spend years struggling to find their calling in life. I was one of them. I spent years doing other things that I was pretty good at, but I always felt something was missing."[6] There are many lives that intersect with yours and you either bump them in a direction towards their temporal and eternal flourishing or you inhibit them from walking that direction. Please look into your heart as you read this book and ask yourself how this applies to you. Ask yourself what these themes imply for you, how you live your life and the choices you make each day.

---

[6] The Way of the Shepherd, 39

Chapter 1 helps you understand the cultural landscape in which we live. Looking at the big picture of life, we better understand ourselves and clearly glean the importance of leadership. Chapter 2 is dedicated to leadership theories. It provides an introduction to the ways of leading which are being taught in academia as well as in corporate development programs. Chapter 3 presents different principles and best practices from leaders throughout the ages. The chapters on the Judeo-Christian worldview, Jesus as the source and summit of leadership and a Christian leadership model provide a synthesis of how God sees the world, humanity and leadership. It provides you with a roadmap for your own leadership that harmonizes the human and divine. The final chapters of the book apply this to several areas of your life such as: virtue development, building blocks for leadership problem solving, as well as how to lead in the various sectors of society.

Where are the leaders? It is easy to keep asking this question and point fingers at others for not being the type of leaders they should be. It is easy to distrust leaders. This includes yourself. Well known socialist and activist Eugene Debs said, "I never had much faith in leaders. I am willing to be charged with almost anything, rather than to be charged with being a leader. I am suspicious of leaders, and especially of the intellectual variety. Give me the rank and file every day in the week."[7] We might feel like this at times. This book, however, is about pointing That finger back at yourself and recognizing that you are called to lead. You need to own it. If something needs to change for the better, you are part of the solution. A leader does not pass the buck. "A leader does not blame others for the problems. Leaders must own everything in their world. There is no one else to blame."[8] The leader asks himself what he can do to contribute to the good. That person is you.

My prayers are with you as you delve into this book. May this book serve you on your life journey and be one small contribution, one link in the chain of your leadership for others. Discover your call to lead.

---

[7] Debbs, Eugene, "The Canton, Ohio Speech, Anti-War Speech" in The Call (16 June 1918)

[8] Willink, Jocko, *Extreme Ownership: How U.S. Navy SEALs Lead and Win*

ACKNOWLEDGMENTS

Building a home or skyscraper takes time and a team: architects, designers, carpenters, electricians, masons and plumbers just to mention a few. This book is also the result of many men and women who have influenced me over the years. My parents and grandparents helped lay a deep foundation. Friends and professors at Rensselaer during my engineering studies broadened my appreciation for leadership including the importance of teamwork and deep relationships. Coworkers at Xerox reminded me that a leader needs to be humble and balanced. Those responsible for my 12-year formation as a Legionary of Christ priest showed me the patience, care and belief in others required when accompanying others in their leadership development. During the past 10 years of priesthood, many business and cultural leaders shared their experiences, highs and lows, joys and sorrows with me; they taught me what leadership looks like in the trenches.

In particular, I want to acknowledge Fr John Connor (General Director of the Legionaries of Christ) for his mentorship and support. Fr Shawn Aaron, Fr David Daly, Fr Mark Haydu, Fr Thomas Montanaro, Fr Michael Sliney, Fr Feargal O'Duill and Fr Daniel Brandenburg (all members of the Legionaries of Christ) have supported me through my leadership journey. Donna and Jeff Garrett were instrumental by reviewing and encouraging the publication of my first book which led to this new work. My sincere gratitude extends to Bob Dill (National Managing Director of the Lumen Institute), Chris Donahue (CEO, Federated Investors and Chairman of the Lumen Institute) and Dan D'Aniello (Founder, The Carlyle Group) who have supported me on this quest. A special mention goes to New Fire Evangelization which has helped with the editing and publication of this book. I extend my prayers and gratitude for the many unnamed friends and acquaintances who have supported me and this book.

Last but not least, I acknowledge Jesus Christ who has been the beginning and culmination of my journey. He has showed me the depths of what leadership can be. The experiences and insights presented in these pages are a small testimony to what I have received from him and pray enriches you as well.

PART I
THE STATE OF LEADERSHIP

CHAPTER 1
THE LEADERSHIP LANDSCAPE

The battle of our time is in the final analysis a battle for hearts and minds and souls.[9]

Good intentions are not enough to engage the world well...God save us from Christians who are well-intentioned but not wise[10]

Thomas had a lot on his mind one morning. Sitting down for coffee, he quickly launched into All the concerns he had about the world. His comments were like those of so many others. 'Politicians are greedy.' 'The media is so negative.' 'Young people don't take life seriously.' The list went on and on. The conversation then turned to solutions. I asked him, 'so what do you think we should do about this?' Like many others, Thomas did not know. It is hard to move forward if you do not have good leaders to model the way. It is also very easy to feel stuck when you face so much negativity. Having this conversation with Thomas over a cappuccino was a reminder that you need to understand your cultural reality in order to chart the course.

How do cultures change? Do masses shape culture? What is the role of influential leaders? How do institutions contribute to culture? "Ideas are important, of course, but without understanding the nature, workings, and power of the institutions in which those ideas are generated and managed, one only understands half of what is going on in culture. It is better to think of culture as a thing, if you will, manufactured not by lone individuals but rather by

---

[9] Hyde, Douglas, *Dedication and Leadership*, 35.

[10] Hunter, James, *To Change the World*, see Kindle ed., Oxford University Press, 2010, 275.

institutions and the elites who lead them."[11] According to Dr James Hunter's research, institutions have much greater power and influence to change culture compared to individuals . It should be no surprise to us since we see cultural revolutionists targeting and taking-over powerful institutions in media and education.

By studying history, it is possible to identify cultural realities and challenges. The perennial issues permeate our past , hence the field of leadership. These are issues that need to be faced in every age and society. If we do not take stock of them from the beginning, it is hard to imagine being a leader who will effectively impact society for the good. On the other hand, the modern day has particular predicaments that haven't been present in all ages and cultures. They're often dictated by modern technology, sociological phenomenon or absence of religion, transcendent thought and self-reflection.

In this chapter, my intent is not to give an exhaustive analysis of culture. There are other books that cover this theme in more depth. My hope in the following lines is to give the reader a summary of the main issues and behaviors that influence how leadership and leaders in particular often operate either for good or for evil. By understanding these things, the reader will be in a much better position to see his or her own leadership with greater objectivity.

A. Perennial Culture and Leadership Realities

What are the things that endure? Do you ever think about the undeniable facts of life? You are born. You live. You die. You hunger and thirst; you eat and drink. You breathe air. You are healthy at times and sick at others. These are perennial realities. You cannot deny them. Similar realities exist at moral, spiritual and social levels. Including leadership.

The first perennial culture and leadership reality is the quest for happiness. In all ages and all times, men and women have sought happiness. It means different things to different people, but is often described as fulfillment, completion, life at its best, harmony and virtue. Great theologian Thomas Aquinas wrote that "virtue's true reward is happiness itself."[12] When citing the greatest leaders in human history, it is not uncommon to see Gandhi's name on the list. He said "happiness is when what you think, what you say, and what you do are in harmony."[13] As a leader and someone who is interested to grow in leadership, it is important to recognize happiness as the deep-down driving force of people. Many might think of happiness and connect it to different things such as power, money, pleasure, virtue or relationships. A leader

---

[11] Ibid, 34.

[12] Thomas Aquinas, *Summa Theologica*

[13] Mahatma Gandhi, as quoted in Humor, Play, & Laughter : Stress-proofing Life with Your Kids (1998) by Joseph A. Michelli, p. 88.

who is focused on others will always keep in mind their desire for happiness and will leverage this both in terms of how they act towards them as well as how to motivate them.

The second perennial culture and leadership reality is the distrust of leaders. Whether we speak of thousands of years ago in places like Greece, Babylon, Egypt or speak of modern day United States, countries in Latin, South America, Europe, Asia and Africa, you read articles about distrust and cynicism towards leaders. It's a general attitude that we cannot ignore when we talk about leadership. It undermines the way people think and feel about aspects of their life. How can we lead in a positive direction (often going against the grain) if so many people inherently distrust and are skeptical of anyone with a title or role of influence in society? Keep this in mind for your leadership.

While it is clear that there is not a widespread aversion to leadership in the 21st century, we do need to keep in mind that there are ideological currents operative in every age that try to discredit the role of leadership. Isabel Paterson was a Canadian-American journalist, novelist, political philosopher, and a leading literary and cultural critic of her day. She expressed her sentiments on leadership saying, "when the word leader, or leadership, returns to current use, it connotes a relapse into barbarism. For a civilized people, it is the most ominous word in any language."[14] This utopian vision of a society without leaders seems to recur in different societies. It indicates that the world and hence each one of us will be better off if there was no one with authority to influence us. It might sound appealing on the surface, but it is totally unscientific. It's not based in reality. The human reality is that every society and human being needs an organizational principle which we often call authority. Authority is either vested in someone because the greater body chose them, because we defer to them due to their charisma or knowledge, or because they take power with power.

Why do people distrust leaders? This leads us to the third topic we need to understand when we speak of leadership. Many people distrust and are skeptical about leaders and leadership because they see the role of power and its tendency to corrupt those who wield it. Lord Acton was a 19th century English Catholic historian, politician, and writer who famously commented "power tends to corrupt, and absolute power corrupts absolutely. Great men are almost always badmen, even when they exercise influence and not authority: still more when you superadd the tendency or the certainty of corruption by authority. There is no worse heresy than that the office sanctifies the holder of it."[15] We can all think of people throughout history who have demonstrated it.

As a stark reminder, I had the opportunity to have lunch several years ago with one of the most powerful politicians in the United States government. The longer I sat and listened to him, the

---

[14] Isabel Paterson, *The God of the Machine* (1943)

[15] Lord Acton, in a letter to Mandell Creighton (5 April 1887), published in Historical Essays and Studies (1907).

clearer I saw that this person was full of conviction and drunk on power. There was no room for dialogue. Power and the drug-like effect of accumulating it was looking me straight in the eyes.. It was a healthy reminder that you can easily blind yourself to believe you see clearly. As Austrian-Israeli philosopher, Martin Buber, wrote, "when we see a great man desiring power instead of his real goal we soon recognize that he is sick, or more precisely that his attitude to his work is sick. He overreaches himself, the work denies itself to him, the incarnation of the spirit no longer takes place, and to avoid the threat of senselessness he snatches after empty power. This sickness casts the genius on to the same level as those hysterical figures who, being by nature without power, slave for power, in order that they may enjoy the illusion that they are inwardly powerful, and who in this striving for power cannot let a pause intervene, since a pause would bring with it the possibility of self-reflection and self-reflection would bring collapse."[16] Leadership thus becomes a vehicle to acquire power.

We cannot underestimate the role and influence of power in the life of leaders and leadership. It is a reality and we must each grapple with it. Scripture commentator Erasmo Merikakis says "we have long since witnessed the dangerous triangulation that occurs between a powerful person in authority, the people under him, and an individual from among the people who threatens that authority… unenlightened authority is all about control by force, protection of the *status quo*, and safeguarding acquire privileges and influences at all cost. What underlies most motivations of a self-serving authority is, quite primitively, the fear of losing the power that has been acquired by any and all means. Whereas virtuous statesmen look to God or moral philosophy or wise counselors for light and guidance, weak and greedy rulers at bottom believe only in the laws of expediency and force."[17] Power is neither good nor evil in itself, but it quickly turns against mankind when it is pursued and held for its own sake.

As a final reflection on the reality and role of power, it is useful to consider three insights offered by Dr James Hunter. "First, power tends to become an end in itself. There are many reasons why power grows and why people want to keep it but mostly it is because of the material, social, and symbolic advantages that accompany it…Second, it is not something that is exercised exclusively by the mighty against the vulnerable and defenseless with the latter always complying. Even the weak possess the power to challenge, subvert, destabilize, and oppose… Third, power always seems to carry with it unintended consequences. For one, the exercise of power is always hard to undo. It tends to act back on those who have it and use it."[18] In our modern, pluralistic society without a common 'cultural DNA', power is often the path chosen by leaders to attempt to unite or coerce people.

---

[16] Martin Buber, Between Man and Man (1965), 151.

[17] Leivi-Merikakis, Erasmo, Fire of Mercy: Heart of the Word (Volume IV), Ignatius Press, San Francisco, 2021, 65-6

[18] Hunter, James, *To Change the World*, see Kindle ed., Oxford University Press, 2010, 179.

The Leadership Landscape

A fourth leadership reality is celebrity status and scandal. "Status can be defined as social approval or disapproval and it is organized according to an often rigid, even if unformalized and unspoken, hierarchical system of ranking."[19] It is important to think here of celebrity status not just in one sector of life. There has been celebrity status in entertainment, sports, business, politics and even members of the clergy. Why the interest in celebrity status? It is a deeper question with psychological underpinnings, but American novelist Siri Hustvedt gives a succinct answer: "celebrity is life in the third person."[20] It is a tantalizing opportunity (perhaps as an escape from your own reality) to live your life emulating those who you admire.

This perennial theme has two sides. The first side is simply status or celebration of celebrity of these individuals. In a given time and culture, celebrity might be automatically given to certain figures in a specific sector of society. In other cases, it is a much broader and far-reaching conversation. Commenting on contemporary obsession with celebrity, actor Jack Gleeson(actor in *Game of Thrones* television series) says, "celebrity worship syndrome ... is indicative of a kind of a complete dissolution of the self in favor of another. ... Whether it's a mob mentality or a desire to be controlled by something higher than you, these cases are indicative of how charisma can replace the ego."[21]

Celebrity status carries with it a form of affirmation which implies it is good. Celebrity and celebration are related words. If we are celebrating celebrity status, we are implicitly acknowledging that there is something good here. Is there really something good? Is the person society anoints as a celebrity really a good role model and leader? Have they done something to deserve the status? This is dubious, at best, in many cases. Celebrity status is almost automatic in different culture and sectors of society. You get drafted into the NBA or NFL and suddenly you are considered an amazing person. You sing a hit song that makes it to the music charts and you are regarded as a credible authority on what's good and right. You act in a TV show or movie and now you should be the reference point for how our children should think and behave. What have such celebrities done to warrant being a reference point other than perhaps a certain skill, talent, or simply working hard to get what they want? In some cases, celebrity is primarily due to their parents' or influential connections.

The other side of this reality is scandal. By scandal I am referring to the negative and sometimes horrific evil example given by people who hold a celebrity status. The impact of scandals runs deep and erodes confidence in those we see in these positions of influence. As the second century Roman poet, Juvenal, writes: "and there's a lust in man no charm can tame of loudly publishing our neighbor's shame; On eagles' wings immortal scandals fly, while virtuous actions

---

[19] *Ibid*, 257.

[20] Siri Hustvedt, The Blazing World (2014), "Harriet Burden: Notebook D". London: Sceptre, 2014, p. 346

[21] Jack Gleeson, Speech at Oxford Union (2014)

are but borne to die."[22] Scandal and celebrity often go hand-in-hand and we are all too often eager to drink it in as evidenced by tabloids and news programs. A good reminder can be found in the *Catechism of the Catholic Church* which speaks of scandal saying "anyone who uses the power at his disposal in such a way that leads others to do wrong becomes guilty of scandal and responsible for the evil that he is directly or indirectly encouraged."[23] William Shakespeare adds "for greater scandal waits on greatest state."[24] These should serve us as a reminder that although any human being can cause scandal, it is magnified by their level of leadership, celebrity, and status. A fifth cultural and leadership theme which has been perennial through the ages is the quest for novelty. Human beings like what is new. Look at the modern day phenomenon with cell phones, computers and other forms of technology. They are changing at a rapid pace with new features and abilities. Novelty in philosophy. Novelty in fashion. Novelty in music and art. The human mind and heart is fickle; it has a hard time settling down and being satisfied with anything that doesn't change or stays constant. As Dean Inge expressed it, "there are two kinds of fools: one says, "This is old, therefore it is good"; the other says, "This is new, therefore it is better.""[25] As Greek philosopher Aristotle would probably comment, we get caught up on accidentals instead of focusing on the substance of life. Accidentals tend to change and they are not what matters most.

As you look at the world and your leadership, you will inevitably see this trait in humanity. The leader often needs to harness this weakness of seeking novelty and channel it towards what is good and lasting. Recognize with author and satirist Douglas Adams that "anything that is in the world when you're born is normal and ordinary and it's just a natural part of the way the world works. Anything that's invented between when you're 15 and 35 is new and exciting and revolutionary and you can probably get a career in it. Anything invented after 35 is against the natural order of things."[26] As you've probably heard from various sources, there is nothing new under the sun even if the latest pop-up ad or one of your friend tells you the contrary.

The sixth and final cultural and leadership reality to consider is the desire for material security. In all ages and cultures of the world, there is a natural need for a minimal level of material security to provide for food and housing. This is a basic human need and all leaders should be aware of this. It is important to remember that "the international community ... allows nearly 3 billion people—almost half of all humanity—to subsist on $2 or less a day in a world of

---

[22] Juvenal, Satires (early 2nd century), IX. Harvey's translation.

[23] Catechism of the Catholic Church (1992), § 2287

[24] William Shakespeare, The Rape of Lucrece (1594), line 1,004.

[25] Dean Inge, More Lay Thoughts of a Dean (1931), p. 200.

[26] Douglas Adams, The Salmon of Doubt: Hitchhiking the Galaxy One Last Time (2002), p. 95.

unprecedented wealth."[27] We also know, however, the desire for material security can go way beyond what is strictly needed to survive. In fact, there is a tendency to acquire wealth and material security in a disordered and exorbitant manner.

It is interesting to note that many throughout history equate material well-being with happiness. Aristotle's comments on this are just as valid today as they were over 2000 years ago. "Happiness, whether consisting in pleasure or virtue, or both, is more often found with those who are highly cultivated in their minds and in their character, and have only a moderate share of external goods, than among those who possess external goods to a useless extent but are deficient in higher qualities."[28] One of the perennial dangers for a leader is avarice which blinds them and makes their own security the focus of their leadership, authority, and power. The great orator and personal advisor to Roman emperors, St Ambrose of Milan, openly spoke about this danger. "How far, O rich, do you extend your senseless avarice? Do you intend to be the sole inhabitants of the earth? Why do you drive out the fellow sharers of nature, and claim it all for yourselves? The earth was made for all, rich and poor, in common. Why do you rich claim it as your exclusive right? The soil was given to the rich and poor in common—wherefore, oh, ye rich, do you unjustly claim it for yourselves alone?"[29]

As a leader or an aspiring leader, keep in mind that wealth in itself is not bad. In fact, we need material security at least on a basic level to function and build a society. Famous entertainer P.T. Barnum reminds us that "the desire for wealth is nearly universal, and none can say that it is not laudable, provided the possessor of it accepts it's responsibilities, and uses it as a friend to humanity."[30] This is one of the great challenges of the 21st-century as wealth is multiplied in the global economy. If we are naïve, we can quickly become slaves of wealth in both concept as well as acquisition. Famous Irish statement and political philosopher, Edmund Burke, exhorts us to remember that "if we command our wealth, we shall be rich and free; if our wealth commands us, we are poor indeed."[31] Whenever we are commanded and obey internal base passions without the ability to say 'no', it is called slavery.

As we look back on these perennial themes which affect culture and leadership throughout history, I would like to offer you an example that touches on all the above five themes. The example of Pontius Pilate is well known in the Judeo-Christian tradition and a leadership figure who goes down in history as making an unjust decision. He sacrificed one falsely accused to

---

[27] Kofi Annan, as quoted in Can Globalization Really Solve Our Problems? in Awake magazine (22 May 2002)

[28] Aristotle in *Politics*

[29] Ambrose of Milan, in The Cry for Justice, p. 397

[30] P. T. Barnum, 'Preserve Your Integrity', The Art of Money Getting (1880)

[31] Edmund Burke, Letters on a Regicide Peace

quiet a violent crowd. He was distrusted by the populace. He is well known as a public figure. He valued material security and his reputation. He put self ahead of those he was called to serve. "How contemptible, this option to safeguard one's public and official image above all other priorities! How fallacious this maneuver to purchase a short span of soul's ease at the price of perpetual restlessness! How hollow and insubstantial, this inability (or refusal) to take a firm stand and risk detriment to oneself for the sake of justice! At least a vigorous sinner can be forgiven once he confesses his burden of weighty sin, whereas it is obvious that Pilate will never think he has anything to repent of as he floats off weightlessly—but with thoroughly washed hands—in the galaxies of moral suspension, a mere specter of the man God intended him to become."[32] If we are not aware of the above perennial challenges to leadership, we can just as easily act in the same ways as the bad leaders in history. Although our leadership may not be seen on a global or national scale, it will still be unveiled at the end of history and weighed on the scales of how we impacted those around us.

B. Contemporary Culture and Leadership Realities

As we saw in the previous section, there are several perennial cultural and leadership challenges that influence each one of us. They cannot be ignored. Turning to the modern era, there are also specific challenges we face that contribute to how we lead. Again, my intention is not to provide an exhaustive study on modern day phenomenon or go into great depth on any of them. My intention is the help those interested in growing and improving their leadership to better understand the main influences that impact how the way of seeing their lives contributes to the way we interact with each other.

The first phenomenon is relativism. Simply put, relativism states that there is no objective truth. 'Your truth is just as good as my truth.' 'Believe whatever you want as long as it does not interfere with my life.' These are both statements typical of a relativist mentality. Over the millennia, this school of philosophical thought has come and gone but often resurfaces. For all of the progress in the empirical sciences, we also see an increase in skepticism about life and reality. For Emeritus Pope Benedict XVI, this was a theme of great concern and one which he addressed in various writings and speeches including saying "**having a clear faith, based on the creed of the church is often labeled today as fundamentalism.** Whereas relativism, which is letting oneself be tossed and swept along by every wind of teaching, look like the only attitude acceptable to today's standards. We are moving toward a dictatorship of relativism which does not recognize anything as for certain and which has as its highest goal one's own ego and one's own desires."[33] Do you recognize this way of thinking in your family, friends and coworkers? Do you see it in the way you think?

---

[32] Merikakis, IV, 444-45

[33] **Pope Benedict XVI, Homily** at the Mass for the Election of the Roman Pontiff (18 April 2005); as published in The Essential Pope Benedict XVI: His Central Writings and Speeches (2008) edited by John F. Thornton and Susan B. Varenne, p. 22

The Leadership Landscape

This way of thinking leads to disastrous conclusions. For example, "I was in that ultimate moment of terror that is the beginning of life. It is nothing. Simple, hideous nothing. The final truth of all things is that there is no final Truth. Truth is what's transitory. It's human life that is real."[34] Of the many applications of such thinking, the 20th and 21st century has seen attempts to redefine gender. Consider for example, Austrian physiologist Eugen Steinach who said "between a real man and a real woman there are innumerable others, some of which are significantly characterized as belonging to the intermediate sex."[35] Ideas always translate into actions. It is easy to see how relativism contributed to massacres such as the holocaust when your relativize the value and significance of a certain race or religious demographic. We see the same play out in modern times in school shootings such as Columbine high school. Just listen to what Eric Harris said about his fellow students: "The human race isn't worth fighting for, only worth killing. Give the Earth back to the animals. They deserve it infinitely more than we do. Nothing means anything anymore."[36] For those who think ideas exist in a vacuum, they should listen and ponder very carefully these types of statements and realize that there are consequences to the way we think. Our mentality does not exist in a vacuum but touches how we think and behave towards others.

We are beginning a time in history where leaders need to hold firm and stand up for objective truth. As legal scholar, political philosopher and Princeton professor Robert George teaches, "truth is the ground and condition of freedom. Unless it is true that human beings deserve to have fundamental liberties respected and protected, the tyrant does no wrong in violating them. Relativism, skepticism, and subjectivism about truth provide no secure basis for freedom. We should honor civil liberties because the norms enjoining us to respect and protect them are valid, sound, in a word, true."[37] Anyone interested in leading now or in the future should strongly and firmly choose objective truths based in the reality of what they are. American philosopher Allan Bloom puts it this way: "The highly ethical economist who speaks only about gain, the public-spirited political scientist who sees only group interest are symptomatic of the difficulty of providing a self-explanation for science and a ground for the theoretical life, which has dogged the life of the mind since early modernity but has become particularly acute with cultural relativism."[38] Each one of us is challenged to recognize the relativism around us.We are

---

[34] Paddy Chayefsky, in Altered States (1980)

[35] Eugen Steinach as quoted in "Eugen Steinach: The First Neuroendocrinologist" Endocrinology, March 2014, 155(3):688 –702.

[36] Eric Harris, as quoted in 12 Rules for Life, an Antidote to Chaos (2018), by Jordan B. Peterson, Random House Canada, p. 147

[37] Robert P. George, Twitter post (1 January 2018)

[38] Allan Bloom, The Closing of the American Mind (New York: 1988), pp. 203-204

challenged to reject it as an incomplete picture of reality and to articulate a different vision of reality for those we serve.

A second leadership point which should not be forgotten is the limited role that religious groups have to shape culture. This is not to deny the powerful witness and selfless service given by many clergy and lay men and women to society in the name of their religion and their beliefs. When commenting on this point, I do so from the standpoint of western civilization where Christianity is the dominant religious tradition that has had the most exposure among the religions. Dr James Hunter's research shows that Christians dedicate little effort to the various networks of influence. "Since the 1960s, none of the movements in contemporary Christianity have been prominent in creating, contributing to, or supporting structures in the arts, humane letters, the academy, and the like…they have been absent from the arenas in which the greatest influence in the culture is exerted. The culture-producing institutions of historical Christianity are largely marginalized in the economy of culture formation."[39] This effort has been further hampered by scandals within religions which have a destructive, delegitimizing impact on them as a whole and on their leaders. "His life as a pope was so vile, so foul, so execrable, that I shudder to think of it."[40] We should recognize the increasingly limited role of religion.

In fact, it can be argued that Christians (and followers of other religions) do not take their faith seriously enough and are afraid to propose it as a path of happiness and fulfillment. As former communist leader turned Christian Douglas Hyde comments "to the Christian there is an element of sheer tragedy in this—that people with such potentialities should give so much energy, zeal and dedication to such a cause, whilst those who believe that they have the best cause on earth often give so little to it. And their leaders are so often afraid to ask for more than the merest minimum. The Christian may say that the Communists have the worst creed on earth. But what they have to appreciate is that the Communists shout it from the house-tops; whilst too often those who believe they have the best speak with a muted voice when they speak at all."[41] Leaders need to recognize and encourage the practice of transcendence and formal religion. One of the important dimensions of it is instilling a sense of mission and grandeur in living by your beliefs. "I can think of many a lapsed-Catholic Communist who has told me that when he was practicing the Faith the greatest responsibility he was every given was to help, along with others, to move the chairs in the parish hall 'for Father'. Inside the Communist Party he was made to feel that he had something better than that to offer. And events proved that this was so."[42] It is very possible that the small mindedness and mediocre way of seeing life that permeates many societies has infiltrated and influenced men and women

---

[39] Hunter, James, *To Change the World*, see Kindle ed., Oxford University Press, 2010, 88-9.

[40] Pope Victor III on Pope Benedict IX, Pope (1934), Monumenta Germaniae Historica, Libelli de lite p. 141

[41] Hyde, Douglas, *Dedication and Leadership*, 32.

[42] *Ibid*, 71.

of faith as well. Leaders in any time and place need to break this open and encourage transcendence and religious belief. A leader is a sower of a mission mindset.

A third factor for leaders to consider today is the influence of globalization. Part and parcel with this theme is capitalism. Globalization creates ties and influence between nations and people. It has operated at an unprecedented level throughout history. As evolutionary biologist Jared Diamond says, "globalization makes it impossible for modern societies to collapse in isolation, as did Easter Island and the Greenland Norse in the past. Any society in turmoil today, no matter how remote...can cause trouble for prosperous societies on other continents, and is also subject to their influence (whether helpful or destabilizing). For the first time in history, we face the risk of a global decline. But we also are the first to enjoy the opportunity of learning quickly from developments in societies anywhere else in the world today, and from what has unfolded in societies at any time in the past."[43] The leader needs to keep in mind the interconnectedness among people in the world and be aware of how it affects our mindset. For example, it might be tempting to think that truth is relative just because different cultures have diverging beliefs on certain topics. This reality is made all the more clear given the international exchange of information.

Capitalism continues to be debated in our globalized world. What is capitalism? "Capitalism is a mode of socio-economic organization in which a class of entrepreneurs and entrepreneurial institutions provide the capital with which businesses produce goods and services and employ workers. In return the capitalist extracts profits from the goods created. Capitalism is frequently seen as the embodiment of the market economy, and hence may result in the optimum distribution of scarce resources, with a resulting improvement for all; this optimism is countered by pointing to the opportunity for exploitation inherent in the system."[44] Just as there is no absolutely perfect form of government, there is also different economic system with pros as well as cons. There has been a fascination for socialism as opposed to capitalism in. It is nothing new. Leadership guru Peter Drucker offers an important perspective. "As for the explanation that fascism is a last desperate attempt of capitalism to delay the socialist revolution, it simply is not true. It is not true that 'big business' promoted fascism. On the contrary, both in Italy and in Germany the proportion of fascist sympathizers and backers was smallest in the industrial and financial classes. It is equally untrue that 'big business' profits from fascism; of all the classes it probably suffers most from totalitarian economics and Wehrwirtschaft."[45] I don't propose to take sides on the capitalism versus socialism issue in this book, but I encourage every leader to better understand the benefits and the weaknesses of both economic systems. From a Christian perspective, the human person and his holistic good must be at the center of any economic system. Any system that would use, exploit, or reduce

---

[43] Jared Diamond, *Collapse: How Societies Choose to Fail or Succeed* (2005), (Prologue)

[44] Simon Blackburn ed. (1996) Oxford Dictionary of Philosophy. Lemma "Capitalism"

[45] Peter Drucker, *The End of Economic Man*, The John Day Company, (1939) p. 7

the human person to a cog in a machine needs to be purified and freed of such impoverished thinking.

A fourth contemporary leadership reality is the political polarization of every sector of society. I cannot count how many conversations over coffee, one way or the other, come back to politics. It has managed to creep into every sector of society: sports, religion, medicine, education, sexuality, and so much more. "What is implied here should not be passed over too quickly. Politics has become so central in our time that institutions, groups, and issues are now defined relative to the state, its laws and procedures. Institutions such as popular and higher education, philanthropy, science, the arts, and even the family understand their identity and function according to what the state does or does not permit. Groups (women, minorities, gays, Christians, etc.) have validity not only but increasingly through the rights conferred by the state. Issues gain legitimacy only when recognized by law and public policy."[46] You've certainly experienced this and I invite you to take a few moments to reflect how this has happened around you. For example, "there is the politicization of the news media. It isn't just that media organizations position themselves and are judged by the public by their ideological orientation (e.g., the New York Times is liberal and the Washington Times is conservative; CNN is liberal and Fox News is conservative). Unless the topic is a human interest story buried at the end of the newscast or in the back pages of the newspaper or news magazine, news reporting on almost any issue is framed in terms of who is winning and who is losing in the contest for political advantage."[47] As you evaluate your own leadership, it is important to avoid one dictated by politics. Leadership needs to be rooted in virtue, not limited to a particular political party.

A fifth cultural leadership phenomenon is pluralism. While this can easily lead us to relativism, it is not the same thing. Pluralism is a result of different cultures and traditions coexisting in a given society. Leaders in the 21st-century must be ready to act within this context. "A secure pluralistic society requires communities that are educated and confident both in the identity and depth of their own traditions and in those of their neighbors."[48] This is the ideal for which we as leaders should strive, but in practice it will be difficult.. "By its very nature, pluralism juxtaposes culture, each with its own definition of words or perspectives on the meaning of words. God, love, family, faith, courage, loyalty—the entire lexicon of signs, gestures, utterances, speech acts, ideals, and beliefs—mean different things within different social and cultural contexts. Confidence in the meaning of words cannot help but be undermined."[49] As leaders, listen carefully to respected leadership expert Peter Drucker when he says, "all earlier pluralist societies destroyed themselves because no one took care of the common good. They

---

[46] Hunter, James, *To Change the World*, see Kindle ed., Oxford University Press, 2010, 102.

[47] *Ibid*, 104

[48] Aga Khan IV, in an address at the Leadership and Diversity Conference Gatineau, Quebec, Canada (19 May 2004)

[49] Hunter, James, *To Change the World*, see Kindle ed., Oxford University Press, 2010, 207.

abounded in communities but could not sustain community, let alone create it."[50] Leadership looks at the needs of the group, society, and the world. We need to be careful and realistic in pluralistic societies; it is easy to be focused on your own culture and abjure the common good.

A sixth phenomenon is the rise of soft and hard totalitarian regimes which either embrace or imitate Communism and Marxism. This has been an attractive yet deceptive ideology during the past 100 years and, like Nazism, has contributed to the deaths of tens of millions of individuals as well as incalculable suffering for others. Surprisingly, , this political philosophy still attracts young people to its ranks. "No-one could claim that in the period in which Communism has been in our midst they have had anything like its success…I am talking about their ability to fire the imagination, create a sense of dedication and send their followers into effective, meaningful action."[51] Communism flies the flag of trying to change the world. "That slogan of 'change the world' has proved to be one of the most dynamic of the past 120 years. Many years after Frederick Engels was dead and buried, Communist parties throughout the world made it their slogan."[52]

Communism also attracts good men and women. "Part of the tragedy of Communism is that it takes good men, with good intentions, and uses them for a bad cause. Because its approaches to God, to the nature of man and to the world, are false, it starts off on the wrong foot. The consequences is that the idealists, and natural rebels who join the Communist Party, set out to be the saviors of mankind and instead become men's jailers. Communism stands condemned, not only for what it does to the masses, but also for what it does to the Communists themselves."[53] Established as well as emerging leaders should be aware of the attractive nature of Communism and be able to explain why it is not a path for the common good of society.

The reality and dangers of Marxist ideology are real. The proponents of Marxism are alive and well in the United States and other western countries. If you doubt this, read 2021 best-seller *American Marxism*. In this telling Marxism assessment, author Mark Levin says "the counterrevolution to the American Revolution is in full force. It can no longer be dismissed or ignored, for it is devouring our society and culture, swirling around our everyday lives, and ubiquitous in our politics, schools, media and entertainment."[54] It is easy to sit back and think Communism is not active in our midst. "In America, many Marxists cloak themselves in phrases like "progressives," "Democratic Socialists," "social activists," "community activists," etc., as

---

[50] Peter Drucker, in The New Pluralism Leader to Leader, No. 14 (Fall 1999)

[51] *Dedication and Leadership*, Hyde, Douglas, University of Notre Dame Press, Notre Dame, IN, 1966, 12

[52] *Ibid*, 30-1

[53] *Ibid*, 148

[54] Levin, Mark, *American Marxism*, 1.

most Americans remain openly hostile to the name Marxism."[55] Marxist-inspired groups appeal the disenfranchised and those who are easily manipulated (such as young people looking for meaning, purpose, and an ideal for which to fight), the poor, and fringe groups.

They try to discredit history, tradition as well as anyone in the mainstream culture labeling them as oppressors, bigots and racists. Do I see through this smokescreen? Am I caught up in the confusion?

Ideological groups (such as Marxism) infiltrate government and academia systems for their own purposes. "Indeed, America's college and university faculties have turned their classrooms into breeding grounds for resistance, rebellion, and revolution against American society, as well as receptors for Marxist or Marxist-like indoctrination and propaganda. Academic freedom exists first and foremost for the militant professors, and the competition of ideas is mostly a quaint concept of what higher education used to be and should be. But Marxism is not about free speech and debate, it is about domination, repression, indoctrination, conformity, and compliance."[56] Leaders must recognize the intentional, hostile takeover of culture through vehicles such as education, media and politics. These noble and morally neutral institutions are susceptible to the virtue or vice of those in them.

A seventh area to consider is the militant atheist movement. Since the Enlightenment, there has been a growing trend (often associated with the empirical sciences and humanist movement) to promote an atheistic outlook. In recent years, militant atheists such as Christopher Hitchens, Richard Dawkins, Sam Harris and Lawrence Krauss have continued to advance the paradigm that religion hurts humanity and only a global, unified approach to life without God will help us progress. Their arguments cannot refute the proposal of an all transcendent and all loving God. Their caricatures of God are one in which God is imminent and limited to the confines of this universe. They dismiss the belief in an all transcendent loving God as childish and contrary to science and mature human thought. They draw attention to bad examples of religion and are slow to acknowledge holy lives and immense contribution to culture from those who acted out of love for God and neighbor. Leaders must be aware of the influence of the anti-God movement that shapes much of public opinion. The arguments of atheists have no basis in science.Many of the most recognized scientists throughout history believed in God. Anyone interested in leadership should not forget that it was regimes that ascribed to atheism (for example Nazism and Communism) who were responsible for killing over 100 million people in the 20th century. When we eclipse God, we also eclipse the dignity of the human person.

An eighth phenomenon that leaders need to understand is the woke/cancel culture. In the past 20 years, the increasing sensitivity and desire for "social justice" and progressive activism has led at times to an unfettered retaliation against those who disagree. Woke culture often seeks to

---

[55] Ibid, 1.

[56] Ibid, 32-3.

intimidate and marginalize opponents. While a need for social activism will exist at times, it should always focus on the dignity of each person regardless of race, gender, and religion. Woke culture is characterized by a growing cultivation of resentment among those who perceive themselves as aggrieved. "The sense of injury is the key. Over time, the perceived injustice becomes central to the person's and the group's identity. Understanding themselves to be victimized is not a passive acknowledgement but a belief that can be cultivated…It is often useful at such times to exaggerate or magnify the threat. The injury or threat thereof is so central to the identity and dynamics of the group that to give it up is to give up a critical part of whom they understand themselves to be. Thus, instead of letting go, the sense of injury continues to get deeper."[57] This creates a complex reality by which leaders fear social repercussions for saying anything that is not acceptable to the woke guardians. Leading in a woke culture is challenging. A leader needs convictions to affect appropriate, objectively good social change, but also needs to resist (at times to the detriment of his public image) evil and what harms society. Leaders should remember that their influence is at the service of others and they may suffer for doing the right thing. We will see more of this later when speaking about self-sacrificing leadership.

A ninth cultural phenomenon is the widespread influence of social media. As leaders, we cannot underestimate the power of information, which may be true, partially true or completely false. Of course, there are many positives such communication with loved ones, and brand promotions, etc. yet, there are real consequences. "Many of the parents I spoke to worried that their kids' digital habits — round-the-clock responding to texts, posting to social media, obsessively following the filtered exploits of peers — were partly to blame for their children's struggles."[58] There is overwhelming evidence that social media use increases anxiety and stress especially when it consumes our day. Average TV and social media daily use if extrapolated from your life based on current usage equates to around 15 years. A second danger is the ease in which we can distort, malign and even destroy the good name of others. "We begin by casually disfiguring a persons words, and we end up literally mangling the entire person— face, hands, feet, and heart."[59] Leaders are challenged to be aware of this; speak and act in a way that shows others how to best use social media. Deadwood drifts down stream. Leaders are meant to row upstream.

The tenth and final phenomenon is millennials. These young adults are becoming a mainstay in culture; their unique gifts as well as challenges invite leaders to better understand and work with them. For millennials it is also a moment to invite you to take up the leadership challenge,

---

[57] Hunter, James, *To Change the World*, see Kindle ed., Oxford University Press, 2010, 107.

[58] Benoit Denizet-Lewis, ""Why Are More American Teenagers Than Ever Suffering From Severe Anxiety?", New York Times' Magazine, (Oct 11, 2017); as quoted in "Anxiety is Now the Most Pressing Mental Health Problem For American Teens" Drake Baer, Thrive Global, (October 16, 2017).

[59] Merikakis, IV 322

recognize that you have much more to offer and much more to learn. There are several leadership characteristics that are very important to this generation. First, always help others transcend their lives and be personally enriched. Second, be authentic. Third, work in collaboration with others (especially in teams). And last, a leader needs to be resilient in the ever challenging cultural landscape. A resilient leader encourages and inspires confidence in moments of challenge that enables the others to take heart and continue onward. Millennials look for and are highly encouraged by resilient leaders.

As we conclude this chapter, we have surveyed some of the perennial and contemporary realities in which any leader must operate. As we continue our consideration of leadership, please remember that you were born for this time in history and have a role to play. If contemporary society has the above mentioned characteristics, God has also given you the personal talents as well as his assistance to become the leader the world needs you to be. Faced with confusion, cynicism, loss of hope and often deep suffering, people deep down long for leaders to be a point of light, a roadmap for life— a safe harbor. "Times of great calamity and confusion have been productive for the greatest minds. The purest ore is produced from the hottest furnace. The brightest thunder-bolt is elicited from the darkest storm."[60] Author Anne Frank puts it this way: "In spite of everything I still believe that people are really good at heart. I simply can't build up my hopes on a foundation consisting of confusion, misery and death."[61]

We have all heard the Greek adage *know thy self*, but perhaps we have not deeply contemplated the desires and behaviors of our human nature that translate into cultural tendencies. By knowing the contemporary realities, you are in a better position to be a leader at the service of others. People are often looking up to a leader for direction, safety and protection. Unfortunately, many leaders do not help others flourish. "I'll tell you what else is sad…Every day, hundreds of thousands of people get up and go to work in a fold that looks a lot like this one. They work in a neglected pasture, untended by the very people who are responsible for the health and well-being of the flock. At quitting time, they go home having survived another day, but they haven't thrived. They certainly haven't flourished. On the outside, they look just fine, but on the inside, they look like these poor sheep."[62] As we will see later in this book, a leader at the apex of leadership performance is like a good shepherd who cares for those entrusted to him. Let's continue this leadership journey by taking a quick tour of the most common leadership theories and philosophies.

Questions for Personal Reflection and Group Discussion

---

[60] Charles Caleb Colton, in History of Logan County and Ohio: Containing a History of the State of Ohio …, O.L. Baskin, 1880, p. 577

[61] Anne Frank, in Memorable Quotations: Jewish Writers of the Past, iUniverse, 2003, p. 37

[62] Leman and Pentak, *The Way of the Shepherd*, 55-6

The Leadership Landscape

1. What perennial leadership challenges were presented? Which one do you think is the most important? Why?
2. Can you identify other perennial leadership challenges not covered in this book?
3. What contemporary leadership challenges were presented? Which one do you think is the most important? Why?
4. What other contemporary leadership challenges exist? Why do you consider it a challenge?
5. Of the perennial and contemporary challenges, which one most influences you? What are the obstacles stopping you from overcoming it?
6. What emerging leadership challenges do you foresee in the next 5-10 years?
7. How would you propose addressing them?

CHAPTER 2
THE DILEMMA OF HOW TO LEAD

Leadership is a topic with universal appeal; in the popular press and academic research literature, much has been written about leadership. Despite the abundance of writing on the topic, leadership has presented a major challenge to practitioners and researchers interested in understanding the nature of leadership. It is a highly valued phenomenon that is very complex. Through the years, leadership has been defined and conceptualized in many ways.[63]

Over the course of several years, I had a wonderful opportunity to participate in national gatherings convoked by the International Leadership Association (ILA). These gatherings include over 100 leadership educators from academia (such as from Harvard and Northwestern), leadership consultants, experts in corporate leadership training programs as well as others practitioners. They were wonderful moments to attend lectures, workshops, meals, and coffee. I was truly impressed by the zeal and dedication of the women and men who devoted their lives to training the next generation of leaders. I benefited from them by including me, helping me in my own leadership, as well as giving me a better understanding of the complexity of this field.

if you are reading this book, you are interested in leadership. On the human level, leadership presents us with a challenge:how to best define it and what approach should we use to teach it. This is a complex area with 101 different theories. The book, *Leadership*, by Northouse is a

---

[63] Northouse, *Leadership*, 463

standard used in many leadership programs. It mentions "after decades of dissonance, leadership scholars agree on one thing: They can't come up with a common definition for leadership. Because of such factors as growing global influences and generational differences, leadership will continue to have different meanings for different people. The bottom line is that leadership is a complex concept for which a determined definition may long be in flux."[64]

Since this book is written to give you a basic understanding on leadership from various dimensions, I think it is important for you to have a cursory picture of the main schools of leadership. This will prepare you and give you the context to listen to the best insights on leadership over centuries, as well as till the ground of your understanding for receiving insights from God on this theme.

It is important to propose a working definition of leadership. Northouse says, "despite the multitude of ways in which leadership has been conceptualized, the following components can be identified as central to the phenomenon: (a) Leadership is a process, (b) leadership involves influence, (c) leadership occurs in groups, and (d) leadership involves common goals. Based on these components, the following definition of leadership is used in this text: Leadership is a process whereby an individual influences a group of individuals to achieve a common goal."[65] This definition neither names the factors behind influence nor the qualitative good or evil of the influence. For now, it is enough to recognize the basic definition of leadership and what it involves.

Leadership is a bigger field than leadership theories. As described in the definition above as well as the book *Knowing, Doing, Being Leader* (a summary of 40 of the most highly regarded leadership courses and programs presented at a Harvard symposium), leadership implies intellectual knowledge and the development of habits and practices required to lead as well as self-belief. The concept of 'Know, Do and Be' leadership was coined by the US Army in 1999. The central components of this model are linked to three areas of psychology: cognition, behavior and attitudes. According to the Army, "*Be* describes physical, mental and emotional attributes. *Know* implies knowledge of their people, equipment and profession. *Do* means providing purpose, direction and motivation while seeking to accomplish a mission and improve the organization."[66]

The book, *The Future of Leadership*, highlights three important leadership theories. The following pages cover those three while adding several other mainstream theories. The theories that follow include: toxic leadership, servant leadership, transformational leadership, adaptive leadership, and values-based leadership. As we survey these theories, you might be wondering

---

[64] *Ibid*, 276

[65] *Ibid*, 290.

[66] *Army Leadership: Know, Do, Be*, FM 22-100, August 1999, forward.

if one is born a leader, destined to be a leader or follower. Major Dick Winters comments that "I am not sure there is such a thing as a natural born leader. Some leaders are born with special aptitude's or talents, but any success I might have had was the product of good upbringing, intense study and preparation, and physical conditioning that set me apart from many of my peers. I was also surrounded by a group of men who were disciplined and highly trained to accomplish any mission."[67]

Toxic Leadership

The past century calls to mind images of Hitler, Stalin and Mao Zedong. In the 21st century, we can think of Fidel Castro, Hugo Chavez and Nicolas Maduro in Venezuela, as well as Kim Jong-un in North Korea and Vladimir Putin in Russia (his war in Ukraine is still unfolding as this book is being published). "Toxic leadership highlights the deliberate destructive and self-serving misuse of power; it describes a relationship which undermines the effective functioning of the organization and destabilizes sound working relationships."[68] It is a form of leadership focused on the individual leader and on their egotistic goals.

This form of leadership has triggered a radical reaction in leadership studies and development. Many contemporary theories of leadership are aimed at distributed leadership and not concentrating power in any one person. This can go to the extreme of denying the existence of authentic authority based on man's social nature. It is important to dwell for a moment on the root problem behind toxic leadership. Sin and personal weakness afflict all mankind to some degree, but toxic leadership is the fruit of pride, which is the most dangerous vice that can enter the human heart— the TH ultimately the source of many global problems. It corrupts leaders and makes them bad examples for others. "What they lack is authentic humility, which is able to submit to what is greater, but also authentic courage, which leads to belief in what is truly great."[69] When making this comment, Emeritus pope Benedict XVI was contrasting the humility of Jesus, our servant leader and King Herod whose jealousy murdered little children out of fear.

Sometimes we fall into toxic leadership behaviors. Remember, the shipwreck of bad leadership on the global stage is just a public showing of many toxic attitudes and choices that led to what we see in its catastrophic effects. One example that might help us is Major Dick Winters who comments that "what bothered Easy Company's officers, me included, was not his emphasis on strict discipline, but his desire to lead by fear rather than example…If infractions of discipline were not found during inspections, he manufactured deficiencies to prove a point or emphasize

---

[67] Winters, Dick, *Beyond Band of Brothers*, 284

[68] *Leadership: The Key Concepts*, edited by Antonio Marturano and Jonathan Gosling (quoting Greenleaf, Robert, The Servant as Leader, Paulist Press, New York, NY, 1970, 13), Routledge, New York, NY, 2008, 150.

[69] Pope Benedict XVI, Homily on Feast of the Epiphany, January 6, 2011.

his authority as company commander...At other times, our commander deliberately embarrassed the platoon leaders in front of other men. Not surprisingly, he rapidly emerged as the central target of hate and scorn within Easy Company."[70] While most readers will have never experienced war first-hand, we all are in situations where we can be on the giving or receiving end of leadership that is imposed through fear and belittling others.

A final comment on toxic leadership: it often manifests in men and women who see leadership as a reward. Leadership expert and consultant, Pat Lencioni, addresses this theme at length in his latest book, *The Motive*. "When leaders are motivated by personal reward, they will avoid the unpleasant situations and activities that leadership requires. They will calculate the personal economics of uncomfortable and tedious responsibilities—responsibilities only a leader can do —and try to avoid them. This inevitably leaves the people in their charge without direction, guidance, and protection, which eventually hurts those people and the organization as a whole."[71] How does this look in my heart? How often do I look for rewards? How do I see positions of influence especially those I would like to fill? Do I see them as a service to others or something which serves my interests and desires?

Servant Leadership

Servant leadership is an extremely popular and inspirational concept of leadership. It brings to mind the image of Jesus Christ as the 'suffering servant' described by the Prophet Isaiah. For 20 centuries, Christians followed Christ's footsteps carry their cross each day as well as imitate Simon of Cyrene by serving Jesus Christ. While a true and beautiful image, this is not the origin of the modern concept of servant leadership. Nonetheless, there is no doubt that this new strain is tending towards the example of Jesus, who freely laid down his life to save others.

The 20th-century concept of 'servant leadership' was founded by Robert Greenleaf in 1970. According to this author, servant leadership "begins with the natural feeling that one wants to serve, to serve first. Then a conscious choice brings one to aspire to lead."[72] This concept is focused on the individual and their feelings. It is not centered on oneself. According to a recent definition, servant leadership is "an understanding and practice of leadership that places the good of those led over the self-interest of the leader. Servant-leadership promotes the valuing and development of people, the building of community, the practice of authenticity, the providing

---

[70] Dick Winters, *Beyond Band of Brothers*, 26

[71] Pat Lencioni, *The Motive*, 132

[72] Leadership: The Key Concepts, edited by Antonio Marturano and Jonathan Gosling (quoting Greenleaf, Robert, The Servant as Leader, Paulist Press, New York, NY, 1970, 13), Routledge, New York, NY, 2008, 147.

of leadership for the good of those led, and the sharing of power and status for the common good of each individual—the total organization and those served by the organization."[73]

Considering this understanding of servant leadership, we see an approximation to a Christian understanding of the human person and the command of Jesus Christ to love your neighbor as himself. A final quality to mention about servant leadership is its transformational power (not to be confused with transformational leadership). "As a transformational force, servant-leadership has the potential to move leaders and followers toward 'higher levels of motivation and morality'."[74] This is one of the strongest points of this theory. As one would expect, there is a justification for a 'higher level of morality' based on the religious and philosophical framework held by those subscribing to servant leadership. Christians find a natural affinity and justification for this style of leadership based on the example of Jesus Christ who came to serve. For those without Christ as the concrete, singular norm (following von Balthasar's terminology) of existence, servant leadership has been practiced for various reasons: human, philanthropic, win peoples' favor, climb the 'corporate ladder', et cetera.

Values-Based Leadership

Values-based leadership is popular in sectors such as business and education. It is often used as a guide for teamwork. What are the basics of values-based leadership? Harry Kraemer tells us in his popular book, *From Values to Action*, "leadership, simply put, is the ability to influence others. Values-based leadership takes it to the next level. By word, action, and example, values-based leaders seek to inspire and motive, using their influence to pursue what matters most. What matters most, of course, depends somewhat on personal choice."[75] This last sentence is very telling— it should remind us as leaders that values-based leadership can quickly turn into relativism. What matters most to you? This can easily be confused with 'what is the right thing to do' and 'what matters most for others'. This leadership style can help us understand how to lead with values but needs to be coupled with a moral objective framework that transcends 'individual values'.

In Kraemer's case, he proposes four over-arching values. "I believe that the path to becoming a values-based leader begins and ends with what I call the four principles of values-based leadership. These principles are self-reflection, balance, true self-confidence, and genuine humility. The principles are interconnected, each building on and contributing to the others.

---

[73] Ibid (quoting Laub, J., 'Assessing the Servant Organization: Development of the Servant Organizational Leadership Assessment (SOLA) Instrument', Unpublished Dissertation, Florida Atlantic University, 1999, 81), 147-48.

[74] *Ibid*, 150

[75] *From Values to Action: The Four Principles of Values-Based Leadership*, Kraemer, Harry, Jossey-Bass, San Francisco, CA, 2011, 2

Together, they form a solid foundation for values-based leadership."[76] As in so many other mainstream leadership books, the author does not provide a transcendent grounding or a foundation for these. It is an approach of 'these tend to work in practice' so they are recommended. In reality, these four act as a roadmap to 'clarify your values' but do not guarantee the values held by individual or organization are good. It is important for a leader (and an organization) to have clearly defined values. These values clarify what one stands for and provide a starting point for plans of action and accountability.

Transformational Leadership

Since its inception, this theory has shaped leadership studies and development programs worldwide. In 1978, James MacGregor Burns wrote the book, *Leadership*. In 2011, it is still considered to be the seminal text in leadership studies. What is transformational leadership? Its main idea: "Transforming leadership is normative in the sense that it does not simply describe how leaders do in fact behave but, rather, prescribes how they ought to behave. Burns claims that leaders must do more than cater to whatever wants and desires people happen to have. Transforming leadership thus aims to move beyond people's wants and desires, thereby engaging their real needs and values."[77] Does this also sound similar to servant leadership? There is an overlap because both focus on doing the right thing for those being led or served.

Unlike other leadership theories, transformational leadership stresses the normative dimension of a leader. The leader should be a man or woman of moral backbone and not a 'weather vane' that moves according to public opinion. The normative aspect herein is not simply an ideal or slogan called upon by followers of this theory. "No normative conception of leadership comes close to transformational leadership in terms of conceptual sophistication and empirical analysis. Moreover, its influence extends across leadership contexts: politics, business and nonprofits."[78] The idea is to have a leadership theory based on objective reality and not on subjective opinion.

Norms are at the core of transformational leadership. This leads many of its followers to espouse a comprehensive moral framework to ensure good leadership. In this respect, Burns correctly understood that men and women seek the good and ought to act for the good. Because it is part of human nature, it carries an obligation. What is the nature of the moral obligation according to the founder of transformational leadership? "According to Burns, then, good leadership implies a moral responsibility to respond to people's needs and values in a way that is conducive to the highest forms of human relations. How does transforming leadership

---

[76] Ibid,-5.

[77] Leadership: The Key Concepts, edited by Antonio Marturano and Jonathan Gosling, Routledge, New York, NY, 2008, 171.

[78] Ibid, 174.

move beyond potentially suspect motivational and moral states to discharge its moral responsibility? With respect to motivation, Burns appeals directly to Abraham Maslow's (1954) hierarchy of needs...With respect to morality,...morally responsible leadership transforms individuals to make their good consistent with the good of the group."[79] This is very good for two reasons. The first is that leaders are always in relation to others. Secondly, norms and moral actions are proposed in the context of a leader's responsibility. In contemporary society when many speak about rights and few about the corresponding duties-responsibilities, this is a breath of fresh air. Leaders are indeed responsible to society and must administer their role in the service of others.

Although transformational leadership has its strong points and moves in the right direction, it has a gaping hole at its center: there is no absolute moral standard upon which it stands. The previous quote spoke about making the moral good consistent with the good of the group. Within transformational leadership, there is, however, no objective, absolute, and unchanging good of the group that serves as a reference point for the leader. Without this absolute good, it is impossible to say one is a good or bad leader (only an ethical or unethical leader according to the group's established standards). In other words, "to say that leadership is inauthentic simply means that it is unethical. Moral authenticity is not necessary for the conceptual authenticity of transformational leadership unless we assume that morality is itself part of the concept of transformational leadership. Defenders of transformational leadership cannot make this assumption because so doing begs the question."[80] Transformational leadership, therefore, distinguishes ethics and morality. Morality is not part of the discussion; If it were, it 'begs the question' of its source and foundation. Only God can provide the foundation for an absolute and unchanging moral standard of action. This is what transformational leadership aspires to do, but it falls short by limiting the source of responsibility to seek the subjective good of the majority. It is clear that this theory of leadership can be 'transformed' by inserting the reality of absolute, unchanging morality founded on God.

Adaptive Leadership

This is a more recent and popular leadership theory. "The adaptive leadership model was introduced by Harvard professor Ronald Heifetz and Marty Linsky. Heifetz defines it as the act of mobilizing a group of individuals to handle tough challenges and emerge triumphant in the end."[81] This vision of leadership is both attractive and effective in a rapidly changing world with often complex problems without roadmaps (for example, the Coronavirus Pandemic that began in 2020). "What is the recipe for success? In truth, there are no simple solutions, just as there is no average day in combat. Each situation is different and requires a leader to be flexible in

---

[79] Ibid, 172.

[80] Ibid, 173.

[81] https://corporatefinanceinstitute.com/resources/careers/soft-skills/adaptive-leadership/

adapting his or her particular leadership style to the specific circumstances required to accomplish any mission."[82] Professor Heifetz wrote that leadership is too often equivocated with skills or traits rather than focusing on the problem to be solved. For him and those ascribing to this theory, leadership is primarily about the goal and how you help others get there.

This theory invites leaders to do what is necessary. "I don't believe a persuasive visionary leader can step in and solve the adaptive challenges people are facing. The difficult work of deciding how to interpret and balance overlapping values, which losses to accept, which ways of doing things to change, which new capacities to build, and how to do so-- that's the work that must be done to meet an adaptive challenge. Leadership then, as we will use the term in this course, is this practice of adaptive work. Creating with people new capacity to meet the challenges they face to thrive in our changing and challenging world."[83]

Adaptive leadership centers on the challenge, the goal, and the change needed to achieve it. "The success of your leadership depends on your ability to distinguish challenges that are technical-- problems that can be solved by authoritative and managerial expertise-- from challenges that are adaptive, and thus require the building of new capacities. When people make this mistake, they approach an adaptive challenge in a problem-solving mode, failing to recognize that what they need to provide is the mobilizing and organizing of people to create new capacity to meet the challenge."[84] For this reason, adaptive leadership involves recognizing people are part of the issue. Meeting the challenge often involves facilitating attitude changes and the mindsets of your team.

A challenge provokes disequilibrium in a group. The group must respond through conflict resolution to reach stability. "With an adaptive challenge, the high level of disequilibrium does not go away quickly because the new adaptive solution takes a longer period of time to create. But as people get organized to deal with the adaptive challenge, the disequilibrium can be reduced into the productive range. Now what happens next depends on how conflict is orchestrated. In a system where stakeholders do not have the stomach for conflict, disequilibrium might spike again and then decrease rapidly as individuals employ conflict avoidance."[85] Working through disequilibrium caused by the adaptive challenge is an essential part of leadership.

---

[82] Winters, Richard, Beyond Band of Brothers, 284.

[83] Ronald Heifetz, Senior lecturer in Harvard Kennedy School, Harvard Online Course, April 2021.

[84] Ibid.

[85] Adapted from Ronald Heifetz, Alexander Grashow and Marty Linsky, *The Practice of Adaptive Leadership: Tools and Tactics for Changing Your Organization and the World* (Boston, MA: Harvard Business Review Press, 2009), 30.

As an existing or up-and-coming leader, I recommend becoming familiar with this style and theory of leadership. One of the important qualities of a leader in the 21st century and beyond is the adaptability and flexibility to lead through complex and shifting situations.

Conclusion

We have discussed five popular leadership theories. There are others you may study such as trait leadership, behavioral leadership, authentic leadership and others. My hope in sharing these five is to wet your appetite to know more and realize that your philosophy and view of leadership will chart your course. As described, no theory fully captures all aspects of leadership. There is no 'unified theory' of leadership. As we progress through this discussion of leadership, I pray you will better understand how you currently see leadership and expand your vision to encompass the full spectrum of reality (both human and divine).

Questions for Personal Reflection and Group Discussion

1. Which leadership theories resonated with you? Why?
2. "   "   did not resonate with you? Why?
3. What leadership theory most describes your way of leading and influencing?
4. "   "   would most positively impact culture in your opinion? Why?
5. What are 2-3 examples of toxic leadership in society? Why are they toxic?
6. Which leadership theory do you plan to study to learn more to improve your leadership?

PART II
VALUABLE INSIGHTS ON LEADERSHIP

CHAPTER 3
INSIGHTS FROM GREAT LEADERS

I suppose men are born with traits that can be cultivated in the direction of leadership. But there is also no doubt that leadership can be cultivated. The idea of any man being born an army commander or being born to be a theater commander, such as General Eisenhower, just isn't so. The characteristics of leadership, necessarily has to have certain decisiveness and confidence come from knowledge based on studies and training. The fundamental thing is your basic knowledge, the development of your mind, and your ability to apply this knowledge as you go along your military career.[86]

We simply need to expand our self-image by seeing ourselves as influencers; it's the one job that cuts across every domain of our life. In addition, like any dedicated person, we need to study the works of the influencers who are already good at the job.[87]

---

[86] Lucian Truscott, as quoted in *Nineteen Stars: A Study in Military Character & Leadership* (CA: Presidio, 1971), by Edgar F. Puryear, Jr.— in answer to the question of whether leaders are born or made posed by author.

[87] *Influencer: The Power to Change Anything,* Patterson, McGraw-Hill, 2007, 21.

*Leadership is the art of accomplishing more than
the science of management says is possible.*[88]

'Walk the time-tested path'. This is the opening message of John Eldredge's book on fatherhood and leadership. He recounts visiting Chichagof Island near Alaska. "Our guide led us to a trail of what seemed to be massive footprints, with a stride of about two feet between them, pressed down into the bog and making a path through it. "It's a marked trail," he said. A path created by the footprints of the bears. This one is probably centuries old. For as long as the bears have been on this island, they've taken this path. The cubs follow their elders, putting their feet exactly where the older bears walk. That's how they learn to cross this place."[89] Leadership may involve facing new circumstances or require adaptive solutions, but the fundamentals of leadership do not change through the centuries. If you want to be the best leader possible, you will do well to listen to sage advice from leaders who have gone before you.

This chapter shares the wisdom of those who not only taught leadership, but especially those who lived it. If you are reading this book, I assume you are not looking for affirmation; I assume you have already arrived at the pinnacle of your leadership. My goal is to encourage you to aspire to summit the peak of leadership. If you want to climb Mt Everest, you speak to expert climbers who have successfully climbed the peak— hearing their experiences prepares you for the challenges of training and climbing those heights. The same principle applies to scaling the heights of leadership. This chapter is a compilation of insights and best practices from proven leaders, organized by leadership themes.

Vocation

This word comes from the Latin word, *vocare*, meaning to call. Leadership is a calling associated with an inner stirring for greatness, to serve, to make a difference, to change the world. This is not to say the calling is only for 'great people', an elite crowd or those who win the 'leadership lottery'. No, leadership is a calling for each person. Why? At the most basic human level, we are wired to go beyond ourselves, to improve ourselves, and the lives of others. As we will see later, this can be understood at the deeper level as being created, out of love, by God out and to give love to others.

Me? Be a leader? This is a recurring question from people who consider themselves little, unimportant, or unfit to lead others. Do you feel this way? It is not true. You are called to lead others. The world with its physical, emotional and spiritual challenges calls you to step forward. "For years I stood on the sidelines watching the fight, admiring the Party members for all they were doing, but without being directly involved. Then some crisis in national or international

---

[88] Colin Powell, *The Powell Principles* (2003)

[89] Eldredge, John, *Fathered by God*

affairs blew up and I came to believe that, feeling as I did, I had no right at such a time to be just a spectator when others were giving so much. I felt compelled to come in and join them in the struggle. I would have been betraying myself had I not done so."[90] You are called to enter the struggle of leadership.

Yes, you are in so many ways 'ordinary'. At the same time, can we not say this about everyone you know? None of us are Superman or Wonder Woman. We each have limitations and blind spots. You can still make the choice to answer the call of leadership. "I've also seen relatively ordinary people lead their organizations to greater heights than anyone expected because they believed it was their responsibility to do the most mundane and uncomfortable jobs and tasks."[91] Deep down we connect with this reality— we watch shows and read stories about the 'little guy' who does not come from riches or nobility; he is called to make a difference. Each of us can make a difference by stepping into our leadership calling.

Embrace the idea of leadership as a vocation. This is the opposite of seeing it as 'my right' or 'I earned it'. Unfortunately, many of your contemporaries are blinded or confused about the purpose and meaning of their leadership. You must be wary about falling into this trap. "Like so many people, I never stopped to consider why I should be a leader. As it turns out, the primary motive for most young people, and too many older ones, is the rewards that leadership brings with it. Things like notoriety, status and power. But people who are motivated by these things won't embrace the demands of leadership when they see little or no connection between doing their duties and receiving those rewards. They'll pick and choose how they spend their time and energy based on what they are going to get, rather than what they need to give to the people they're supposed to be leading. This is as dangerous as it is common."[92] He goes on to comment that "they believe that being a leader is the reward for hard work; therefore, the experience of being a leader should be pleasant and enjoyable, free to choose what they work on and avoid anything mundane, unpleasant, or uncomfortable."[93] The pursuit of leadership often starts with good intentions, but it can quickly become a shipwreck—self-centered. We need to be crystal clear that leadership is a calling. It is a responsibility that is difficult, demanding and challenging. You should not expect anything less.

Influence

Influence is the bread and butter of leadership. The simplest definition of leadership is 'to influence others'. We are speaking about interacting with others— affecting their behavior. Think about how you nudge people into one direction through your interactions. Think about how your

---

[90] Hyde, Douglas, *Dedication and Leadership*, 38.

[91] *The Motive*, Pat Lencioni, John Wiley & Sons, Inc, Hoboken, NJ, 2020, 138-39.

[92] Ibid, x.

[93] Ibid, 135.

parents influenced you through their words, support, and love (or lack thereof). Reminisce, for a moment, the influence of good friends over the years and the people with with authority who impacted you. Our relationships and behaviors always form and inform others: the way they think and act. As a leader in training you need to influence intentionally. This often involves helping others alter or channel their behavior. "When it comes to altering behavior, you need to help others answer only two questions. First: Is it worth it? (If not, why waste the effort?) And second: Can they do this thing? (If not, why try?)."[94] Leaders are behavior focused; they cannot be satisfied with nice ideas and intentions. Are people listening and following? Are they working together towards the desired goal? Are there behaviors that are obstacles to what we need to accomplish? Ask yourself these questions every day to form an influence mindset.

It is not enough to have the desire to intentionally influence others — to be behavior focused. Leaders must go further to identify what needs to be harnessed or changed. "Perhaps the most important discovery from Wiwat's work is the notion that in addition to focusing on behavior, you should give special attention to a handful of high-leverage behaviors. Principle number two: Discover a few vital behaviors, change those, and problems-no matter their size-topple like a house of cards."[95] The men and women who demonstrate optimum human leadership are able to hone in on key issues and practices linked to success.

Best-selling author Malcolm Gladwell speaks about influence in his book, *The Tipping Point*. His research reveals that far-reaching influence (which he calls 'epidemics') requires three dimensions: 'The Law of the Few', the Stickiness Factor and the power of context. "The Law of the Few says that Connectors, Mavens, and Salesmen are responsible for starting word-of-mouth epidemics, which means that if you are interested in starting a word-of-mouth epidemic, your resources ought to be solely concentrated on those three groups."[96] The Stickiness Factor says that "there is a simple way to package information that, under the right circumstances, can make it irresistible. All you have to do is find it."[97] Lastly, the power of context tells us that circumstances and personal emotions (not only inner dispositions and convictions) drive decision and action. These three are equally important for leaders who want a far-reaching influence.

Jim Collins ranks among the most influential leadership researchers in the past 100 years. His book *Good to Great* is a classic read by leaders in all sectors of influence. He demonstrated through his research that maximum influence is shown by what he calls the 'Level 5 Leader.' "The eleven good-to-great CEOs are some of the most remarkable CEOs of the century, given

---

[94] Influencer: *The Power to Change Anything*, Patterson, McGraw-Hill, 2007, 50.

[95] Ibid, 28.

[96] Gladwell, Malcolm, *The Tipping Point: How Little Things can make a Big Difference*, Back Bay Books, New York, NY, 2002, 256.

[97] Ibid, 132.

that only eleven companies from the Fortune 500 met the exacting standards for entry into this study. Yet, despite their remarkable results, almost no one ever remarked about them! ... The good-to-great leaders never wanted to become larger-than-life heroes. They never aspired to be put on a pedestal or become unreachable icons. They were seemingly ordinary people quietly producing extraordinary results. ...It is very important to grasp that Level 5 leadership is not just about humility and modesty. It is equally about ferocious resolve, an almost stoic determination to do whatever needs to be done to make the company great."[98]

Can you be trained to have this type of influence? Can you transform into a Level 5 leader? Asked about this possibility, Jim Collins responds saying "my hypothesis is that there are two categories of people: those who do not have the seed of Level 5 and those who do. ... The second category of people—and I suspect the larger group—consists of those who have the potential to evolve to Level 5; the capability resides within them, perhaps buried or ignored, but there nonetheless. And under the right circumstances—self-reflection, conscious personal development, a mentor, a great teacher, loving parents, a significant life experience, a Level 5 boss, or any number of other factors—they begin to develop."[99] It is noteworthy that the heights of influence are built upon a humble, open spirit who's willing to learn, and change for the good of others.

Of the many aspects of influence, I would like to highlight storytelling. This influential skill has gained popularity in business, politics and university classrooms. Are you an expert storyteller? If not, you need to work on this. From Socrates and Demosthenes to Jesus Christ as well as contemporary leaders , storytelling is an art capable of multiplying your influence capability through communication. How do you do it? There are books written about this this as well as good YouTube videos sharing best practices. In short,

> **The first step is to make your reader or viewer identify your character as someone he knows. Step two-if the author can make the audience imagine that what is happening can happen to him, the situation will be permeated with aroused emotion and the viewer will experience a sensation so great that he will feel not as a spectator but as the participant of an exciting drama before him. Concrete and vivid stories exert extraordinary influence...**
>
> **Tell the whole story. Make sure that the narrative you're employing contains a clear link between the current behaviors and existing negative results. Also make sure that the story includes positive replacement behaviors that yield new and**

---

[98] Collins, Jim, *Good to Great* (quoted from - https://www.jimcollins.com/concepts/level-five-leadership.html)

[99] Ibid.

better results. Remember, stories need to deal with both "Will it be worth it?" and "Can I do it?" When it comes to changing behavior, nothing else matters.[100]

We all know from experience the power of a good story. It not only captures our imagination, but makes us associate ourselves with it. It let's us see paths and possibilities that were previously unopened.

I offer you a concluding thought on influence: as you think about the problems you're trying to resolve, don't be afraid to draw on the power of intrinsic satisfiers. As Don Berwick so aptly stated: "The biggest motivators of excellence are intrinsic. They have to do with people's accountability to themselves. It's wanting to do well, to be proud, to go home happy having accomplished something."[101] Leaders will always grow when they connect their vocation to leadership with intrinsic motivations. Keep this in mind around those you serve as a leader: family, friends, coworkers and anyone under your charge—Influence by connecting with the inner motivations of others.

Power

Leadership is power? "Power" is pejorative in today's culture. Leadership includes the exercise of power (authority), but is not limited to it. It is not uncommon to see men and women in roles of authority drunk with power. Let us not confuse these bad examples with the neutral nature of power. Power is inextricably part of human life: "The reason is that power is inherent to our nature as human beings and is part and parcel of human experience. I come to this broad conclusion from the scholarly insights of philosophical anthropology. Human beings have a peculiar relationship to nature and the natural world—one of indeterminacy, an indeterminacy so great that it threatens our very existence."[102] Let us accept that power and authority are allotted more to some than others in our society. This is a neutral reality. What matters is how we use power.

Some ideologies claim it possible to organize a society without power concentrating in certain people. History shows that it is not possible.

> **Power is not just an expression of the relationship of human beings to nature but of human beings to each other. Human beings are constituted and continually formed by the relationships we have with others. And yet human beings have differing capacities to act in the world and to influence the environment around them. It is for this reason that interdependency is built into human experience. We**

---

[100] Influencer: *The Power to Change Anything*, Patterson, McGraw-Hill, 2007, 72.

[101] Ibid, 109.

[102] Hunter, James, *To Change the World*, 177.

need each other and the abilities and talents everyone brings to make survival possible. But this fact means that power is inherently asymmetrical. Someone, some group, some institutions will always have more capacity to act than others and someone, some group, and some institution will always have a greater capacity to acquire resources than others. Indeed, part of their power is the capacity—at least the potential—to deprive others of the ability to act or accumulate.[103]

I appeal to the young leaders to whom we entrust the future. Ideological groups have falsely claimed they will transform society by making it more just and equal without the need of power. Look at Communism in the past two centuries; communism in its every manifestation has a small group of power-hungry men and women at the top, brutally imposing their ideology with ruthless destruction upon the populace. Let us cease and desist from the quest for the utopia of a society where power is not held by certain individuals. The best option history offers us is to train virtuous leaders and to distribute power in such way that it is not held by small groups of elites. A series of checks-and-balances is needed no matter the organization.

Culture Change

Leadership implies change. Change what? Ideas, behaviors and attitudes. One word describes these three: culture. Change in leadership and culture go hand in hand. This plays out in family, work, and social life— it touches what we teach in school to youth and informs what they value. "The first responsibility of a leader is to define reality. The last is to say thank you. In between the two, the leader must become a servant and a debtor. That sums up the progress of an artful leader."[104] Have you thought about the consequences of your words and decisions? Do you realize that you are responsible for culture change? Are you making an intentional effort to make a positive impact?

An important dimension of leadership and culture change is to recognize that it starts at the top of the influence pyramid. Influential leaders make the most significant impact on culture changes. Leadership and culture expert, Dr James Hunter, says "the deepest and most enduring forms of cultural change nearly always occurs from the "top down." In other words, the work of world-making and world-changing are, by and large, the work of elites: gatekeepers who provide creative direction and management within spheres of social life. Even where the impetus for change draws from popular agitation, it does not gain traction until it is embraced and propagated by elites."[105] This is an important concept to understand and internalize. Many of us are naïve; convinced by the modern myth that we can all change culture together. This is

---

[103] Ibid, 177.

[104] Max De Pree, in Leadership Is an Art (1989), p. 9

[105] Hunter, James, *To Change the World*, 41

true but primarily limited to our collaboration with small groups of elites who 'nudge' us into the direction they want.

This is an uncomfortable subject for many. It is easier to live in the paradigm; believing each of us has equal influence and opportunity to change culture. It is not reality. "The reason for this, as I have said, is that culture is about how societies define reality—what is good, bad, right, wrong, real, unreal, important, unimportant, and so on. This capacity is not evenly distributed in a society, but is concentrated in certain institutions and among certain leadership groups who have a lopsided access to the means of cultural production. These elites operate in well-developed networks and powerful institutions. Over time, cultural innovation is translated and diffused. Deep-rooted cultural change tends to begin with those whose work is most conceptual and invisible and it moves through to those whose work is most concrete and visible."[106]

There is a pattern for culture change. It starts with networks of influential leaders who have access to institutions such as politics, business, media, education and journalism. "In a very crude formulation, the process begins with theorists who generate ideas and knowledge; moves to researchers who explore, revise, expand, and validate ideas; moves on to teachers and educators who pass those ideas on to others, then passes on to popularizers who simplify ideas and practitioners who apply those ideas. All of this, of course, transpires through networks and structures of cultural production. Cultural change is most enduring when it penetrates the structure of our imagination, frameworks of knowledge and discussion, the perception of everyday reality. This rarely if ever happens through grassroots political mobilization though grassroots mobilization can be a manifestation of deeper cultural transformation."[107] This insight is sobering; might make us feel helpless. History shows us that many changes in culture are out of our hands—controlled by small groups of influential men and women. These individuals control culture shifts from a human perspective. I highlight this here since the above perspective does not directly account for the role of the divine and supernatural in culture change. We will look at this in more depth in subsequent chapters.

Culture seems to be changing at an accelerated rate. Technology, views on family life, roles in society and expectations about life are morphing within generational time periods. Why is it happening now? "When networks of elites in overlapping fields of culture and overlapping spheres of social life come together with their varied resources and act in common purpose, cultures do change and change profoundly. Persistence over time is essential; little of significance happens in three to five years. But when cultural and symbolic capital overlap with social capital and economic capital and, in time, political capital, and these various resources are directed toward shared ends, the world, indeed, changes."[108] Clearly, a globally connected

---

[106] Ibid, 41.

[107] Ibid, 42.

[108] Ibid, 43.

world facilitates rapid change. There is, however, an intentional effort between networks of influencers in various sectors to change the way we think and act about certain issues: freedom without constraints; rights; diversity; gender fluidity; marriage as something that can be redefined; democracy and capitalism as evil; tolerance of evil as an absolute good that should be enshrined in law; conscience and religious protection as something to be rejected.

So where does this leave us? Is there anything I can do as an average leader or person who aspires leadership? Please do not lose motivation because of the above. Culture change is a fact and leaders have a central role in it. As God's plan would have it, the 'little guy' (you and me) does play a big part in history;Culture landscapes are not to be measured simply by large scale changes on the world scene. The first culture you can change is your own destiny by taking responsibility of your life, how you think and see reality, as well as how you behave and treat others. This will, in turn, affects others. Our measure of leadership should not be solely focused on big picture culture change, but on the life changes of those around us who have been direct recipients of our influence. We should start there and trust our impact is making a difference in the big picture of history.

Self-Reflection: Know Yourself, Know Others

Leaders are busy people. With many concerns; many activities; many goals. Many people to help. During a Houston Business Journal executives evening, I was struck by a speaker who had interviewed hundreds of business and cultural leaders around the world. One of them said that less than 5% of these leaders spent 10 minutes or more each month to quiet their minds and reflect on what they had lived in past weeks.

When you read leadership books and hear experts speak about key leadership traits, self-reflection is often mentioned. "Here's a simple way to think about the connection between self-reflection and leadership: If you are not self-reflective, how can you truly know yourself? If you do not know yourself, how can you lead yourself? And if you cannot lead yourself, how can you possibly lead others?"[109] It is a key factor for distinguishing true and effective leaders from those who simply inherit or bulldoze their way into positions of influence.

We are not referring to prayer here. Self-reflection is the capacity for and habit of going inside yourself and reviewing past experiences, memories, your thoughts, and actions. This is an ability unique to the human race. Animals act out of instinct and sensual memory but the human person (thanks to the immaterial soul) can go 'outside' the limits of materiality and examine oneself. Famous philosopher and author of the *L'Encyclopédie* project, Denis Diderot, comments saying "grace causes the Christian to act, reason the philosopher. Other men are carried away by their passions, their actions not being preceded by reflection: these are the men who walk in darkness. On the other hand, the philosopher, even in his passions, acts only after

---

[109] Kraemer, Harry, *From Values to Action: The Four Principles of Values-Based Leadership*, 5

reflection; he walks in the dark, but by a torch."[110] This habit is not innate. Like so many other leadership habits, it must be formed and developed— we are all capable of being self-reflective . Be aware that the noise and distraction of media, music and frenetic activity will keep you from being a person of self-reflection. If you want to develop this habit, it is critical to find time every day to be still, quiet— without filling minutes and space with activities. This happens when you remember events in your heart and even journal to help you recall and record your experiences.This is a challenge and a habit that all students of leadership must embrace in the 21st Century if they are to be true leaders .

Know yourself. Know others. This is sage advice and key to leadership. A powerful summary of this theme is given in the book *The Way of the Shepherd*. The authors recommend five dimensions for self-reflection on self and others using the acronym SHAPE: strengths, heart, attitude, personality and experiences.

Strengths. Do you know your strengths? The strengths of others? What are they? Do I lead with my (and others') strengths in mind? "Always try to place people where they can operate out of their strengths and not their weaknesses. The first step is to understand the strengths of the people on your team, or the people who are about to join it."[111] Clifton Strengths is a wonderful tool to better know yourself. It would be a good investment only worth a few dollars and the time to take this self-knowledge test.

Heart. We often focus on our heart, our wants, our passions. Do I know the passions and desires of others? Do I place those things front and center when I lead? "It doesn't matter how strong you are in a given area if you're not motivated to exercise that strength, so I want to know what my people are passionate about. If I put them in areas that reflect their passions…They'll begin to think of their job more as a cause than a place to draw a paycheck. That's a big difference!"[112] This is a big step for many. Our work trains us to be self-centered; we find it difficult to live constantly thinking about the others' desires, needs, and passions. It is a big attitudinal conversion. It requires an about-face in the way we think and where we focus. Get this right, it will change your leadership and command the respect and loyalty of those you influence.

Attitude. Is your attitude habitually positive? Negative? Take a moment to think about this because others know it. They see your leadership based on your attitude. If you have a habitually negative attitude, you are limiting your leadership. Next, look at the attitude of those you influence. "I can't emphasize this one enough. You want positive, can-do people. Given a choice between talent and attitude, I'll take attitude every time…people with a good attitude are

---

[110] Denis Diderot in the article on Philosophy, Vol. 25, p. 667, in L'Encyclopédie (1751 - 1766).

[111] Pentak, Leman, *The Way of the Shepherd*, 33.

[112] Ibid, 34.

usually team players. For another, they usually have a teachable spirit. People with negative attitudes tend to be lone rangers."[113] I am not advocating to give up on or write off the people with a negative attitude. I am, however, inviting you to know those around you and recognize the limitations of those with negative attitudes; they're i harmful both for themselves and others. Negativity is an internal cancer that harms the individual. Be realistic with people who are habitually negative, though it is not easy, you sometimes need to give them space, recommend coaching (or even a good therapist). As a last resort, be ready to remove them from your team after taking the appropriate steps to warn them about the consequences for repeated negativity.

Personality. What is yours? Have you stopped to think about the personalities of those you serve as a leader? Your spouse's personality? Your child's? Your coworker's? "Some are extraverts, others introverts. Some people love repetition…others would sooner crawl down into a hole and die if they can't have some variety. Some people thrive on structure. Some thrive on change. The point is to put a person in a position that reflects his or her personality."[114] Why do teams and organizations fail? Why are there so many problems in marriage and family dynamics? One reason is not paying attention to personality differences. We want and expect others to think and react the way we do. We look at others through the lens of our personality. An important step in your leadership is reflecting on the personality of those around you: speak to their personality— motivate and entrust tasks that resonate with who they are. .

Experiences. Think of your life for a moment. Your life has a rich history of experiences. Yes, there are many good ones but also some you wish did not happen. There are some things which give you a rough edge and perhaps even traumatized you. These experiences affect your leadership. It is important to come to grips with them and integrate them so your life is harmonious and not divided. If not properly integrated, you will find yourself full of self-loathing, thinking you are not loveable, believing you are a mistake or will always fall short. It can even lead to depression, despair, and suicide when the downward spiral is not stopped. Please do not hesitate to speak with a trained therapist who is also open to the transcendent and God's role in our healing. The above is equally true for those you lead. "Each person you meet is a product of their life experiences. Often the key to understanding an individual and the key to knowing where to place him or her on your team is to learn something about the person's various experiences."[115] Spend time with those you lead. Ask them open-ended questions about their life story. Take time to learn about them. This is not a superficial show in order to get them to do what you want. Be authentic. Be there with them. If you take the time to know those you serve, you will understand their story and be in a better position to help them find their place —their mission at hand. You will be able to encourage them to go towards what will be most helpful for them. True leaders get to know their people, which includes knowing the experiences that most shaped their lives.

---

[113] Ibid, 34.

[114] Ibid, 37.

[115] Ibid, 38.

Clear Hedgehog Concept

This concept applies no matter your sector of leadership. For-profit or non-profit businesses. Schools. Churches. Political action. Historical research demonstrates that leaders and organizations with a clearly defined mission and a focused organization are more effective. Jim Collins is a good reference in this area. *Good to Great* speaks about the Hedgehog concept. This concept combines three critical questions. First, what are you deeply passionate about? Second, what can you be the best in the world at? Third, what drives your economic (or resource) engine? Collins says "a Hedgehog Concept is not a goal to be the best, a strategy to be the best, an intention to be the best, a plan to be the best. It is an understanding of what you can be the best at. The distinction is absolutely crucial. Every company would like to be the best at something, but few actually understand—with piercing insight and egoless clarity—what they actually have the potential to be the best at and, just as important, what they cannot-be the best at. And it is this distinction that stands as one of the primary contrasts between the good-to-great companies and the comparison companies."[116] According to Jim Collins, the most effective leaders are not just 'Level 5', but also operate from within their Hedgehog. These leaders and their organizations have clear answers to the three questions above. Their decisions, time allocations, and resources are driven by the it.

There are consequences of a clear hedgehog. Yes, it will bring focus. Yes, it will make you more effective. It will, however, require you to cut-bait with certain lines of business—programs that are ineffective, and good things that are not consistent with your hedgehog. Collins says "to go from good to great requires transcending the curse of competence. It requires the discipline to say, "Just because we are good at it—just because we're making money and generating growth—doesn't necessarily mean we can become the best at it." The good-to-great companies understood that doing what you are good at will only make you good; focusing solely on what you can potentially do better than any other organization is the only path to greatness."[117] This aspect of leadership is not about going around saying 'I'm the best', but rather making a serious investment of time, talent and treasure. It is to commit to good stewardship and pursue excellence in your endeavors.

Motivating Others to Accomplish a Goal

Along with influence, this is perhaps the most simple and common definition of leadership. "Leadership is the art of accomplishing more than the science of management says

---

[116] Collins, Jim, Good to Great (quoted at https://www.jimcollins.com/concepts/the-hedgehog-concept.html)

[117] Ibid.

Insights from great leaders

is possible."[118] Working with others to accomplish a goal is part-and-parcel of leadership. The first and most important goal for leaders to accomplish is to help those they influence to maximize their potential and fulfill their destiny to love and be loved. They commit to the improvement of those under their charge. Pat Lencioni teaches that "all of my people have their issues…Everybody has something…And it's my job to help them get better."[119] I cannot stress enough that our focus as leaders should be on others before we consider generic, 'cold' goals. Goals can and often are laudable, necessary in their respective sectors of society (such as tasks at work). We each should examine our hearts, however, to see if we are focused on the good of others. This is the most important goal. If we are focused on others and their overall good, things will go well long-term. People we lead will know they are respected, known for who they are and valued. They will be motivated to work together and strive for greater excellence in the goals we set before them. This is summarized well by leadership legends, Peter Drucker and Warren Bennis, who remind us that "**management is doing** things right; leadership is doing the right things."[120]

This translates into the way leaders see their people. Again turning to Peter Drucker, who tells us "successful leaders don't start out asking, "What do I want to do?" They ask, "What needs to be done?" Then they ask, "Of those things that would make a difference, which are right for me?" They don't tackle things they aren't good at. They make sure other necessities get done, but not by them. Successful leaders make sure that they succeed. They are not afraid of strength in others. **Andrew Carnegie wanted** to put on his gravestone, "Here lies a man who knew how to put into his service more able men than he was himself.""[121] Great leaders see the inherent worth of others and empower them towards the goals at hand. We can, indeed, accomplish great things but we cannot do it alone. We need the collective genius and talent of others to achieve our goals. Speaking of Andrew Carnegie, he was known to have said "no man will make a great leader who wants to do it all himself, or to get all the credit for doing it."[122] Are you this type of leader? One who tries to do it all alone, who wants the credit for himself?

'Let's take that hill.' This is not necessarily the rally cry in a war. It is the spirit behind each goal, each deliverable a leader asks of his team. We know from experience that it is not enough to indicate a hill to take, but a goal to achieve. True leadership implies those with us want to go

---

[118] Colin Powell, *The Powell Principles* (2003)

[119] *The Motive*, Pat Lencioni, 48-49

[120] Peter Drucker, and Warren Bennis, as quoted in *Seven Habits of Highly Effective People* (1989) by Stephen R. Covey, p. 101

[121] Peter Drucker, as quoted in "'What Needs to Be Done', Peter Drucker On Leadership", an interview with Rich Karlgaard in Forbes magazine (19 November 2004)

[122] Andrew Carnegie, as quoted in Managing Software Development Projects : Formula for Success(1995) by Neal Whitten, p. 63

there. It is not about motivation alone, but rather about the follower's heart desiring what the leader asks. President Eisenhower said "the essence of leadership is to get others to do something because they think you want it done and because they know it is worthwhile doing -- that is what we are talking about."[123] Think about times you worked for or collaborated with someone in a leadership role. Did you do your part because it was expected as your job? Did you really believe in what you were doing? Did you make the goal your own? Something you believed in?

The former emperor of **Ethiopia, Haile Selassie I**, said "the art of leadership is in the ability to make people want to work for you, while they are really under no obligation to do so. Leaders are people, who raise the standards by which they judge themselves and by which they are willing to be judged. The goal chosen, the objective selected, the requirements imposed, are not mainly for their followers alone. They develop with consummate energy and devotion, their own skill and knowledge in order to reach the standard they themselves have set."[124] This is what true leaders seek. They want those they steward and influence to embrace the goals and the work required. Once again, I encourage you to embrace putting the good of others at the center of your leadership. This is the first and most critical step for others to embrace your leadership.

Embrace Challenges

Think of a leader you admire. Who is it? Did they have challenges? Be crystal clear. They did, many of them. Think about Admiral William McRaven. This contemporary military leader was responsible for thousands of anti-terrorist operations around the world. Now take just one mission. An unforgettable mission. To capture terrorist Osama bin Laden after he engineered the September 11, 2001 attack on the Twin Towers and the Pentagon. It was a tough mission that required months of research and surveillance, prudential conversations and silence, debate with military, intelligence and political leaders meetings about the best course of action, ground-air team's training and rehearsal, as well as the actual mission itself. Read McRaven's book, *Sea Stories*, for the full details, but suffice to say it was a mission that required everything from this leader.

A Canadian journalist wrote that ""Safety first" has been the motto of the human race for half a million years; but it has never been the motto of leaders. A leader must face danger. He must take the risk and the blame, and the brunt of the storm."[125] This is the part of leadership that

---

[123] Dwight D. Eisenhower, Remarks at the Republican Campaign Picnic at the President's Gettysburg Farm (September 12, 1956). Source: Eisenhower Presidential Library. Archived from the original on January 25, 2021.

[124] Haile Selassie I, Speech on Leadership in Speeches Delivered on Various Occasions, May 1957-December 1959 (1960), p. 138

[125] Herbert N. Casson in: The Office Economist (1935) Vol. 17-21. p. 145

some (young and old) do not want. They lack the commitment, dedication, and selflessness to embrace the challenges required. Some might say, 'I am a hard worker, I am committed'. This is no doubt true of many, but it is insufficient for true leadership, for the heights and pinnacle of leadership. Why?

The reason is we easily put limits on how much we are willing to give of ourselves. Most leaders and influences work hard but they also tend to draw back when the leadership required asks them to put their ego aside or to sacrifice their popularity to do the right thing. "All of the great leaders have had one characteristic in common: it was the willingness to confront unequivocally the major anxiety of their people in their time. This, and not much else, is the essence of leadership."[126] This rings true, but leaders often stop short of confronting those things which harm and stifle those under their care. Think of the parent who turns a blind eye to the drugs or pornography enslaving their child. Reflect on politicians who strive for popularity and reelection instead of speaking the hard truths about public policies that stifle those they represent. Recall examples of senior business leaders who focused on lucrative payouts instead of the jobs of their employees.

The 21st Century presents leaders with another challenge. They are called to lead in a time when many 'experts' will tell them what they should do. Back-seat leaders with a Ph.D or large social media following can be quick to criticize leadership decisions. These people are often outside their swim lane with little basis for their advice. It would be like an English teacher giving an airplane pilot direction on how to land in bad weather. Those in leadership roles must be able to distinguish those they should ignore and those whose advice is worth considering. Even in the case of listening to true experts, it is sometimes necessary to not follow their guidance. Former prime minister of the United Kingdom, James Callaghan, said "a leader must have the courage to act against an expert's advice."[127] This takes grit and conviction both to seek expert input and to make a well-discerned decision. It is not easy and will require tough nerves as well as openness to make mistakes. As you gain experience and seek experts' advice, you will develop the capacity to know when to go with (or against) what the experts suggest.

Effective Communication

Leadership and communication go hand in hand. It is difficult to think of a leader who cannot communicate. Bad communication is a sure ingredient for disaster in an organization, a family, or a team. Are you a good communicator? I am not just asking about public speaking. Do you share your vision and ideas in a way that attracts others? Do you communicate in a way that is confusing or simply does not connect with others? I have good news for you: you can learn to improve your communication skills as a leader. I was impressed by an example in the book,

---

[126] John Kenneth Galbraith in *The Age of Uncertainty* (1977), Ch. 12

[127] James Callaghan, The Harvard Business Review (1 November 1986)

Dedication and Leadership. The author describes how he trained all types of people to speak in front of groups. He even had one man with a severe stutter who, through training and practice, became a group organizer and speaker at his workplace.

Communication requires diligent work and effort. George Patton gives us a healthy reminder when he says that "wars may be fought with weapons, but they are won by men. It is the spirit of the men who follow and of the man who leads that gains the victory."[128] The quest for leadership requires you to make the commitment to dedicate yourself to be a good communicator. This dedication implies you seek feedback on it. . It means you must be the first one to go out and talk with your people and engage them in their mission. Good communication starts with you showing interest in others and their realities.

Communication also implies follow-up and accountability. A good leader does not leave anything to chance. He repeats the key messages over-and-over again. He reminds people of their vision, mission, and they need now. He reminds them of his belief in them. "I'm talking about being a constant, incessant reminder of the company's purpose, strategy, values, priorities. I like to say that you're not only the CEO, you're the CRO…the chief reminding officer. Constant reminders which includes updates and stories. There is no such thing as communicating too much about the important stuff."[129] We do not want to annoy people, but it is the leader's job to safeguard the key messages of the mission at hand. He must own it and lead by example. If there is confusion about the vision, mission and expectations, the leader must own this as his fault. When there is subpar performance and even abject failure, the leader should be the first one to take responsibility, apologize and present a plan of action for the organization to change.

Conclusion

In this chapter, we examined several perennial leadership themes and behaviors. This was by no means exhaustive.The selection was chosen by consulting many recognized leaders and texts. Before proceeding to the next chapter, take a few minutes to re-examine what you just read. Which area struck you the most? In which one do you need to improve your attitude and behavior to be a better leader? Vocation? Influence? Power? Culture change? Self-reflection? Motivating others to accomplish a goal? Embracing challenges? Effective communication? Having a clear hedgehog concept?

Take some time to think on a strategy to grow your awareness of one of these. How do you do this? Several options include: read a seminal book on that theme; consult one or two leaders and a them to share their experience on the theme you chose; ask someone you trust to give you regular feedback on how you are improving in that area. Leaders are proactive and do not

---

[128] George S. Patton, in Cavalry Journal (September 1933)

[129] Pat Lencioni, *The Motive*, 100.

leave things to chance. If you recognize a blind spot or area for growth, embrace and lean into this opportunity.

Questions for Personal Reflection and Group Discussion

1. What leadership insights were mentioned in this chapter?
2. Which one struck me the most? Why?
3. What does 'leadership as a vocation' mean to you?
4. What are some examples of influence? Of power? How can they be used for good or evil?
5. What is your greatest obstacle to making time for self-reflection? When, where and how do you do this?
6. Are you an effective communicator? What would help you improve?
7. What motivates you? How do you motivate others? Do you ask them for feedback on how well received (or not) is your style of motivating?
8. Do you have a clear hedgehog concept? What is it? What changes (if any) do you need to make to adhere to it?

CHAPTER 4
DIFFERENT WORLDVIEWS

World views, as related to the sciences, ethics, arts, politics and religions, are integral parts of all cultures. They have a strongly motivating and inspiring function. A socially shared view of the whole gives a culture a sense of direction, confidence and self-esteem. Moreover, interactions between cultures change constantly.[130]

Both Religion and science require a belief in God. For believers, God is in the beginning, and for physicists He is at the end of all considerations... To the former He is the foundation, to the latter, the crown of the edifice of every generalized world view.[131]

Imagine being at a networking function at a beautiful club in Washington DC. There are business leaders, politicians, young professionals and nonprofit sector representatives presenting for this important occasion. I was also there as a Catholic priest and business ethics representative for US Hispanic Chamber of Commerce. After the champagne toast, I turned

---

[130] Diederick Aerts, Leo Apostel, Bart De Moor, Staff Hellemans, Edel Maex, Hubert Van Belle & Jan Van der Veken (1994) World views. From Fragmentation to Integration. Vrije Universiteit Brussel, VUB Press. p. 8.

[131] Max Planck Religion and Natural Science (Lecture Given 1937).

and stood in front of me was a woman with a scowl on her face— before I could say anything, she asked "why are you here"? I extended my hand and introduced myself. I then proceeded to explain that I was the business ethics advisor for the Chamber. The scowl on her face remained as she said; " you have no business being here". This led to an interesting discussion. She admitted she had travelled to Washington DC not only for this event, but also for an atheist convention. This was one of those moments when the importance of worldview hit me head on. It was through her worldview that she saw the event we attended and my presence there.

We continue our exploration of leadership by considering the importance of your worldview. Why is this so important? Is it arbitrary? Is this not something at 40,000 feet up the air and leadership on the ground, practical living? Our answers to these questions greatly influence the quality of our leadership. Our worldview is the lens by which we interpret reality. The worldview we hold is affected by several things such as our cultural background, personal habits, traditions, philosophical view of reality, and, of course, religion. As we saw earlier in this book, relativism is an example of a popular philosophical view of reality, which conditions your worldview. If you had the experience of a close-knit family who played board games and ate meals together, you probably have a worldview that sees strong family life as important and valuable. These and many other experiences come together to help you see your place (and others) in reality.

According to author David Noebel, there are six major worldviews present in the 21st century: the Christian worldview, the Islamic worldview, the secular humanist worldview, the Marxist worldview, the cosmic humanist (or New Age) worldview, and the post-modern worldview. Each of these has a perspective and position on the following disciplines that make up a worldview: theology, philosophy, ethics, biology, psychology, sociology, law, politics, economics, and history. I will add the Hindu worldview as a seventh since it has about 1.3 billion adherents (mostly in India).

Let's take a quick look at each of these worldviews. Secular humanism and Marxism are present in many educational institutions and influence the formation of future generations. Despite clear intellectual flaws, they continue to be popular— younger generations are easily manipulated into subscribing to their ideology. Postmodernism represents a form of cultural relativism touching on subjects such as truth, reality, reason, and the meaning of language. The New Age worldview is an eclectic smattering of eastern religious traditions with other religions that produce a 'whatever you decide for yourself is right as long as it is not too exclusive or narrow-minded' outlook on life. Islam claims 1.8 billion adherents and offers a worldview informed by the claims of Mohammed to be the last prophet sent by God to reveal his will.

The final worldview is Christianity. It is the worldview I will unpack at some length in the following pages. Why highlight this worldview and not the others? First, it is the worldview shared by the greatest percentage of human beings on the planet (around 2.4 billion), including many in North and South America as well as Europe. Secondly, the other worldviews are newer than Christianity. Third, many things we value in Western civilization began with (or at least were promoted by) Christian culture: modern science, universities, hospitals, the free market economy and international law. Each of these examples was highly influenced by the Christian worldview (for reference, see the book *How the Catholic Church Built Western Civilization*). Postmodernism, New Age, and Marxism are 'worldview fads' that only for about a century, propagated in certain sectors by intellectual and social elites. Existing 14 centuries, Islam has been concentrated in the Middle East and Africa where sharia law often enforces social adherence.

Secular humanism owes much of its worldview to the Enlightenment period and further developed in the 19th century. Among the current worldviews, Christianity is the largest as well as had the longest tradition. Although the following thoughts will be about the Christian worldview, it is important to note that some of what follows is also part of the Jewish faith tradition since there are many consistent views between these two divinely inspired religions. For greater study, I recommend the *Bible* (especially the New Testament) and the *Catechism of the Catholic Church*. This second reference provides a systematic summary of Christian teaching on belief, worship, behavior, and prayer.

The Christian worldview starts with creation; God makes everything that exists out of love and for the good of mankind. "Creation is the foundation of all God's saving plans, the beginning of the history of salvation that culminates in Christ. Conversely, the mystery of Christ casts conclusive light on the mystery of creation and reveals the end for which "in the beginning God created the heavens and the earth": from the beginning, God envisaged the glory of the new creation in Christ."[132] The created universe and its materiality are good. Contrary to dualistic philosophies, Christianity posits the physical (including the human body) as good and in no way contrary to the spirit. The physical is not a 'prison' for the human spirit. "Because creation comes forth from God's goodness, it shares in that goodness - "And God saw that it was good. . . very good" for God willed creation as a gift addressed to man, an inheritance destined for and entrusted to him. On many occasions the Church has had to defend the goodness of creation, including the physical world."[133] Despite some opinions, Christianity offers a very positive view of the physical dimension of reality. It readily defends the validity of the physical sciences as well as the beauty and dignity of human sexuality.

God and all he has created is good. Mankind, however, experiences brokenness, a tendency towards selfishness, hate, violence, and dominating others. Our freedom is weakened and easily moved towards evil. We, leaders included, often succumb to choices beneath the goodness we are called to practice.

---

[132] Catechism of the Catholic Church, 280.

[133] Ibid, 299.

> **God is infinitely good and all his works are good. Yet no one can escape the experience of suffering or the evils in nature which seem to be linked to the limitations proper to creatures: and above all to the question of moral evil. Where does evil come from? "I sought whence evil comes and there was no solution", said St. Augustine, and his own painful quest would only be resolved by his conversion to the living God. For "the mystery of lawlessness" is clarified only in the light of the "mystery of our religion". The revelation of divine love in Christ manifested at the same time the extent of evil and the superabundance of grace. We must therefore approach the question of the origin of evil by fixing the eyes of our faith on him who alone is its conqueror.[134]**

Most religions have a name for evil choices—sins in Christianity. They are choices that are either against the love of God, love of other people, or against ourselves. Leaders need to keep this tendency in mind as they lead others. Everyone (including the greatest saints) sin. None of us is perfect. You will need a healthy dose of realism about our human weaknesses as you lead others.

Why do we sin? Why do we choose evil? As a leader, you need to have an answer to these questions. Evil is mysterious. "Only the light of divine Revelation clarifies the reality of sin and particularly of the sin committed at mankind's origins. Without the knowledge Revelation gives of God we cannot recognize sin clearly and are tempted to explain it as merely a developmental flaw, a psychological weakness, a mistake, or the necessary consequence of an inadequate social structure. Only in the knowledge of God's plan for man can we grasp that sin is an abuse of the freedom that God gives to created persons so that they are capable of loving him and loving one another."[135] Each one of us needs to come to grips with our choices. No one makes choices for you. Ultimate finger-pointing for your actions must come back to yourself. You and you alone make choices. This includes those that are evil and, as a leader, you need to own this.

The ultimate origin of sin and personal weakness is explained in many religious traditions. In a Judeo-Christian belief, human freedom is weak due to our first parents' turn against God's will. "The account of the fall in Genesis 3 uses figurative language, but affirms a primeval event, a deed that took place at the beginning of the history of man. Revelation gives us the certainty of faith that the whole of human history is marked by the original fault freely committed by our first parents."[136] Mankind's knowledge of the Creator, as well as his desires, over the course of history, has become debased. . St Paul speaks to this reality in his Letter to the Romans saying "while claiming to be wise, they became fools and exchanged the glory of the immortal God for the likeness of an image of mortal man or of birds or of four-legged animals or of snakes.

---

[134] Ibid, 385.

[135] Ibid, 387.

[136] Ibid, 390.

Therefore, God handed them over to impurity through the lusts of their hearts for the mutual degradation of their bodies. They exchanged the truth of God for a lie and revered and worshiped the creature rather than the creator, who is blessed forever. Amen."[137] This tendency lives in us today. As a leader, it is important to recognize the trend towards disobedience to God and the created moral order.Love God above all, and love your neighbor as yourself.

Leaders need know what they are up against. The quest for leadership is a confrontation with human weakness. Yes, each person we lead can be selfish, vane, or a slave to power and pleasure. We need, however, to keep in mind that there is a more sinister intelligence at work, bent on our destruction. Look at the history of the world. What do you see? Death and destruction; the manipulation of nations and peoples' lives. This is not random chance. You can see the finger print of an intelligence behind this. Many religions identify the source and embodiment of evil as a spirit. In the Judeo-Christian worldview, "behind the disobedient choice of our first parents lurks a seductive voice, opposed to God, which makes them fall into death out of envy. Scripture and the Church's Tradition see in this being a fallen angel, called "Satan" or the "devil". The Church teaches that Satan was at first a good angel, made by God: "The devil and the other demons were indeed created naturally good by God, but they became evil by their own doing.""[138] Your role as a leader includes confronting this evil one—"the deceiver", as Jesus called him. He is the 'father of lies' and desires only division, destruction, and misery . A true leader says 'begone, Satan. I reject you.' Being a good leader is difficult not only because of the formation required as well as the inherent challenges of human relationships, but also due to the opposition and interference of this intelligent spirit who wants you to fail.

For leaders seeking a worldview that corresponds reality, the Judeo-Christian understanding brings clarity and peace. You will feel an interior freedom when you know the truth of reality, which includes recognizing that life includes spiritual combat. "The whole of man's history has been the story of dour combat with the powers of evil, stretching, so our Lord tells us, from the very dawn of history until the last day. Finding himself in the midst of the battlefield man has to struggle to do what is right, and it is at great cost to himself, and aided by God's grace, that he succeeds in achieving his own inner integrity."[139] This should not surprise us. Look at the challenges of our daily life. Look at what movie genres appeal and inspire us. Good versus evil is a perennial theme that resonates. Leaders embrace the call to combat for the good of others. Leadership is much more than simply leading a team or getting what you want; true leadership involves clutching the flag of your inner freedom and charging forward against the inner forces that try to subjugate you into selfishness, vanity, and pleasure-seeking. True leadership is helping others do the same against the forces of evil that will try to corrupt their hearts.

The Judeo-Christian worldview would not be complete without mentioning the fulfillment of all

---

[137] Romans 1:22-25.

[138] Catechism of the Catholic Church, 391.

[139] Ibid, 409.

desire. The entire world needs a savior, a messiah. Christianity proclaims Jesus Christ as the one savior who came among us 2,000 years ago. Christians believe God spoke over through various prophets throughout the ages, but chose Jesus as the definitive Prophet. "Christ, the Son of God made man, is the Father's one, perfect and unsurpassable Word. In him he has said everything; there will be no other word than this one."[140] This is why Christians proclaim Jesus as God's definitive revelation. Do you want to know who God is? Do you want to know what he thinks of the world? Do you desire to understand your place in the universe and in God's eyes? Christianity says look no further: Jesus reveals all of this to you. Christians do not see Jesus as simply an ethical teacher, wonder-worker, or spiritual guru. He is not just one more incarnation of a series of wisemen. No. This is not what Jesus believed about himself and it is not what Christians believe about him. Christians believe Jesus Christ is God made man and the savior of the world. He is the love of God made manifest for all to see giving himself freely in sacrifice crucified on a cross. Risen from the death on the third day, Jesus opens the doors of eternal life to all who embrace him as well as a life lived in the truth following an upright conscience.

The Christian worldview reminds leaders they do not have to confront evil on their own. Jesus Christ has defeated evil, sin, and death. A Christian worldview sees daily life permeated with the presence of a loving God who stands by his children who struggle through the pilgrimage of life. With Jesus Christ, a leader finds strength and support to make God his first love and to embrace all people as those created out of love by God. He embraces the stewardship of leadership with the heart of Christ. This is the theme of the next chapter.

In summary, leadership is directly tied to worldview. Your worldview is a roadmap for interpreting and navigating reality. The quality of your leadership depends on how accurate your worldview matches objective reality. Remember, reality is not what you make it. If you doubt that, look at the physical laws of the universe such as the Law of Gravity. You can deny this law and say it is not an objective reality, but if you jump off a bridge, you will fall and get hurt. As a leader, you need to ensure your worldview is accurate to reality. Christianity offers a robust worldview which has positively contributed to the history of the world. It has the largest following of any worldview and arguably conforms to and explains reality in an accurate and consistent manner. What worldview do you follow? Is it accurate to reality? Does it really answer the deep questions of life such as: who am I? Where do I come from? Why am I here? What is my purpose? Is there an afterlife? Who is God? What has he said and revealed to (and about) humanity? I would propose you do a deeper study on the Christian worldview. You might find yourself surprised by the beauty of what you will find.

---

[140] Ibid, 65.

Different Worldviews

Questions for Personal Reflection and Group Discussion

1. What is a worldview? How would you describe it to a friend who asked?
2. What are the main worldviews presented in this book? Which one most describes your way of interpreting reality?
3. Why was the Christian worldview explained in greater depth?
4. What are the main components of the Christian worldview? Would you add something more than what was written? If so, what and why?
5. What beliefs are common between the worldviews? What are different? You could consider topics such as: God, afterlife, human nature, family, law and order, education, sexuality and leadership.

CHAPTER 5
A JUDEO-CHRISTIAN UNDERSTANDING OF LEADERSHIP

Worldly power expects to be served, while divine omnipotence expects only to serve. Worldly greatness wants to crystallize around itself as much of mankind as possible, wants to become the center of a self- created universe. Divine greatness, already the true center of the universe and now manifest in human flesh, enjoys the freedom to put itself at the periphery, to bow down under the feet of others, to spend its substance in meeting every need it encounters.[141]

I still remember as if it were yesterday the example Fr Daniel. This generous priest was committed to give me advise and support me during my years of seminary training. At one point, I traveled from California to Connecticut for an eight day retreat. To my surprise, Fr Daniel decided to fly cross-country to visit me for a one hour conversation and immediately fly straight back to California. Seeing him there, grasping his selfless, servicial act of support, I better understood Christian leadership. Christian leadership is not about imposing one's beliefs on others. It is certainly not taking over the state, enacting harsh laws, or dominating others. As we will see, Christian leadership is focused on serving others with the love of God.

We have thus far examined perennial and contemporary trends and beliefs that are important for leaders. We then looked at some of the mainstream leadership theories as well as historic leadership insights. Now, after highlighting mainstream worldviews and centering ourselves on the one offered through a Judeo-Christian understanding of the world, it is time to dive deeper

---

[141] Merikakis, Erasmo, *Fire of Mercy, Heart of the Word*, Vol 3, 292.

into a specific Judeo-Christian view of leadership. Given both the widespread nature of the Judeo-Christian worldview and its global impact on the history of culture for thousands of years, it is important to now grasp how this worldview sees leadership. Leadership in its essence. Leadership as an art. Leadership in roles of authority and influence. This chapter aims to provide a succinct summary to help inform your understanding of leadership. Please note that a Judeo-Christian understanding of leadership does not contradict contemporary leadership theories and practice. A Judeo-Christian understanding helps us understand the 'why' behind these theories.

As an introduction to this theme, it is important for the reader to clearly grasp that a Judeo-Christian view of life values the good in everything authentically human. God made all things good. This includes the soul and body. It includes our sexuality. It includes our intellect and will as well as desires. Food, sports, rest, and friendship are all good in themselves. Naturally, this understanding applies to the field of leadership. Leadership is an eminently positive reality and should be treated as such. This implies a responsible living of leadership roles and positions as well as commitment to develop leadership capacity for the maximum good of humanity.

Dr James Hunter provides a good summary of the Judeo-Christian view of leadership in his book, *To Change the World*. It is useful to note that this view is consistent with many of the generally accepted ideas of leadership. He writes that "leadership is, in part, a set of practices surrounding the legitimate use of gifts, resources, position, and therefore influence (or relational power). But leadership is not simply one half of a dichotomy that divides the world between leaders and followers. Nor is leadership a one-dimensional or "zero-sum" property, which is to say it does not operate on a single continuum where more influence for one person or group will mean less for another. The fact is, our lives are constituted by multiple spheres of activity and relationship—not just one—and, in each of these, we have varying kinds and evolving degrees of influence."[142] Secondly, he highlights that each one of us is meant to lead and follow. "In short, everyone exercises leadership in varying degrees since we all have some influence in the wide variety of contexts in which we live. Using the same logic, we can say that we are all followers in a sense, for even where we exercise leadership, we are held to account—we follow the dictates, needs, and standards of others. We are accountable to our spouses, children, and parents, to our neighbors, to employers, and to those for whom we volunteer. Even the most powerful are held to account."[143] The Judeo-Christian understanding of leadership is eminently positive, sees us all as protagonists and encourages us to take responsibility of our leadership.

Dr Hunter is not naïve to reality. There is a disparity between those with more influence and those with less. "Leadership, then, like power, is relative. With that said, I do not want to imply naively that social influence does not operate on an absolute basis as well. Obviously, some people have more influence than others and a small number have incalculably more influence

---

[142] Hunter, James, To Change the World, 255.

[143] Ibid, 255.

than the majority. Likewise, there are some who have next to nothing by way of life-chances or influence, and the disparities between the most influential and the least can be deplorable."[144] This is a reality often decried by leadership gurus, minority groups, and Christians alike. Rather than trying to create an ideology that paints dreams of eliminating this (as does Marxism and woke culture), leaders need to recognize inequalities and work constructively to include marginalized and forgotten in societies.

A final, introductory thought is about leadership as a universal reality. Leadership is not for a select few. Each one of us has influence and the capacity to increase and improve that influence. "A simple dichotomous view that divides people into leaders and followers either with influence or without it is, like the concept of power itself, mostly useless, for it does not describe the reality of the world or our lives in it. Leadership, then, is an issue not for the clergy alone, nor for the "rich," the "powerful," or the "talented." Everyone is implicated in the obligations of leadership. In varying degrees and varying ways, all Christians bear this burden."[145] Each one of us…not just clergy…have leadership responsibility. Whether you hold a formal leadership position or not, you are called to lead and influence others.

Let us now take a quick look at insights on leadership from a Christian perspective as seen through the Bible, holy men and women, as well as Church teaching.

Leadership from perspective of the Bible

Every religion offers a holy book that summarizes its teachings. For Jewish and Christian faiths, it is the Holy Bible. Jews and Christians believe that the books of the Bible contain God's revelation to mankind. It shares what God wanted to make known about himself as well as his plan for our lives. There are dozens of references to leadership through examples and teaching all throughout the Bible. Let's go through some of these here to give an idea of what the Bible teaches about leadership.

First, the Bible tells us that leadership is a call to service. Jesus Christ himself spoke about being a servant. "But among you it will be different. Whoever wants to be a leader among you must be your servant."[146] This biblical teaching stresses that leadership is not about coercion, domination, or manipulation. Leadership is a gift to be exercised at the service of others who are seen as equals and deserving of your love and respect. God backs up this teaching through his own freely chosen acts of service— closely related to the insight that we should see goodness and strength in those we serve. "Don't be selfish; don't try to impress others. Be humble,

---

[144] Ibid, 256.

[145] Ibid, 256.

[146] Matthew 20:26

thinking of others as better than yourselves."[147] Over and over again, the Bible reminds those of influence that they are not at the center. The clear message is that God is the center of all creation; any influence that we exercise is meant to be on his behalf. It should be lived with kindness and respect while still accomplishing the goal and mission required through your leadership.

Another common teaching on leadership found in the Bible is fairness and honesty. It is interesting that this is also affirmed by leadership researchers and large scale surveys that analyze good leaders' top traits. Honesty and fairness are usually in the top five traits of most admired leaders. "If a king judges the poor with truth, His throne will be established forever."[148] This particular quote reminds us that fairness and honesty are not selective. You are not a good leader if you are honest only toward your friends and those you like. You are not a good leader if you treat those in your inner circle with fairness but do not act the same with strangers and those who are most vulnerable. Your leadership is most on display when you do not have anything to benefit from those you serve. When you go out of the way to serve those who are most needy. When was the last time you went out of your way to show interest, care, or concern for someone who is not your friend? Can you say you are honest and fair with all people who you influence ? Or is it selective and measured based on a caste system of importance to you?

As we will see in a later chapter, prudence is a critical virtue for a leader. The Bible comments on this from different perspectives. In first place, a leader moderates his speech. "A fool vents all his feelings, but a wise man holds them back."[149] Since prudence involves saying and doing the right thing at the right time and in the right measure, it would be nonsense for a leader to speak on impulse or on emotions as they come. Leadership requires you to moderate your tongue and say only what is needed and necessary. Listen to public figures on TV and social media and notice how they often drone on and on, letting fly many unnecessary (and often hurtful) words. Prudence is a special lacking quality in many leaders today and to which you are called if you want to be a good leader.

Also related to prudence is asking advice. Conventional leadership wisdom agrees with the Bible on this point. "Where there is no guidance the people fall, but in abundance of counselors there is victory."[150] In an age when many are taught to go at it alone, or to think you have it all within you, we can be slow to find good advisors and coaching. It is sad to see that many feel it is beneath them. It is sad to see seeking advice as a betrayal of their true selves. In reality, we do not have it all within us to be successful and good leaders. We all have blind

---

[147] Phil 2:3

[148] Proverbs 29:14

[149] Proverbs 29:11

[150] Ibid, 11:14

spots. Successful leaders form a board of advisors around them to give input on both their leadership and particular decisions.

Leaders inspire others. This is another leadership trait highlighted in the Bible. This does not mean that leaders are better than others. No, this point highlights that leadership is a quest and a growing transformation which inspires others. The Bible tells us "therefore an overseer must be above reproach, the husband of one wife, sober-minded, self-controlled, respectable, hospitable, able to teach."[151] Men and women can possess a harmonious integration of many virtues and develop their strengths at the service of others. Like a bee is drawn to honey, men and women are drawn to authentic and virtuous individuals. "Remember your leaders, those who spoke to you the word of God. Consider the outcome of their way of life, and imitate their faith."[152] Deep down, we all want to be inspiring and to inspire others.

Consistent with this theme and the quality of being a servant, the Bible for also reminds us to be patient and kind to those we serve including the ones who err and are weak. "We urge you, brothers, admonish the idle, encourage the fainthearted, help the weak, be patient with them all."[153] This theme is directly tied to the heart of Jesus the Good Shepherd which we will address at length in the next chapter. Anyone in a leadership role (or in a relationship like friendships or marriage) can testify that it is difficult to be patient and understanding with others, especially in moments of weakness and mistakes. This is where the leader shows both his ability to manage others' progress toward a goal as well as sees through to the heart and the good of the other person. Leaders are constantly challenged to not see people as means but ends. Love and respect is the only dignified response to a person. This includes when they are in a place of weakness or have made a terrible mistake. This does not mean the leader turns a blind eye but responds from a place of love and truth— he tailors accountability measures with this in mind.

The Bible also speaks of leadership as a responsibility. As we see in the parable of the talents in chapter 25 of Matthew's gospel, leadership is a talent and capacity each one of us is called to develop and exercise. We will eventually be held accountable to God for how we lived our leadership. "Be shepherds of God's flock that is under your care, watching over them—not because you must, but because you are willing, as God wants you to be; not pursuing dishonest gain, but eager to serve; not lording it over those entrusted to you, but being examples to the flock. And when the Chief Shepherd appears, you will receive the crown of glory that will never fade away."[154] In the Biblical mindset, leadership as a responsibility is never something

---

[151] 1 Timothy 3:2

[152] Hebrews 13:7

[153] 1 Thessalonians 5:14

[154] 1 Peter 5:2-4

burdensome. It may be tiring, but it is ultimately a gift. This gift needs to be lived with responsibility and seriousness. If you ever see a flock of sheep, the shepherd is never far away. It takes the care and defends his flock very seriously. The Bible exhorts us to have the same attitude in regards to our leadership.

I will finish mentioning two other traits highlighted in the Bible. They go together. Integrity and being steadfast. As it is with honesty, integrity is consistently at the top of most admired leadership traits and is often on the list of corporate core values. The Jewish and Christian faiths have extolled integrity for thousands of years. "It is an abomination for kings to commit wicked acts, For a throne is established on righteousness."[155] Unfortunately as mentioned earlier, the bad examples of leaders has corrupted and discouraged many. Integrity has to be consistent both in word and action. It has to live up to the expectations of the influence you have. Closely related to integrity is the trait of being steadfast. It is not enough to have good intentions about being a person of integrity; you need to be a leader who actually follows through and sticks to your guns through thick and thin. "But those who wait on the Lord, shall renew their strength; They shall mount up with wings like eagles, they shall run and not be weary, they shall walk and not faint."[156] Although secular men and women extoll the human value of perseverance, the Bible unabashedly reminds us that we do not have it within ourselves to remain leaders of integrity without the grace of God. It is important for leaders to lean on God for strength each day. This is not a weakness but rather wisdom and realism for the person who wants to remain steadfast in leadership. The Bible tells us over-and-over again that we need God at the center of our lives if we are going to live up to are calling as leaders.

Leadership from perspective of Holy Men and Women

We have just surveyed the basic teachings of the Bible on the theme of leadership. It is useful to do the same from men and women who lived these teachings in practice. 'Saints' is the term given by Christians to those who lived their faith in Jesus Christ to the point of conforming their lives to his own in a heroic degree. Many of us have witnessed in our own lifetime the examples of Saint Mother Teresa of Calcutta and Saint John Paul II. Just as many consult and reference leadership gurus of the 21st century, Christians put forward the example and advice of the saints. These men and women challenge us to embrace and live our call to leadership in a deeper way. For the sake of brevity, I will share leadership insights from three saints: St Augustine, St Mother Teresa of Calcutta, and St John Paul II.

St Augustine and his leadership journey have been detailed and discussed for 1600 years. There are many books about him and his teachings. As an accomplished philosopher and

---

[155] Proverbs 16:12

[156] Isaiah 40:31

orator, he influenced western civilization to our own day. A convert to Catholic Christianity, he continues to be a pillar and example for us all. Speaking about rulers and leaders,

> **We call those Christian rulers happy who govern with justice, never forgetting that they are only human. They think of sovereignty as a ministry of God, and they fear and worship God. They are slow to punish and quick to forgive. They temper with mercy and generosity the unavoidable harshness of their commands. They are all the more in control of their sinful desires because they are freer to indulge them. They prefer to rule their own passions more than to rule the peoples of the world. They rule not out of vain glory but out of love for everlasting bliss. They offer to God the humble sacrifice of their repentance and prayer. In this life they are happy in their hope and are destined to be truly happy when the eternal day comes for which we all hope.[157]**

As one who dealt with secular Roman leaders as well as leaders in the Church, St Augustine knew first hand the truth of the above. He does not wish away the difficulty of living up to this high bar, but puts it forward with confidence that we will embrace our leadership calling with excellence.

St Augustine affirms the Bible's teaching on being a servant. "The first thing good superiors must realize is that they are servants. They should not consider it beneath their dignity to be servants to many. Indeed, the Lord of lords did not consider it beneath His dignity to be a servant to us."[158] Contrary to the wisdom of the world, Christianity glories in the grandeur and the identity of being a servant. It means walking in the footsteps of God himself who did not deem it below himself to be among us in our own flesh and give up his life for us.

What about more recent saints? Although it is inspiring to think of great men and women from centuries past, there is nothing quite like witnessing a real life saint during your own lifetime. If you ask around, the most recognized modern saint is probably St Mother Teresa of Calcutta. She is known by people of all walks of life and admired for her selfless service to the poor, sick, and suffering. She served the poorest of the poor while also advising world leaders. What does this humble saint and leader advise us?

She was often known to speak about true success and accomplishment. One of her most popular sayings was "God has not called me to be successful. He has called me to be faithful." This is an important insight for leaders since we can be preoccupied about goals, accomplishments, and milestones. For St Mother Teresa, true success was not the ideal of eliminating poverty or reaching a certain number of people. Her life mission was to be faithful to what Jesus Christ asked of her. Everything about her life can be understood through this lens.

---

[157] St Augustine, City of God, 5.24.

[158] St Augustine, Sermon 340A.1

She frequently spoke about God's calling to her heart— her life project was a daily response to this call. Do I see my leadership this way? Do I have that same purity of intention?

Another insight on leadership from her life is related to the scale of impact. As leaders, we dream about changing the world and making a big impact, but sooner or later, become discouraged because we do not see immediate results; we finally realize the world and its problems are much bigger than our influence. St. Mother Teresa was often known to say "I alone cannot change the world, but I can cast a stone across the waters to create many ripples." This is a leader who knew the long term impact of helping in little ways every day. She saw all acts of kindness as an opportunity to serve God and her neighbor. Love reverberates throughout the 'moral intranet' of the world and changes lives in ways we cannot fathom or predict. She was content as a leader to give in the small and unpretentious ways. We can all learn from her example. No one can claim their leadership is insignificant. Every single one of us can make the commitment to serve and help those around us. Who in my family needs extra attention, patience, or care? Who at my workplace has few friends, is often misunderstood, and needs my care and concern? Start with these people. You might be surprised by the difference it makes in their lives. This, in turn, will have a ripple effect through the world.

A third saint and someone many in the 21st century saw first hand was St John Paul II. As a pope of the modern era, he had unprecedented exposure on the global stage. Along with President Ronald Reagan and Prime Minister Margaret Thatcher, he is attributed with the fall of Soviet communism. Regular gatherings of youth numbering in the millions were commonplace during his papacy. He had an electrifying personality, was a known to be a mystic, and a man of deep prayer and union with God. A philosopher and prodigious writer, his thoughts on theology, the human person, sexuality, and marriage as well as the nature of truth and reason continue to be studied and discussed. Being an advisor to national leaders and frequently speaking and writing on the theme of leadership, he offers contemporary leaders much food for thought.

At the center of his life experience, St John Paul II taught that "a person's rightful due is to be treated as an object of love, not as an object of use."[159] As we have already seen in other places, the person under our leadership and affected by our influence is never a tool nor someone to be manipulated. They deserve our care and respect. Without this in mind, our leadership will always be detrimental and not fulfill its mission at the service of others. It will easily degenerated into self serving, making other people feel used.

St John Paul II was also known to be a leader who stressed the importance of hope and not giving in to fear. "I plead with you — never, ever give up on hope, never doubt, never tire, and never become discouraged. Do not be afraid." As the Third Millennium approached, he regularly reminded humanity to not be afraid. This is the result of being a leader whose heart and mind's eye was rooted in the experience and reality of the risen Jesus Christ who he

---

[159] Pope John Paul II, *Love and Responsibility*.

constantly beheld and relied upon. As you may know from experience already, leadership is something we can start practicing with great enthusiasm, hope, and a vision with wide horizons. Over time, however, this can be eroded through failures and disappointments. We can find ourselves upset, discouraged, even cynical. We can start to believe that the journey was not worth it and contemplate abandoning the effort to lead in a selfless, loving, and humble way. This saint has walked the walk as a leader. He reminds you and me to keep our eyes on God. God alone is the ultimate source of strength and reason to rejoice even in the midst of what appears in the eyes of the world as failure.

St John Paul II also encouraged youth. "Dear young people, let yourselves be taken over by the light of Christ, and spread that light wherever you are."[160] This saint was convinced that leaders need to give special attention to the future generations. He knew that youth have a great capacity for an ideal and desire to be part of a great quest. They are open and desirous to be heroic. Young people deep down do not want to be mediocre. This is why he dedicated himself to many encounters with young people including the famous World Youth Days, which drew millions of young people. Like St John Paul II, each one of us need to ask ourselves if we are paying attention to the future generations. Do we see them as a nuisance or as an asset? What am I doing in this regards? What could I do as a leader to serve the future generations? We will look at this theme in the next chapter dedicated to a Christian leadership model.

Leadership from the Perspective of Church teaching

In addition to learning directly from the Bible as well as the life example of saints, leaders can also receive insight from official Church teaching. These teachings are based on the Scripture and Tradition of Christianity and often published after a major conference or gathering of experts. Once again, my goal is to give you a snapshot of the insights on leadership offered from the Christian perspective that are often not published in mainstream media or books. You will not likely hear many of these insights at business schools or in leadership books. It is, however, important to consider these as part of a holistic presentation of leadership.

Pope Francis made international news as a world influencer in his early years as pope. He has spoken on various occasions regarding leadership as a service. One of his first addresses to Church leaders detailed 10 leadership 'sicknesses'. He recommended steps for clergy and laity to live up to their leadership. "For leadership there is only one road: service. There is no other way. If you have many qualities, the ability to communicate, etc. , but you are not a servant, your leadership will fail, it is useless, it has not power to gather [people] together… Leadership must enter into service, but with a personal love for the people."[161]

---

[160] Evening Vigil with Young People, Address by the Holy Father John Paul II, Toronto, Downsview Park, Saturday July 27, 2002

[161] Pope Francis, Address, 12th May 2014

A critical aspect of leadership is the formation of conscience. Conscience is like a moral GPS that orients us towards what is true and good. It helps us to recognize and embrace good and avoid evil. Speaking on this theme, St. John Paul II said "the Church needs to pay greater attention to the formation of consciences, which will prepare the leaders of society for public life at all levels, promote civic education, respect for law and for human rights, and inspire greater efforts in the ethical training of political leaders."[162] This is an aspect of leadership that you do not find in most mainstream training programs. At best, you will find references to ethics and diversity training. The Christian vision is much greater. It goes to the level of not only acknowledging the importance of respecting conscience, but also the task of forming it in truth—according to our calling and mission in life. Modern society stresses freedom of conscience, but falls very short in acknowledging and offering guidance on training our conscience to help us achieve our flourishing.

Another Church teaching on leadership is the importance of serving both the poor and influential. Jesus Christ, God made man, associated himself to our lowly humanity and gave special care to those who were marginalized and suffering. For this reason, the Catholic Church teaches the importance of a preferential option for the poor. This means we should give special care and concern to those who are suffering in mind, body, or spirit. Leaders with a well formed heart and conscience are attentive to alleviate others' sufferings. At the same time, the Church teaches that this preferential treatment towards the poor is not everything. Those in roles of leadership are important to God and the Church as well. "Love for the poor must be preferential, but not exclusive. The Synod Fathers observed that it was in part because of an approach to the pastoral care of the poor marked by a certain exclusiveness that the pastoral care for the leading sectors of society has been neglected and many people have thus been estranged from the Church. The damage done by the spread of secularism in these sectors—political or economic, union-related, military, social or cultural—shows how urgent it is that they be evangelized, with the encouragement and guidance of the Church's Pastors, who are called by God to care for everyone."[163] This is an important reminder not only for Christian clergy, but also for all men and women. We have neglected the intentional formation and accompaniment of those in leadership roles for too long. Instead of complaining about the state of the world, we should acknowledge our omission to grow as leaders and help train other leaders.

The evangelization and organization of social structures and institutions is central to this theme. At the service of the Church, congregations of priests and lay movements such as the Legionaries of Christ and *Regnum Christi* help men and women discover their call to Christian leadership at the service of others. "In order to further the work of evangelization, structures and institutions need to be organized and governed in accordance with Christ's truth. This is done through their *leaders*, individuals who by their natural gifts and by their positions, can exercise exceptional influence over the direction of their structures and institutions. So,

---

[162] Saint John Paul II, *Ecclesia in America* (1999), 56

[163] Ibid, 67.

evangelization of society includes the evangelization of leaders in all sectors of society. *Regnum Christi* has always been called to pay close attention to this "existential periphery".[164]

Following this line of thought, Church teachings include the intentional support and guidance of leaders in all strata of society. Business. Sports. Politics. Entertainment. Science. Higher education. The list goes on. Christianity's ideal includes the intentional accompaniment of men and women in these different sectors of society helping guide them in their roles of leadership. "A very important task is the formation of thinkers and people who occupy decision-making positions. To that end, we must employ effort and creativity in the evangelization of businesspeople, politicians, and opinion makers, the world of labor, and union, cooperative, and community leaders."[165] While some might think the Christian Church is limited to social work helping the suffering, its vision goes beyond serving and supporting those in roles of leadership. It should be mentioned that those in roles of leadership often suffer misunderstanding and feel isolated in carrying their burden of leadership. We've all heard that it is lonely at the top— any person in a role of leadership will feel this to some degree. . The Church believes and teaches that all leaders deserve to be listened to and supported in their role; no one needs to go through their leadership journey alone, unsupported.

Another aspect of the Church's role in leadership is to shape culture through ideas and art. Leadership is greatly influenced by ideas. This can play out in a good or evil way. Look at the intellectual fallacy's behind Nazism and Communism and see the practical consequences, including millions who died because of a dream built on illusions that were not consistent with the human dream. The Church understands the power of ideas and the importance of transmitting them. "God is not only the highest Truth. He is also highest Goodness and supreme Beauty. Hence, 'Society needs artists, just as it needs scientists, technicians, workers, professional people, witnesses of the faith, teachers, fathers and mothers, who ensure the growth of the person and the development of the community by means of that supreme art form which is "the art of education.""[166] How should we do this? How do we inform the minds and hearts of leaders? The Church offers the following thought: "Optimize the use of Catholic media, making them more active and effective, whether for communicating the faith or for dialogue between the Church and society…Work with artists, athletes, fashion professionals, journalists, communicators, and media hosts, and with those who produce information in the media, such as intellectuals, professors, community and religious leaders…Restore the role of the priest as opinion shaper."[167]

---

[164] Bartunek, Fr John, *What is Regnum Christi?*, 64.

[165] CELAM, Aparecida Concluding Document 2007, 492

[166] Ibid, 496.

[167] Ibid, 497.

When it comes to the Church, many think it's teachings and ideals are oriented for and towards clergy. The reality is the opposite. The vast majority of believers are not part of the clergy. They live their lives as mothers and fathers, professionals and students. The past 50 years of Church thought has increasingly focused on the role of the lay person and their calling to leadership both in the Church and in society. In recent times, Pope Francis has spoken and written on this theme at great length. He has also involved laymen and women in roles of leadership both inside the Church as well as in society focused ministries.

> **Lay people are, put simply, the vast majority of the people of God. The minority – ordained ministers – are at their service. There has been a growing awareness of the identity and mission of the laity in the Church. We can count on many lay persons, although still not nearly enough, who have a deeply-rooted sense of community and great fidelity to the tasks of charity, catechesis and the celebration of the faith. At the same time, a clear awareness of this responsibility of the laity, grounded in their baptism and confirmation, does not appear in the same way in all places. In some cases, it is because lay persons have not been given the formation needed to take on important responsibilities. In others, it is because in their particular Churches room has not been made for them to speak and to act, due to an excessive clericalism which keeps them away from decision-making. Even if many are now involved in the lay ministries, this involvement is not reflected in a greater penetration of Christian values in the social, political and economic sectors. It often remains tied to tasks within the Church, without a real commitment to applying the Gospel to the transformation of society. The formation of the laity and the evangelization of professional and intellectual life represent a significant pastoral challenge.**[168]

The Church is on the forefront of encouraging all men and women to embrace their leadership calling.

I would like to close this portion of the chapter by highlighting Christianity's great esteem for promotion of the dignity of women. Without a doubt, women throughout the world owe a great debt of gratitude to Christianity for ushering in an appreciation their equal human dignity with men. Jesus Christ revealed this dignity in a time when women were considered second class citizens in every respect. God gives women many gifts and talents that are not in competition with men but show their complementarity to men. "There is also a special need to accompany young women showing leadership potential, so that they can receive training and the necessary qualifications. The young people who met before the Synod called for 'programs for the formation and continued development of young leaders. Some young women feel that there is a lack of leading female role models within the Church and they too wish to give their intellectual

---

[168] Francis, *Evangelii Gaudium*, 102

and professional gifts to the Church."[169]   Contrary to the tendency of a secular worldview, Christianity and the Church present a healthy and positive view of the complementarity of male and female leaders. Instead of painting a picture of struggle between men and women to dominate, the Church exhorts us and reminds us that men and women are equal in dignity before God and this is the most important thing. They each have different gifts which compliment the other. There is room for both of them at the table of leadership. While this does not mean that every role of leadership within the Church is open to both men and women based on the revealed and willed plan of God in Jesus Christ, it does mean that men and women should be allowed to exercise their leadership to their fullest potential according to God's plan for both the Church and society.

Leadership and Elitism

Before closing, I would like to address a topic that might be on the mind of both Christians and non-Christians. I am regularly asked about the danger of leadership and elitism. Is striving to be a leader elitist? Is dedicating yourself to train and accompany leaders on their difficult journey fueling and fostering elitism? If you are in a position of societal leadership, are you elitist? As you think about these questions, your answer might not be a straight-forward 'yes' or 'no'. This is a delicate theme that ultimately requires a balanced understanding.

The specter of elitism overshadows Christianity whenever leadership is discussed. This accusation is leveled at the Church but the same standard is often not applied to those who regularly operate within networks of elites. As regards Christianity and elitism,

> **This point bears some emphasis. The significance of every person before God irrespective of worldly stature or accomplishment and the care for the least are the ethical hallmarks of Christianity, for they mark every human being and every human life in the most practical ways with God's image and therefore as worthy of respect and love. Without these, Christianity is a brutalizing ideology. This is why elitism—a disposition and relationality of superiority, condescension, and entitlement by social elites—is so abhorrent for the Christian. Its foundation is exclusion on the implicit (and sometimes explicit) view that people are not equal in love and dignity before God. Thus, by its very nature, elitism is exploitative. So far as I can tell, elitism for believers is despicable and utterly anathema to the gospel they cherish.[170]**

This is the reality. Elitism is abhorrent for Christianity and it should be abhorrent to you as a leader too. The very concept of elitism is about being closed inside yourself , set apart as

---

[169] Ibid, 245.

[170] Hunter, James, *To Change the World*, 97.

above-and-beyond others. It is being a part of a privileged group that sees itself as better than others, who impose its views and desires on others.

The danger is real; elitism can penetrate and take hold of the Church and groups of Christians. "The dangers are apparent. The most obvious danger is the temptation that Christians who are in positions of leadership will act in a way that is elitist. They will misuse their position to exclude others for the sake of exclusion or to protect their own power and vested interests for no other reason than to aggrandize power and privilege."[171] Unfortunately, Christians themselves can be suspicious of those in roles of authority. In my experience, however, many men and women in roles of influence are people of great integrity, often ardent in their Christian faith. "Just as dangerous are the pressures of duplicity. Because Christianity has lost status in the institutional centers of the modern world, those believers who work and live in the higher echelons of culture, politics, business, and finance are under great pressure to carefully "manage their identities" in part by hiding this discrediting information about themselves. In this case, the consequence of disclosure is to be excluded themselves. The temptation to be deceptive or dishonest about your faith in these circles is enormous."[172] It is terrible when you see people of faith selling their souls to the devil in order to climb the ladder of societal success. We see this in all sectors of leadership. The shipwreck of these Christians should be a reminder of what can happen to any of us if we do not have strong convictions about putting our faith and God ahead of anything else. As the CEO of Waste Management Corporation, Jim Fish once told his board of directors, "my priorities are God first, then my family and then this company. I am the man I am because of this hierarchy of priorities."[173] The challenge for each of us is to stand by these priorities.

The challenge for Christians is to balance the call of being a faithful presence in the world with the achievements and positions that come through good leadership. It is like walking a ridge-line with extremes on each side. If you are not careful, you can compromise your faith in pursuit of societal success. On the other hand, you could refuse leadership in fear of losing your faith or being considered elitist by those inside and outside the Church. "What this tells us is that though the association between leadership and elitism is strong, elitism is not inherent to leadership. Though the pretensions of influence and authority are ever present, and the opportunities for hubris are everywhere, there is a different way modeled on the leadership of Jesus who rejected status and its privileges."[174] This is a dichotomy that has no easy answer. It must be answered by those of us who choose to walk the leadership calling with care and wisdom. The danger does not eliminate the calling to leadership that we must each pursue.

---

[171] Ibid, 258.

[172] Ibid, 258.

[173] Jim Fish (CEO of Waste Management Corporation), Lumen Institute National Speaker Event, 2019.

[174] Hunter, James, *To Change the World*, 259.

A Judeo-Christian understanding of Leadership

The parable of the talents (Matthew 25:14-30) is a powerful reference point on the theme of leadership. "Each one of us, as a follower of Christ and a sharer in his mission, is called to develop our natural and supernatural gifts. In doing so, we not only experience more fulfillment ourselves, but we also are better able to influence others in a positive way. We help others to know, love, and follow Christ by direct, one-on-one contact, and indirectly, through our example and through work that fosters the true good of our communities and of the larger society all around us."[175]

In this chapter, we have looked at a Christian understanding of leadership and considered insights from the Bible, Christian saints, as well as official teaching documents of the Church. We have also considered the temptation and reality of leadership and elitism.

Questions for Personal Reflection and Group Discussion

1. What leadership insights were mentioned in this chapter? What did you learn?
2. What insights on leadership does the Bible offer you?
3. " "   "   "   can you learn from holy men and women?
4. " "   "   "   does Church teaching offer you?
5. What is elitism? How can you answer the call to leadership and avoid elitism?
6. Where do you fall into elitism? Where does your family, company, religious or social groups?
7. What more can you do to better understand the Christian view of leadership? Read more on the subject? Invite a Christian leader you know out for coffee or lunch to talk about his experience?

---

[175] Bartunek, Fr John, *What is Regnum Christi?*, 66.

PART III
TOWARDS A MORE ROBUST LEADERSHIP MODEL

CHAPTER 6
THE SOURCE AND SUMMIT OF LEADERSHIP

What distinguishes a great leader from a mediocre one is that a great leader has a heart for his people.[176]

I came not to be served but to serve and give my life as a ransom for many.[177]

No greater love has a man than to lay down his life for his friends.[178]

As a novice in the Legionaries of Christ, I was just beginning my studies for priesthood in 1999. Shipped off to study at our house in Dublin, Ireland, I was quickly introduced to the beautiful countryside and natural beauty of the Emerald Isle. I still remember it like it was yesterday; visiting the iconic Dingle Peninsula, going for a hike with several other seminarians. We had a topographical map, our enthusiasm, and all day to explore. Looking at the map, I noticed an interesting valley surrounded by a ridge with indications of possible waterfalls. We set off at sunrise making a good clip and ascended from the south up to the ridge hoping to get a good glimpse of the valley below. When we arrived, we were not disappointed. I beheld one of the most beautiful sights I have ever seen on this side of heaven. Near the top, a waterfall emanated from the mountain and cascaded down the hillside to the valley that was several thousand feet below. Though risky, we began our downward descent, following the waterfall and seeing with ever greater clarity the beauty of the stream— how it watered the lush green valley

---

[176] *Way of the Shepherd*, 101.

[177] Matthew 20:28

[178] John 15:13

below. It was one of those moments where you admire the beauty of creation on every step of the way with a certain feeling that someone upstairs made this just for you to see.

I was inspired to name this book *The Source and Summit of Leadership*. It is a title full of meaning. The vision in my mind was similar to my experience in Ireland. Leadership is both like a mountain's peak and a lush waterfall. I say a mountain's peak in that it is something many look up to and also a quest to ascend and acquire. On the other hand, it is like a majestic waterfall that gushes forth to nourish and sustain all it touches. I chose this title not only because of the beauty of mountains and waterfalls. In the Christian tradition, Jesus Christ is "the source and summit of the Christian life."[179] All comes from him. All is oriented toward him. Christians believe and propose to the world that he is the one to whom all our transcendent desires point. We were created to be united to him in this life and the next. He is the destiny of each man and woman.

In the previous two chapters, we discussed a Christian worldview and then delved a bit deeper into insights on leadership. It is now time to focus on the heart, which animates and gives life to leadership from a Christian perspective. I would be so bold as to propose that it is really this reason that undergirds the metaphysical and existential foundation for leadership. Just as there are the physical constants that explain the structure of the physical universe, there is also a moral, animating principle at work behind the human person and our interactions with each other. This animating principle is not simply a philosophical idea, but a person. His name is Jesus Christ.

In my first book, *The Future of Leadership*, I summarized this theme from the perspective of Emeritus Pope Benedict XVI. This pope gave succinct summaries and insights on the reasons Jesus Christ is the source and summit of leadership on many occasions. In this book, I would like to give you a cursory view of the Christian reason that Christ is indeed the foundation and reference point for all leadership. The next chapter will leverage these insights as well as previous chapters to present a Christian leadership model.

Jesus used the example of the Good Shepherd to describe his leadership. This is an image from both the Old and New Testaments of the Bible. Although you have probably never shepherded an animal like sheep, the image is still apropos in the 21st century. The image of the Good Shepherd brings to mind the tender care and steadfast leadership that God takes towards us. Contrary to the image of a shepherd for hire, Jesus reminded his listeners that he would not just take care of his sheep but that he would literally lay down his life in sacrifice for them. This should astound us since even a good friend would be hard pressed to lay down his life for you.

For the purpose of this book, I am going to assume you will take me at face value on the claim that Jesus Christ is God in the flesh. There are many writings and speeches ranging from past

---

[179] Catechism of the Catholic Church, 1324

centuries all the way to the modern era that delve into the why of this claim. For example, the book *The Case for Christ: A Journalist's Personal Investigation of the Evidence for Jesus* (written by professional journalist Lee Strobel) discusses many proven facts about Jesus and the New Testament. As many sound thinkers have summarized, Jesus Christ was either a madman and lunatic or he was what he claimed to be: God in the flesh who gives his life as a ransom for each one of us. Ponder the radicality and weight of this claim. God loves you so much that he would go to this length to be with you, to teach you about your destiny, and sacrifice himself so this destiny would be available to you. This is the Good Shepherd heart that is at the center of Christian leadership, the hidden moral force behind all leadership when lived in truth and love.

Let's stay with the image of the Good Shepherd for a moment. Since this is central to our understanding of leadership, and a Christian vision of our lives and our world, we could greatly benefit from reading at length Jesus' words about himself and his heart:

> **I am the good shepherd, and I know mine and mine know me just as the Father knows me and I know the Father; and I will lay down my life for the sheep. I have other sheep that do not belong to this fold. These also I must lead, and they will hear my voice, and there will be one flock, one shepherd. This is why the Father loves me, because I lay down my life in order to take it up again. No one takes it from me, but I lay it down on my own. I have power to lay it down, and power to take it up again. This command I have received from my Father.**[180]

What do we see here? First of all and contrary to militant atheist explanations of the universe, we are not simply an insignificant speck of dust . In reality, each person is the apple of God's eye. He knows and sees you at every moment of your day with love and a twinkle in his eye. He is constantly looking out for you and takes personal interest in the daily realities of your life. Contrary to the late Christopher Hitchens' arguments about God as a dictator and overseer, Jesus presents God as one who is intimate, close, and eminently valuing of even the smallest things of your life. I think we can relate to this especially through the analogies of marriage and best friends. In a marriage or very close friendship, it is natural to lovingly share and be concerned about things that would be insignificant to other people. Lovers appreciate the care and concern shown for one another by valuing the details of their lives. This does not mean being overbearing or nit-picky toward the other, but having a shared interest in the other.

A second characteristic of Jesus' heart in this passage is his universal love for all mankind. His love, care, and concern is personalized towards each one of us, yet also reaches out to everyone including our enemies. Jesus' heart is also for those of other religions including Muslims, Jews, Hindus, and those who follow different belief systems. This universal love implies that Jesus wants to lead us all to heaven, to our final destiny of happiness and

---

[180] John 10:14-18

flourishing. This is a magnanimous heart. Writing about the shepherd heart of Christ, St Asterius of Amasea says "we should not look on men as lost or beyond hope; we should not abandon them when they are in danger or be slow to come to their help. When they turn away from the right path and wander, we must lead them back, and rejoice at their return, welcoming them back into the company of those who lead."[181]

Imagine for a moment that you are the leader responsible for the entire world population in this moment of history. Think of the effort involved to just do the minimum; trying to help as many people as possible. God has continued doing this for all human history, gently guiding us to follow him.

The Gospel passage about the Good Shepherd highlights God's commitment to lay down his life for us. Since we value freedom so much, I would like to stress the words of Jesus that no one takes his life from him. He freely chooses to come among us as well as to sacrifice himself for our sake on the cross. Freedom is at the heart of history and leadership.

Let us now take a walk through some of moments that show the Good Shepherd heart of Jesus.

Leadership by becoming one like us

Most of us can probably recall special memories during Christmas. I still remember with fondness running down the stairs as a child and finding a race car set under the Christmas tree. The big meals. Visits from grandparents and relatives. Time off school. These Memories fill the minds and hearts of billions of men, women, and children around the world evert year. Do we ever stop to think about what is behind all this? In the West, more and more people greet each other with the phrase 'happy holidays' instead of the reason for the season. Christ's birth on Christmas Day. This is the reason Christians and so many others celebrate December 25th with such joy.

God becoming man, taking flesh and bone is traditionally known as the Incarnation. He was in flesh, literally speaking. The all transcendent, the all powerful, the all knowing and loving God assumed human nature without losing his divine nature. This is a great mystery that cannot be picked apart by science but accepted as revelation and communication from a God who wanted to be up close and personal with us. As I said in my previous book, "the Incarnation of Jesus Christ means that God has definitively assumed human nature to himself and now invites all men and women to participate in the divine life of the Holy Trinity. The *kenosis* of Christ is truly amazing since it implies that God humbles himself to take on human flesh so as to let us share in his glorious divinity."[182] This reality implies a truly magnanimous heart. A heart of a shepherd

---

[181] Hom. 13: PG 40, 355-358, 362

[182] Haslam, Nathaniel, *The Future of Leadership*, 25.

that literally wants to become one of his sheep so he can reveal his love and care in a language that they can understand. God literally comes down to our level.

The implications of this are truly staggering— they boggle the mind. Contrary to those who base their interpretation and vision of the human person on chaotic, unguided evolution, this revelation helps us understand that each one of us is important, not a random occurrence, or a cosmic mistake. You and I are not here by chance. You and I are here because we were willed and wanted. Going further, it means that every aspect of human life is shared and given meaning by God himself. "This implies that he also fully assumed, experienced, and understood the role and importance of leadership. He knows the importance of influence in the life of a leader, the role of charisma, service, heroism, bringing out the best in others, eloquence and communication, organization, and time management, just to name a few. Since Christ is the reference point, beginning, end, and perfection of the human person, it is necessary to look to him as the point of reference for being human and for being a leader."[183] Leadership is not something that is existentially relative. It is anchored to an objective and fundamental truth. Jesus Christ is leadership itself. He shows it to us through his person; he reveals how it can be developed and deployed. He instructs us on how it is not to be used and abused. Finally, he exhorts us to find strength and direction for leadership by coming to him.

Leadership in teaching us to love

Think of the stories you have heard about Jesus:opening the eyes of the blind, healing a woman with the hemorrhage, forgiving the adulterous woman. Restoring full health to the paralytic. Raising up dead children. Patiently training the disciples who were often focused on themselves, on who was the greatest. Washing the apostles feet. Giving his Body and Blood in Holy Communion at the Last Supper. These and so many other examples give us insight into the leadership heart of Jesus.

His entire life on earth was a teaching moment. He went about doing good, teaching us about God's heart, and how he sees each one of us. He taught us that love is at the heart of leadership.

> **All people are called by God to share in his divine life. The Holy Trinity is a relationship of love. The vocation of each man and woman is nothing less than this: to love God with all one's heart, mind, soul, and strength and their neighbor as themselves. Being called to an intimate relationship of love with God and all other human beings implies there can be no separation between faith and morality, between what one professes and how one lives his daily life. This means that leadership entails and must be guided by love. The nature and measure of this love can only be that shown by Jesus Christ: serving the other for who they**

---

[183] Ibid, 25.

are and not to get anything for oneself to the point of giving one's life for them. Jesus Christ is, therefore, the universal and concrete norm for the human person and action.[184]

Love is the animating force behind and in the universe. It is the reference and end goal of human freedom. As the Bible attests, Jesus knows human nature through and through including the possibility of having a twisted, selfish heart. From his birth to his freely chosen death, Jesus went about teaching love as the meaning and goal of human life. When we speak about leadership, we must frame it in the context of love.

As this implies, it is possible to live leadership and life without love, wrapped up in your own selfishness, vain pursuit of popularity, as well as addiction to pleasure and power. Jesus dedicates significant time and effort to teach, correct, and admonish religious and secular leaders who do not base their influence on their love for God and their neighbor. "A leader who lives without love of God and his neighbor falls short of his vocation as a human being. This is true mediocrity. This is true failure. The one who does not love has lost and never really lived. A person can appear externally as a leader due to fame, fortune, and position, but without love, they are nothing; they are no true leader. The key to life as a leader is love."[185] This is a gentle but firm reminder that those who teach leadership have a special responsibility to exhort their students to excellence.

In the case of complacency and error, Jesus teaches the need for fraternal correction. We need to be careful not to fall into relativism. A complacent 'let's just get along' is no basis for leadership. Jesus Christ knew when it was time to bring out the rod of discipline to correct the sheep that were stubborn or going astray. We should not be surprised when he does this to us. "Discipline isn't about handing out punishment or assigning blame; it's about instruction. It's about instructing your people in the direction they should go by helping them see further down the path they're currently treading. That's far different than calling someone in because they 'fouled up.'"[186] Leadership requires you too see the big picture and help others embrace it. We wanted to make course corrections at times. As a leader, you are guilty of an omission when you do not teach others what is required for their full human flourishing.

Leadership in service and sacrifice

Jesus Christ, the Good Shepherd, also teaches us that leadership is both service and sacrifice. At the beginning of this chapter, we heard him say that he came to serve and not be served. This is very difficult for us to grasp since our lives are a blend of selfish and selfless desires and

---

[184] Ibid, 26.

[185] Ibid, 37.

[186] *The Way of the Shepherd*, 90.

actions. In the case of Jesus, who is God, his entire life in flesh was a selfless giving to you and me. He did not mix words when he challenged his disciples saying, "you know that those who are considered rulers of the Gentiles lord it over them, and their great ones exercise authority over them. But it shall not be so among you. But whoever would be great among you must be your servant, and whoever would be first among you must be slave of all."[187] These are radical words that challenge us today just as it challenged the first followers of Christ. Leadership is not about being first in position or in the regard others have for you.

Service. Is that how you see your leadership? How you see your call to leadership? As Pat Lencioni teaches, "at the most fundamental level, the first motive to become a leader is because one wants to serve others, to do whatever is necessary to bring about something good for the people they lead. They understand that sacrifice and suffering are inevitable in this pursuit and that serving others is the only valid motivation for leadership. This is why it annoys me when people praise someone for being a "servant leader," as though there is any other valid option."[188] Service is one of those words that is paid much lip service, but, in practice, does not run very deep in the heart of many leaders or those who speak about it. How often do you think this word is mentioned in business schools, during discussions among politicians, or in public school board meetings? For you as a leader, service needs to become a way of life and not simply virtue signaling or a core value you put on your business card.

Our concept of power directly influences our understanding and attitude toward service. In an unforgettable and deeply penetrating commentary about power and service, Erasmo Merikakis says "Jesus stands human logic on its head by saying that precisely the one holding greatest authority and power must use these for the benefit of all rather than for self-gain; and he extends universally what God does in his creation and what he, Jesus, will now do in his passion, so that the divine principle of loving service is proclaimed to be henceforth the moving force and wellspring of all human activity."[189] As source and summit of all creation, Jesus himself defines leadership. His service heart is the permanent reference point, archetype, and blueprint for any and all leadership. If you and I lead anyone, the quality and fruitfulness of this leadership will be directly tied to and proportional to its union with the ideal and person of Jesus Christ.

This power in service is ultimately grounded upon and proven in his freely embracing his suffering and death. "In his crucifixion, Christ disarmed all forms of worldly power and in his resurrection, he triumphed over them and by so doing, made it possible for those who believe to

---

[187] Mark 10:42-45.

[188] Lencioni, Pat, *The Motive*, 131.

[189] Merikakis, *Fire of Mercy*, Volume IV, 68.

be liberated from them and to participate in the reality of his kingdom."[190] The power of God is a complete service to you and me. This is the exact opposite of a God and leader who is domineering, despotic and abusive.

This leads us to the theme of sacrifice. This is a key aspect and consequence of a Good Shepherd's heart. Anyone in or pursuing a leadership role knows from experience that sacrifice is part of this journey. Climbing the summit of leadership implies sacrifice and hard work. Leadership without sacrifice would be a daydream. We might miss, however, that we can easily fall into selective sacrifice. I would highly alert you about this reality. Selective sacrifice means we will take the hit when it is a means to an end— It means a tainted and self-centered vision of leadership. The sacrifice Jesus made shows us as a leader is pure and unconditional.

The reality of Jesus' suffering is documented by both Jewish and Roman authorities. This is not a fictional story. Have you taken time to think about the magnitude of suffering endured by Jesus? Him sweating blood before his arrest (a very painful experience that doctors attest can happen under great stress), struck and spat upon by Jewish religious leaders and temple guards. His flesh was torn and ripped from his body through torturous scourging (many died from shock and blood loss from this inhuman torture). His brain was pierced when Roman guards put a crown of thorns on him. After carrying a heavy wooden cross, he was nailed to it, nails pierced the nerves below his hands and above his feet. He hung on a cross for hours, unable to breathe, putting weight on the nails to pull himself up for quick breaths. This is serious suffering. It was a sacrifice intentionally offered to you.

This is true sacrifice. Jesus shows himself a leader who is willing to pay the price for you and me. He is willing to pay the price to help us achieve temporal and eternal good. "The price you're willing to pay is relative to the value you attribute to something. That man who neglected his own refused to pay the price, not because he thought it was too high but because the value he put on his sheep was too low. Shepherds call a person like that a 'hireling.'"[191] Where do I act like a hireling? Where do I put conditions on my willingness to sacrifice for others? Am I afraid to lose my reputation over a leadership decision? Over standing up for what is right? When am I not standing my ground before evil ideas and actions which are infiltrating and hurting family, friends and coworkers? In our day and age, the cancel culture is like a bulldozer and many well intentioned people hide and do not risk standing up for their beliefs and convictions out of fear of the boogeyman of being 'cancelled'.

Jesus as a leader was not afraid to confront evil and pay the sacrificial cost required to lead us to heaven. He was willing to pay the cost so that we would get to know God's love and learn to love one another with the same Good Shepherd heart that he showed us. "The practice of leadership for the Christian is sacrificial in character. The quality of commitment implied in

---

[190] Hunter, James. *To Change the World*, 188.

[191] *The Way of the Shepherd*, 101.

faithful presence invariably imposes costs. To enact a vision of human flourishing based in the qualities of life that Jesus modeled will invariably challenge the given structures of the social order. In this light, there is no true leadership without putting at risk your time, wealth, reputation, and position."[192] Jesus challenges us to ask ourselves if we are truly committed to be a sacrificial leader who acts for the good of others. Am I committed?

There is an important assumption behind the concept of power above, service, and sacrifice: we, and everything we are and have, belong to God. Everything originates from him and his desire for us to exist. How can our leadership not also belong to him? "The reason that leadership is sacrificial and selfless is because its practice is an expression of "power under submission."[193] The gifts, resources, and influence we steward are not our own to use as we wish but belong to God: they exist under his authority. Believers are held to account for how they steward them.

Jesus invites each one of us to be leaders of sacrifice. With the authority invested in him as God made man, he exhorts us to take up our own cross and follow him by sacrificing our lives for him and neighbor. "Jesus Christ is the model, example, and reference point for sacrificial leadership. He not only comes among mankind to teach the divine truths and open the way to salvation. His invitation is breathtaking: he wants to save us but invites each person to live out his act of redemptive love in their life."[194] Our destiny and flourishing hinge upon being sacrificial leaders like Jesus. We are not spectators up high in the grandstands of history. You and I are on the playing field. No one can take your place sacrificing your life, energy, and heart for the good of others. For most of us, this does not imply a physical death at the hands of evil forces. It does, however, imply the often hidden interior suffering and death that is part of sacrificial leadership one person, one situation at a time. Jesus looks at you with love and says, 'what about you? What will you do?'

Many today answer by taking the road of indifference or cynicism. Few are willing to take responsibility for their leadership calling and the sacrifices that it demands. Jordan Peterson (Canadian professor of psychology, clinical psychologist, YouTube personality, and author) covered this theme in his book *12 Rules for Life*. "To stand up straight with your shoulders back is to accept the terrible responsibility of life, with eyes wide open. It means deciding to voluntarily transform the chaos of potential into the realities of habitable order. It means adopting the burden of self-conscious vulnerability, and accepting the end of the unconscious paradise of childhood, where finitude and mortality are only dimly comprehended. It means willingly undertaking the sacrifices necessary to generate a productive and meaningful reality (it

---

[192] Hunter, James, *To Change the World*, 259.

[193] Ibid, 260.

[194] Haslam, Nathaniel, *The Future of Leadership*, 43.

means acting to please God, in the ancient language)."[195] May we each embrace the sacrifices asked of us.

Leadership in giving us the power to be leaders like himself

The temptation we face is to intellectually agree and acknowledge the attractiveness of Jesus' example, but go no further. Do we think the call to leadership like Jesus the Good Shepherd is pie in the sky or simply a beautiful ideal? The Good Shepherd heart of Jesus the leader is not satisfied by admiration. He is looking for hearts' unity and life. He is the first one to acknowledge that, without him, nothing good is possible. He is the true vine who enables us (the branches) to bear fruit. His call to come follow him as leaders automatically transmits to any one of us with an open heart the power to be transformed and live the leadership he shows us. In a formal way, we enter the door and journey of Jesus' leadership through what Christians call the sacraments of Baptism, Eucharist (Mass), and Confirmation. These three sacraments are visible signs and rituals that convey an interior, divine transformation and participation in God's power and life. Rooted in these three and supported through daily prayer with God, you and I can resemble Jesus the Good Shepherd more and more.

This is one of the reasons why Jesus Christ and Christianity have always been called the 'Good News'. This is a translation of the original Latin word that was meant to announce an earth-shaking paradigm, defining reality. It was a term reserved to Roman emperors who, at the time, were considered gods. The reality and message of Jesus Christ is truly revolutionary at a heart, mind, and behavioral level. Indeed, it touches the most existential reality of our personhood.

> **Since the dawn of humanity, men and women have aspired to be gods. Now God himself makes sharing his divine life possible through his own initiative. How is this possible for man? It is through living the new commandment of love that men and women come to their complete fulfillment. "The "commandment" of love is only possible because it is more than a requirement. Love can be "commanded" because it has first been given." This commandment applies to leaders as well. Every leadership position (i.e., relationship wherein one influences others) implies an administration of love. The 'instructions' for a leader's administration begin and end with the new commandment of love. While there are often no easy answers in leadership (to paraphrase the title from Ron Heifetz's best-selling leadership book), the sure guide is always love.[196]**

Before such a gift, the only responsible attitude is openness and gratitude. Let us accept the gift of life in Jesus Christ. It is here rooted in him that you can actualize your dreams of leadership to the full.

---

[195] Jordan Peterson, *12 Rules for Life*, 26 (Kindle version)

[196] Haslam, Nathaniel, *The Future of Leadership*, 39.

We live in a time when experience is king. There might be some who are reading this book and say these things are unscientific, childish even. My response would be that their claim is unscientific. Science is based on data, which in turn is a measure of experience. Billions of people have experienced God and met Jesus Christ risen from the dead. Their life transformation and testimony is a robust data set that cannot be ignored. In millions of cases, this claim is backed up by men, women, and children of all races and social classes who chose suffering and death instead of renouncing their belief in Jesus Christ as God. This very large data set of life experience contradicts the most basic human instinct, which is to preserve your life. There was something much greater and transcendent at work for these millions who found strength to persevere in Jesus Christ even under great suffering.

For my part, I also testify that Jesus Christ is God, that he suffered on the cross for me and rose from the dead. I have met him and have a real, daily relationship with him. As a trained engineer and student of the sciences as well as a former atheist, I previously did not believe any of this. God, however, was merciful and very gracious to me— He revealed his son Jesus to me. It is he who called me to the priesthood and a life of servant leadership that I have lived the past 22 years. "The personal encounter with the Risen Christ makes divine love the center of the leader's life. Each person can make this experience. It is not wishful thinking because God has taken the initiative to make it possible."[197] I invite you to ask Jesus Christ the Good Shepherd to teach you and reveal his Sacred Heart to you. You will find all you desire and much more. In him, you will find the source and summit of leadership.

Questions for Personal Reflection and Group Discussion

1. Why is Jesus a good example as a leader?
2. What is the leadership significance of the proposed Christian belief in God becoming human like you? What does this say about leadership and humble service?
3. What comes to your mind when you hear the word 'sacrifice'? How did Jesus live sacrificial leadership?
4. What are 2-3 examples from your life when you were called to sacrifice for the greater good? What sacrifices will you need to make in order to lead more like Jesus?
5. What emotions and convictions do you experience when hearing Jesus gave you power to live leadership as he did?
6. What is your take-away from this chapter?

---

[197] Ibid, 41.

CHAPTER 7
A CHRISTIAN LEADERSHIP MODEL

The critical crossroads at which every would-be disciple sooner or later arrives is the harrowing decision whether to deny his teacher or to deny himself. Such a decision is indeed "harrowing" because the individual human being does not easily acquiesce to following the way marked by anyone other than himself, even if that other is the Word Incarnate.[198]

The rulers of the Gentiles lord it over them, and their great ones are tyrants over them. It will not be so among you; but whoever wishes to be great among you must be your servant, and whoever wishes to be first among you must be your slave; just as the Son of Man came not to be served but to serve.[199]

A Christian leader is an integrally formed apostle who, impelled by the love of Christ and following his example, works with others to make present the mystery of Christ and his Kingdom through inspiring, guiding, and forming others and through the evangelization of society and culture in ways that seek the greatest possible impact.[200]

---

[198] Merikakis, Erasmo, *Fire of Mercy*, Vol IV, 210.

[199] Matthew 20:25-27

[200] Bartunek, John, essay *What is Regnum Christi*

The Curse of Oak Island. Have you heard of it? Previously unbeknownst to me, it is a very popular nine-year series following centuries of old treasure hunts for the famed buried treasure off the coast of Nova Scotia. I first saw an episode flying to visit my family in Pennsylvania. It turns out that my dad had been watching it for several years. It was fascinating to see the enthusiasm and dedication of these men and women, who have given years of study, research, and diligent work to uncover the truth of what happened on Oak Island over the past centuries. Some claim the Crusaders brought treasure and religious artifacts and buried it on this island. Some believe pirates' gold is hidden there. Others claim the English, French, or Portuguese buried the famed riches. Whatever the case may be, various treasure hunters and excavation crews have come to this fame spot over the years.

One of the central details of this show (like any treasure hunt) are treasure maps. There are several old maps that give directions on where the treasure may be on the island. If a treasure map is not accurate, it leads you on a wild goose chase. If accurate, you have a fighting chance to reach 'X' marks the spot. I think this is a good analogy to help us understand the importance of a leadership model. A model is similar to a map that leads us to our ultimate destination, approximating to the path of what we seek. It outlines the scope of the situation at hand.

As we learned in Chapter 2, there are many different leadership models, based on different perspectives such as the importance of leadership traits, leadership behaviors, group dynamics, or approaches to different circumstances which require adaptation. Every of those leadership models (often used in business, education and non profit sectors) show value and merit. My intent with this book is both to reaffirm existing leadership models as helpful and useful, but challenge the reader and to consider there is a much greater panorama and foundation to leadership. I would like to propose a leadership model that is rooted and grounded in Jesus Christ. Practical, surface level leadership models are helpful, but they lack the existential and metaphysical grounding that is required to bridge the temporal and eternal realities of human life. They are decoupled from transcendent meaning-purpose and objective morality-ethics, (which Aristotle rightly claims is directly linked to human flourishing and excellence). As we have already discussed, Jesus Christ is the bridge given to humanity between Heaven and Earth. He is the bridge between human and divine leadership.

A good summary of human leadership theories and development approaches is outlined in the *The Handbook for Teaching Leadership*. This work is a summary of 40 highly regarded leadership programs around the world. The book is a result of a symposium held at Harvard University in 2009. The three-pronged concept of leadership outlined in the book (Knowing Leadership, Doing Leadership, Being a Leader) was originally coined by the U.S. military leadership development program. For all the practical benefits of books like that, we still do not find a deeper understanding and model for leadership at the highest level of our existence.
The following is an outline of the Christian leadership model that I would like to offer the reader based on the Shepherd Heart of Jesus Christ, a Christian worldview, the teachings of the

Church, and my 20 years of experience working in the leadership, both in academic circles as well as in coaching many senior business and cultural leaders.

A Christian Leadership Model:

1. One Foundational Principle: Jesus Christ, the Good Shepherd

2. 4 Leadership Behaviors

- Have a Clear Identity and be a Transmitter of Identity
- Embraces Holistic Virtue Development
- Dedication to the Mission
- Develop the next Generation of Leaders

3. 8 Leadership Virtues

- Humility: to live in the truth of who God is, who others are and who you are
- Prudence: sound judgment in determining actions
- Self-Mastery: controlling your passions amid personal drive for success
- Perseverance: a sound commitment to overcoming obstacles
- Prayer: regular communication with God, humbly seeking his will and friendship
- Integrity: consistency in what one professes to be and how one lives
- Influence: moving others to think and act uprightly through conscientious effort
- Magnanimity: commitment to serve others by putting their needs first

4. 4 Leadership Decision-making Criteria

- Human Dignity: all people are infinitely valuable, worthy of love and deserving of respect and protection (no matter their age, physical- intellectual ability or their perceived contribution to society)
- Common Good: the overall order and stability of society at the service of helping individuals to flourish
- Solidarity: you are your brother and sister's keeper. What happens to others must and should matter to you
- Subsidiarity: let the lower level (be it in politics, education, church, business) do for itself what it can without interference or manipulation by a higher level authority. This fosters responsibility and maturity at all levels

This model can easily incorporate other leadership models, but it goes beyond them to give an existential and metaphysical grounding as well as a moral orientation through love as the object of all leadership.

Let us take some time to go through the first two elements of this model. The second two will be covered in the following chapters.

1. One Organizing Principle: Jesus Christ the Good Shepherd

A treasure map always has a starting and an end point. We should not be surprised that leadership also has an existential starting and ending point. Leadership starts with the loving heart of the Good Shepherd, Jesus Christ and reaches fulfillment when it does all for love of God and neighbor. We each look for an ideal and model to emulate in different facets of our life. It might be someone in our profession or someone who inspired us in our childhood such as a family member or famous public figure. As leaders and those trying to grow in their leadership, it is no surprise that we also tend to seek for those who have climbed the mountain of leadership and stand on its summit as a reference point that beckons us to follow and do the same. Jesus Christ is the one and ultimate ideal for us.

As we read in the last chapter, Jesus defines and is leadership in his very person. As St John the Apostle teaches us in his writings, God is love. It should not be a surprise then that we hear Jesus speaking about himself as the Good Shepherd who lays down his life for his flock. We discussed and covered this theme at length in the last chapter. At this point, I want to reaffirm and emphasize that this is the starting point. We can call it the 'Big Bang of leadership'. Just as the physical universe came into existence out of nothing, so too does all leadership— it finds its underpinnings and beginnings in Jesus. The universe has its internal laws and principles; leadership does as well. One of the mind-boggling revelations we receive in Christianity is that Jesus Christ is the foundation and organizing principle for both the physical, social, and moral universe.

The implications of this ideal and starting point are enormous. No matter what aspect of leadership we want to consider, the starting point is the shepherd heart of Jesus Christ. If we are talking about knowing more about leadership (including the history of leadership and power as well as theories about this subject), we start by looking at the love of the heart of Jesus Christ. On the other hand, we could talk about leadership development programs that focus on concrete skills or habits. Once again, the reference point for how to proceed with such development efforts is Jesus Christ and his shepherd heart. The same applies to developing a leadership conviction and awareness (a 'being leader' mentality). The same is true of circumstantial and adaptive leadership scenarios. In all, we should start with the loving and compassionate heart of Jesus Christ the Good Shepherd.

American writer and artist, Henry Miller, once said "no man is great enough or wise enough for any of us to surrender our destiny to. The only way in which anyone can lead us is to restore to us the belief in our own guidance."[201] Without discounting the importance of discovering your

---

[201] Henry Miller, in *The Wisdom of the Heart* (1941)

own conscience and inner inspiration, God reveals there is an ultimate reference point. The spark of life comes from *Someone*, not from chaos or ourselves in isolation. One of the hallmarks of any age is its clarity on following time-tested, wise principles. We need to go outside ourselves and receive guidance from others. Samuel Rayburn, a former American Congressman considered by many as historically the greatest Speaker of the US House of Representatives, emphasized "you cannot be a leader, and ask other people to follow you, unless you know how to follow, too."[202] For us as leaders in the 21st century and beyond, we need to learn to follow. God has given us good human role models, but the first and ultimate reference point for our leadership is Jesus Christ the Good Shepherd. Let us learn every day how to follow him more closely.

Having clarity on the one foundational, organizing principle, we can now proceed to reflect on the four leadership behaviors.

2. Four Leadership Behaviors

After anchoring our leadership in the Good Shepherd heart of Jesus Christ, we now turn to the main traits that characterize Christian leadership. Unlike some Christian leadership models that rehash and re-present certain virtues that are present in secular theories of leadership (integrity, honesty, perseverance, public speaking skills, small group leadership, ability to delegate, et cetera), this model is based on the Sacred Heart of Jesus the Good Shepherd. The four leadership behaviors that follow flow directly from his loving heart. Different leadership values and virtues can be explained in light of these four.

Clear Identity and Transmitter of Identity

The first part of this leadership behavior is to have a clear leadership identity. One definition of identity is "the distinguishing character or personality of an individual."[203] For the sake of clarity, we should also grasp the difference between objective and subjective identity. Subjective identity is the way you see yourself in relation to others and the universe. This may be more-or-less aligned to your objective identity, which is fixed based on reality and not dependent on what you think and how you see yourself. As an example, I may subjectively see my identity as a human being who is a random fluke of chaotic evolution with no purpose in life other than to get by and make the most of things. This, however, is not very close to the objective identity that God confers on you as a created and willed child who is wanted and

---

[202] Sam Rayburn, The Leadership of Speaker Sam Rayburn, Collected Tributes of His Congressional Colleagues (1961), p. 34. House Doc. 87–247. "A compilation of tributes paid him in the Hall of the House of Representatives, June 12, 1961, and other pertinent material, to celebrate the occasion of his having served as Speaker twice as long as any of his predecessors in the history of the United States: Sixteen years and 273 days" (title page)

[203] Merriam-Webster Dictionary

has a mission on earth as well as an eternal destiny beyond this temporary walk on Earth. A leadership journey requires having a clear identity based in objective reality of who you are and your purpose in life. Subjective identity must be conformed to reflect your objective identity given by God.

How do you find a clear identity? It is very important to know God's revelation about your life and communicate with him. We will discuss this further in the next chapter when speaking about virtue development and prayer. For now, I encourage you to devote time to study the Bible (or the holy book associated with your faith tradition) and give time to God every day to discuss the way he sees you. Identity is never simply how you see yourself, it is subjective and only one part of the equation. You need to anchor your subjective identity based on the objective identity that is rooted in objective reality. Trumpeter and composer, Wynton Marsalis, described this objective reality in his own way saying "I try to find the core values that are so fundamental that they transcend ethnic identity. That doesn't mean I run from it. I embrace African-American culture and I love it and embrace it, but it is a part of a human identity. So I'm always trying to make a larger human statement."[204] We should not run from our experiences and cultural background. They are part of us, yet they must be integrated into an identity grounded in the objective truth of who we are.

Finding a clearer identity also comes through service and acts of love. In the 21st century, many regard Mahatma Gandhi as one of the top 10 leaders of all time. According to Gandhi, "the best way to find yourself is to lose yourself in the service of others."[205] Identity is not something you find by clutching your ego. As Jesus was famously known to say, 'if you want to save your life, you must lose it.' This especially applies to your ego. Writer, Elizabeth Goudge, expressed the importance of identity rooted in love and self-giving when she said "a sense of identity is the gift of love, and only love can give it."[206]

As a leader, how do I see myself? Do I have an identity as a leader? Have I incorrectly assumed that a degree or certain skills makes me a leader? Have I forgotten that leadership starts within based on how I see myself in the world? What in my identity needs to be adjusted and matured? What can I do about this?

The second part of this leadership trait is to be a transmitter of identity. This is often a forgotten aspect of leadership. It is also about passing on identity. Yes, everyone needs to have their own identity, but your job as a leader is to help others discover their objective identity. Since your mature identity is not simply subjective but rooted into an objective reality that touches and influences all of us, you can transmit and pass on identity. Think of Jesus Christ the Good

---

[204] Wynton Marsalis, in Wynton Marsalis gives spirited take on jazz with 'Abyssinian Mass'

[205] Mahatma Gandhi, in The Power of Purpose: Find Meaning, Live Longer, Better, p. 35.

[206] Elizabeth Goudge, The Dean's Watch (1960), Ch. IX.ii.

Shepherd, he had a very clear identity, but went on to help all of us better know and embrace our true identity. As St John Paul II was known to say, Jesus came 'to reveal man to himself'.

Two books that can help us better plumb the depths of transmitting identity are *The Way of the Shepherd* and *Dedication and Leadership*. "Great leaders leave their mark by constantly communicating their values and sense of mission. They tirelessly call their people to engage in the cause. They know people are easily distracted by the many pulls of life, so they are continually calling them back to the mission, back to their purpose for being."[207] Three concrete recommendations on how to pass on identity include "build trust with your followers by modeling authenticity, integrity, and compassion. Set high standards of performance. Relentlessly communicate your values and sense of mission."[208]

Nothing can replace your presence in transmitting identity. "Do not be an absentee shepherd... Nothing reassures the sheep more than the presence of the shepherd."[209] We have all met 'armchair quarterbacks' and seen leaders who rarely come down from their 'ivory tower'. This is ineffective and bad leadership. Do you want to be like this? People will follow you when you transmit clear identity through active presence with them. If you do not invest time and presence with others, "if you give your people halfhearted leadership, you'll get a halfhearted following. But if you invest yourself in them, if you have a heart for them, your people will return your investment with a heartfelt following."[210] This is a first aspect of transmitting identity: stay close to your sheep.

A second aspect of transmitting identity is to frame the others' identity in context of a mission that involves a struggle and a quest. Famous epics such as *The Lord of the Rings* leverage the power of grounding identity in context of a mission involving struggle. In the past 100 years, we have seen first-hand how Communism has mobilized millions based on this principle. The Communist movement has captured the imagination of many and turned them to dedicated action. Christians should not be surprised by this phenomenon since every human being has a heart for an ideal, we all look for a mission. If one is not helped to find their identity in God and his mission, he is susceptible to settle for something second-rate.

As a former Communist leader and trainer, Douglas Hyde, speaks point-blank about instilling a leadership identity in others:it starts with the person himself and then multiplies itself in others. He says "every Communist a leader, every factory a fortress' is one of their slogans. But it is more than a slogan, it is an aim, and one which they set out very determinedly to achieve."[211] As

---

[207] *The Way of the Shepherd*, 49.

[208] Ibid, 50.

[209] Ibid, 64.

[210] Ibid, 106.

[211] Hyde, Douglas, *Dedication and Leadership*, 29.

a Christian, Hyde questioned the average believer's identity and their conviction to transmit it. He noticed reluctance and complacency to transmit a Christian leadership identity. "I believe, as any Christian must, that Christianity has something infinitely better to offer than has Communism…we have something immensely better to sell. Yet it is they who have been able to influence our generation much more profoundly than have we."[212] Why is this the case?

The Communists (and similar ideological movements) give us helpful insights to better understand the gift of a Christian worldview and leadership identity. Communism is based on the false claim that capitalists are the problem, that they need a revolution (bloody if necessary) to right the injustices of the world. There are injustices in the world and there is, indeed, a global (spiritual) struggle for the heart of mankind. This is the struggle of good versus evil. The success of transmitting leadership identity to others is closely connected to anchoring your message in the global struggle and inviting others to play their part. Douglas Hyde elaborates saying "there is a great battle going on all over the world. That this includes his own country, his own town, his own neighborhood, the factory or office where he works. He is made to feel that the period of history in which he happens to be living is a decisive one and that he personally has a decisive role to play. He is part of a great, worldwide movement which is challenged on all sides, confronted by an implacable enemy and involved in a battle which will decide the course of history for generations ahead."[213] When was the last time you heard someone inviting you to be part of the global struggle? Was it from the Gender Ideology movement? The LGBTQ+ movement? The Communist movement? The Woke Culture movement? Some other minority rights group? Have representatives of your faith and Church done the same with equal or more fervor? Have you been encouraged to enter the 'spiritual battle' of our times by leading with the loving shepherd heart of Jesus Christ?

We should not be surprised that transmitting leadership identity can be effective despite the message coming at times from movements with deficient worldviews. As a leader, remember every person's heart longs for an ideal, wants to be part of something greater than itself, and is easily swayed by someone with passion, conviction, and enthusiasm. "To the Christian it may seem extraordinary that an atheist tutor can convince a group of others whom he is instructing in an atheist creed that they are part of a great crusade fighting on the side of good. In fact, this would appear simply to prove man's deep need for a cause, for a faith. It is evidence of modern man's spiritual hunger."[214] If Christians do not transmit their faith and leadership identity, others will fill the vacuum. For the Christian, the mission is to transmit the identity of being a child of God, the call to live as part of the Kingdom of God and share this gift with those you meet. God is the initiator and main driver of transmitting identity, but he asks each one of us to freely collaborate in the effort.

---

[212] Ibid, 12.

[213] Ibid, 52.

[214] Ibid, 60.

Seriously reflect on the great confidence that comes from an encounter with the living Jesus Christ and the power that flows from his resurrection. Christians are bearers of an immense gift to humanity. You might think that you have little to offer others. As a Christ-bearer, however, you have been given a gift that can transform many lives. If you are not Christian but are convinced of the transformative power of love, you will lead at a much higher level of excellence. You will be able to transmit identity and positively change the world one person at a time. "If you are going to turn a man into a leader you must first give him confidence in himself. The second thing is that you must give him something to be confident about. This world is full of people possessed of an overdose of self-confidence but with nothing to back it up. Despite what they may think about the matter, these are not leaders."[215] There is not greater confidence than the one that comes from Jesus Christ. It is his confidence that flows in believers' heart and mind.

The person who effectively transmits identity is living this first leadership behavior. Leaders do not complain about problems but do something about them. Problems start with people and their hearts. Transmitting identity means you take a proactive approach to spread not just a theoretical way of seeing the world and life, but also literally transmit a way of life. "The task of making leaders is really one of creating an attitude of mind. When some new situation arises, the reaction of most people is to ask: when is someone going to do something about it? The spontaneous reaction of the trained leader is at once to ask himself: what do I do in this situation? He comes before his fellows and says: We should do this and that and the other. And they follow him. Partly because he speaks with authority, they respect him and look up to him, but also because they have learned from experience that he has something to offer."[216] A Christian leader is someone who takes initiative to transmit his identity to others.

Embrace Holistic Virtue Development

When I first entered the seminary in 1999, I was struck by their comprehensive growth plan. Rise at 5:45 AM. Make your bed first thing (straight and neat like they do at West Point). Shower and shave. Shine your shoes and walk into the chapel for first prayers by 6:20. Breakfast, then housework. Morning classes, but also time for exercise. Study, exercise, and pray in the afternoon. Dinner and night prayers together. The schedule was rigorous but freeing. Each activity gave us chances to forge different virtues (ie. good habits done with ease) such as: consistent prayer life, spirit of sacrifice, self-mastery, physical fitness, intellectual study and reflection. Think this sounds strange?

I agree not everyone is called to be a priest and live 7-12 years in a seminary preparing for ordination. Virtue development, however, is for everyone. All leaders must embrace holistic virtue formation. 'Holistic' means the parts are closely connected and cannot be understood

---

[215] Ibid, 63.

[216] Ibid, 156-57.

without reference to the whole. In medicine, holistic refers to the treatment of the entire person (not just symptoms). Think about someone who has achieved great earthly success. An Olympic athlete like Simone Biles has formed many habits to support her quest to win gold medals (demanding practice schedule, eating habits, proper rest, emotional boundaries, etc.). Leaders who were not handed a title or achievement forged habits that brought them where they are today. Do you think you can lead without forming good habits?

Formation? Are we speaking about rock formations? A compact military unit of men, planes, or tanks? No. Formation has another meaning: development and growth. I am choosing the word 'formation' because development is often used to indicate fundraising or growth in skills. In Christian circles, we use the terms 'formation' and 'development' to describe growth and training. General Colin Powell said "I believe that leaders must be born with a natural connection and affinity to others, which then must be encouraged and developed by parents and teachers and molded by training, experience, and mentoring. You can learn to be a better leader. And you can also waste your natural talents by ceasing to learn and grow."[217]

My 12-year formation program in the Legionaries of Christ was a blessing. It emphasized virtue formation and provided an organic blueprint of what is possible when the human and divine cooperate. One of our formation texts provides a valuable insight: forming solid virtue requires patient work in the three areas of convictions, attitudes and behaviors.

> **Convictions are the human and supernatural certainties that guide our actions. They also constitute the motives for which a particular way of acting is deemed a personal good, something worth choosing. Attitudes are habitual dispositions of the heart, awakened and sustained by grace, which incline man to act in line with his convictions. Behaviors are the concrete manifestations of one's convictions and attitudes, and, when put into action, also reinforce them: The virtuous life thus builds, strengthens, and shapes freedom.**[218]

Our behavior (virtue or vice) is directly linked to our convictions and attitudes. We cannot undertake virtue formation without keeping these three in mind.

Why the word 'holistic'? The human person is a harmonious union of several dimensions: spiritual, character, emotion, psyche, intellect, sexuality, and biological. You cannot look at a part of yourself and say this part is touched by sexuality and this other one is not. The spiritual reality of your person is not confined to one part of your body. You are one whole and entire being. For this reason, it is important to grasp leadership formation as something holistic (in view of the entire person).

---

[217] Colin Powell, *It Worked For Me: In Life and Leadership* (2012), p. 101

[218] Christus Vita Vestra: Ratio Institutionis of the Congregation of the Legionaries of Christ, Rome, 2017, 120.

A Christian Leadership

This is why Christian leadership formation (development) often speaks of formation on four levels: spiritual, human, intellectual, and pastoral (mission). Spiritual formation refers to our union with God especially through individual and communal prayer, rites of worship, and reading of Scriptures. Human formation focuses on virtue development in areas such as: prudence, perseverance, self-mastery, self-presentation, etiquette, and communication. Intellectual formation addresses the development of the mind, study of the different areas of knowledge, as well as the ability to apply this to modern day circumstances. Pastoral (mission) formation is to help us grow the habits we need for a given mission we've undertaken. Traditional leadership development themes often fall in this last category of mission. Although they are very important, leaders need to keep their eyes on the formation of their entire person.

You may be tempted to react in one of two possible extremes. The first is to reduce formation of one area; this is the type of person who says that leadership skill development is everything. Then there is the intellectual who thinks their book knowledge is enough. You even have spiritual, churchgoing folks who say 'God has everything under control' and they use this as a cover to not do anything about the mission God has given them."The Christian who is trying to train and produce leaders may object that Christians are concerned with the supernatural and must operate at that level…it is theologically sound to say that the supernatural is built on the natural…the natural level which is precisely where the Christian tends often to be at his weakest."[219] God expects Christians and all people of good will to invest their human talents for others. This requires us to train ourselves, be better public speakers, manage groups of people to increase our ability to craft a vision and to strategically achieve it. Formation is needed in all four dimensions.

The second temptation is to be overwhelmed by the task at hand. 'Rome was not built in one day'. Smart generals use the 'divide and conquer' strategy when possible. In virtue formation, you can only intentionally work on 2-3 areas in a given time. Do not let yourself get overwhelmed. Pick a few areas which are critical to your growth and start there. This is a life-long journey.The important thing is to start. We will speak a bit more about this in the chapter dedicated to virtue formation.

Embracing holistic leadership development is not simply a matter for you. As a leader, you are entrusted with caring for others. This includes helping them embrace not only with their identity, but also to take up virtue formation. Many people do not see themselves as leaders and do not realize they can be transformed into one. "Quiet ordinary people with only average potentialities, can be brought to a state of mind where they are anxious to serve their cause by becoming leaders, are made into leaders and are enable to lead effectively."[220] Let us remember that the 'average person' can be a good leader. Believe in the people around you and their potential. "You must believe in the human material you have at your disposal. You must not be

---

[219] Hyde, Douglas, *Dedication and Leadership*, 15.

[220] Ibid, 35.

afraid to make big demands upon it and you must skillfully and intelligently call for sacrifices, following up each such call with another."[221] Leaders challenge those under their charge to live up to their potential. They exhort and rally them in walking towards the best versions of themselves.

The process of walking with others in their virtue formation requires patience and sometimes painstaking work. Douglas Hyde formed thousands of Communist leaders, but he mentions one who was short, overweight and had a terrible stutter. Despite these obstacles, he turned this open and generous soul into a leader of men at his workplace. "First, I inspired him, gave him the clearly-defined goal of a new and better world and the belief that he and others could between them achieve it provided that they prepared themselves sufficiently for the moment of opportunity. I gave him a sense of involvement in a battle, and the conviction that by going to classes he would gain the arms and ammunition required for the fight."[222] How proactive am I in helping others to form virtuous habits? Like Jesus the Good Shepherd, leaders are not self-focused, but centered on the good of others, on helping them achieve their potential and live their mission.

Embrace holistic virtue formation. This is one of the four leadership behaviors. It is something you can do. Leadership guru, Pat Lencioni, exhorts us saying "there is hope for us because we too can become extraordinary leaders if we only embrace the fact that success is not so much a function of intelligence or natural ability, but rather of commitment to the right disciplines."[223] Let us not be afraid to challenge ourselves and challenge others. God invites us to transcend our self-imposed (or societal imposed) narrow visions of our (or others') leadership potential. "The Communists' appeal to idealism is direct and audacious. They say that if you make mean little demands upon people, you will get a mean little response which is all you deserve, but, if you make big demands on them, you will get a heroic response…They work on the assumption that if you call for big sacrifices people will respond to this and, moreover, the relatively smaller sacrifices will come quite naturally."[224] Trust me. If you pursue excellence in holistic virtue formation, you will be a well-rounded leader and be ready to help others experience the freedom of virtuous living.

From a Christian perspective, virtue formation is always seen from a perspective of God's plan of revealing his love to each person and letting that love change them. This is another way of saying and describing the Kingdom of God. "When you distill it to its simplest expression, a "vision of formation" referred to above is nothing more and nothing less than the pursuit of the

---

[221] Ibid, 30.

[222] Ibid, 70.

[223] Lencioni, Pat, *The Four Obsessions of an Extraordinary Executive*, John Wiley & Sons Inc, San Francisco, CA, 2000, 135

[224] Hyde, Douglas, *Dedication and Leadership*, 18.

A Christian Leadership

"Great Commission." It is the task of "making disciples," of being conformed to the image of Christ."[225] As I will describe later, this is a major challenge for Catholic and Protestant churches. They need to transform their formation programs from a 'provide the minimum' approach to a 'forge missionary disciples' approach. Christians have received a great gift, but they need to embrace holistic virtue development if they are to fulfill the responsibility of passing along the gift.

Dedication to the Mission

Visiting a seminary for the first time can be an eye opening experience. In 1999, I made an eight hour drive from Rochester, NY where I worked as an engineer to visit the Novitiate and College of Humanities of the Legionaries of Christ located in Cheshire, CT. I did not know what to expect. It was an eye-opening experience to walk into the chapel and see 150 men under the age of 30. During my two-day stay interacting with these young men, I was inspired by their dedication to the mission of helping others. They had promising lives ahead of them before they entered the seminary. Many were intelligent and also athletic. They could not wait to become priests and give their lives to changing the world person-by-person. They were truly dedicated to the happiness of others, ready to do whatever it takes.

Dedication to the mission. This is the third leadership behavior. It flows directly from the overarching and foundational principle of the loving shepherd heart of Jesus Christ. Jesus was dedicated to the mission. He came to give his life for each one of us. Everything he did was to reveal his father's love for humanity. Every word, every gesture, every act of suffering had purpose and meaning related to his mission. He showed each one of us that dedication to the mission is a hallmark of a true leader. A leader's dedication cannot be to himself. By definition, Jesus' mission was oriented towards others. The same goes for our leadership calling. As the famous slogan goes in the *Mission Impossible* movies, the question is whether you choose to accept it or not.

Look at human examples of leadership and you will find dedication to the mission. "Pick any great leader you can think of. General Patton incessantly demanded that his troops stay on the move. Jesus relentlessly appealed to his followers to spread the good news of the kingdom. Lincoln constantly declared that the Union must be preserved."[226] This is one of the attractive things about true leaders. They are dedicated. Dedication inspires people. Dedication attracts others because, deep down, we all want to be part of something worth sacrificing our lives. Dedication implies achieving something good.

I have referred to Communism in this book. In many respects, you could just as easily substitute these references with gender ideology or cancel culture. The zeal, dedication, and single-

---

[225] Hunter, James, To Change the World, 22.

[226] *Way of the Shepherd*, 49-50.

mindedness of these groups is similar. These insights apply to leadership in general including church leadership. "If you ask me what is the distinguishing mark of the Communist, what it is that Communists most outstandingly have in common, I would not say, as some people might expect, their ability to hate…I would say that beyond any shadow of doubt it is their idealism, their zeal, dedication, devotion to their cause and willingness to sacrifice."[227] Given the powerful example of dedicated men and women, we need to be conscious that leaders who are dedicated have the most influence for good or evil.

We should ask ourselves if we are dedicated or not. Is it to a mission consistent with the shepherd heart of Jesus Christ who sends us on a mission to love one another and build a culture of justice, peace and love? Have I rather become enamored of utopian illusions founded on visions of society, human relations and economy which are not rooted in human reason and God's revelation? Is my dedication rooted in a will to power and implementing my own vision of humanity?

If you are like most people today, you are not dedicated to the mission. Apathy and complacency have been widespread. This is why our human experience revolves around having complacent followers and few leaders. Most of us are content to let others be the change agents; we are satisfied with a life of fulfilling our base desires and petty pursuits. We lack the initiative and commitment to go beyond ourselves and be part of an exciting and life changing cause. This unfortunately includes many Christians. "The number of non-dedicated, non-active members continues to grow. Their minimal Christianity, their lack of dedication and absence of activity becomes the norm. It is a vicious circle."[228] This is both inconsistent an irreconcilable for the Christian who is, by very definition, dedicated to the mission by essence and calling.

There are many positive consequences to being dedicated to the mission. The first is that dedication attracts others. "Like attracts like. Those who are attracted by the dedication they see within the movement will themselves be possessed of a latent idealism, a capacity for dedication. Thus dedication perpetuates itself. It sets the tone and pace of the movement as a whole. This being so, the movement can make big demands upon its followers, knowing that the response will come."[229] When was the last time you saw people attracted to a deflated and unenthusiastic sports team, political party, youth group, corporate culture, or after school high school club? Never. Just like we are not attracted to rancid food, people run away from groups that are unhappy, depressed, or constantly losing members. Groups filled with dedicated members naturally attract more members— a spirit of dedication is contagious.

---

[227] Hyde, Douglas, *Dedication and Leadership*, 15-16.

[228] Ibid, 40.

[229] Ibid, 20-1.

A second consequence of dedication is it galvanizes groups. It creates a spirit of purpose and sacrifice. "If the majority of members, from the leaders down, are characterized by their single-minded devotion to the cause, if it is quite clear that the majority are giving until it hurts, putting their time, money, thought and if necessary life itself at its disposal, then those who consider joining will assume that this is what will be expected of them. If they nonetheless make the decision to join, they will come already conditioned to sacrifice till it hurts."[230] A lack of dedication leads to mediocrity and division. Members can be led to believe complacency and is fine. Dedication to the mission roots out this vice and unifies the members and team.

A third consequence of dedication to the mission is you set a strong foundation for forming other leaders. A leader, team, or organization filled with the spirit of dedication will naturally make this a hallmark in the formation of other leaders in the mission. "It is of course quite possible to produce leaders of some sort by teaching certain techniques. These are not the sort of leaders the Communists are interested in, nor, I suggest, are they the ones the Christian cause requires most today. You can learn certain techniques and so become a leader who leads for himself—if by leadership you simply mean getting to the top whether it be of an organization, a business, a profession or the political system. But the first requirement, if you are going to produce a leader for a cause, is that he should be dedicated."[231]

A fourth consequence of being dedicated to the mission is the immense impact and influence that is deployed. Dedicated individuals exponentially multiply influence by coming together. . "What distinguishes the Communist movement from most others and makes it possible for so small a minority to make so great an impact upon our time is the dedication of the average individual member and the immense and dynamic force this represents when all those individuals collectively make their contribution to the cause."[232] Think about your circle of influence. Do you realize the immense possibilities for positive change and life improvement if those you influence were dedicated to the mission? Are you constrained with a narrow mindset and a limited horizon of what is possible? As a person of faith, have you erroneously capitulated to the idea that God and his Kingdom is irrelevant and has nothing to say to the modern world? Being a true leader means you clearly understand the possibility for change an improvement in your life and others. By being dedicated to the mission and bringing others to share that dedication, you can literally influence an entire city, state and nation. In fact, a few truly dedicated people can influence the history of the world. Think of the 12, insignificant apostles of Jesus who literally influenced the entire world for the past 2000 years.

People of faith have no excuse to be put to shame by members of abortion, Communist, or cancel culture movements. It is a sad day when those who have been given so much in their

---

[230] Ibid, 21.

[231] Ibid, 26.

[232] Ibid, 25-6.

faith sit on the sidelines while those with reductionistic and self-centered ideologies go about, openly proclaiming their false utopias and pseudo-rights. "To the Christian there is something peculiarly poignant about the atheist Communist saying, as so many so often do, from the very depths of their hearts, 'There is nothing too good for the Party' and then going out and making their actions match their words. There is no need to underline what the Christians' positive response should be."[233] Christians in particular should be ready to dedicate their lives to spreading Christ the Good Shepherd's message around the entire world. They should be unafraid to stand up and be heard. "The well-instructed, fully committed, totally dedicated Christian has little to fear. But dedication must be met with dedication. Ideally it should be backed by a genuine understanding of one's own beliefs and of the other man's too. This must be the starting point for any dialogue."[234]

Christian or no Christian, are you ready to dedicate yourself to the mission? A life lived without dedication is a life lived in mediocrity and unfulfilled potential. God created you with a mission to accomplish. I encourage you to pray about this and seek to better understand your mission. When you find it, put your hand to the plow and give it your all.

Develop the Next Generation

The fourth and finally leadership behavior is to develop the next generation. Leaders recognize that all people have dreams and hopes. This is especially true of youth. I have never met a person who did not have a dream for their lives. In many cases, it was to become a veterinarian or engineer, a lawyer or doctor, a wife or husband. Others dream of changing the world by finding the cure to cancer, helping the human race explore outer space, inventing a new technology that will change the way people interact. Others still hope to eliminate poverty or establish greater peace on earth. "Young people have always dreamed of better worlds and we must hope that they always will. The day we lose our dreams all progress will cease. Idealistic young people will want to change the world and will pursue their own idealistic course in any case. If their idealism is not appealed to and canalized within the circles in which they have grown up they will seek elsewhere for an outlet."[235] Jesus the Good Shepherd also recognized this and put special emphasis on training and developing those who would carry his message forward. This is what we see in the Catholic Church for 2000 years. We see generation after generation of leaders passing on their faith by training others to know and love God and others with the conviction that this is also a mission that they must share.

This key leadership behavior means you and I, as leaders, must channel our dedication in a focused way in order to form the next generation. This area of the mission is not something

---

[233] Ibid, 157-58.

[234] Ibid, 21-2.

[235] Ibid, 17-8.

secondary but essential. "Youth is a period of idealism. The Communists attract young people by appealing directly to that idealism. Too often, others have failed either to appeal to it or to use it and they are the losers as a consequence. We have no cause to complain if, having neglected the idealism of youth, we see others come along, take it, use it and harness it to their cause—and against our own."[236] Jesus continually shows kindness, compassion and attention to children in young people. In his time, only adults were considered important. This lack of appreciation and attention seems rampant in every age including our own. Young people are often considered expendable and are treated as consumers to be manipulated. We, as leaders, must always look at young people as God's children who deserve love and respect. They are the future generations and we must dedicate ourselves to help them become the leaders of tomorrow.

More than ever, young people are isolated and neglected. Social media has made it harder to have quality conversations with them. Whether is in the context of business, or even in the Church, leaders need to take the initiative to go out and find young people and show them attention, care, and concern. "Pope Paul VI, when he was still Archbishop Montini of Milan, once said that in the past it was necessary only for the Church to ring its bell for the people to come to it. Now, however, it is necessary for the Church to take the bell to the people."[237] This reality can be disconcerting and even annoying to leaders.

The commitment to develop the next generation implies strenuous effort to be like Christ the Good Shepherd who goes out to find his sheep and show meticulous tender care. "It's your duty to regularly inquire about the progress of your people, because you're responsible for developing them…Periodically call your people in and ask how they're doing. Ask them if there is anything you can help them with, anything they need clarification on…chances are the members of your flock who need help the most will be the ones who are least likely to ask for it."[238] The younger generations are often slow to ask for help. Your job as a leader is to be at their side on a regular basis. This is not a presence of constant correction but supportive presence. "If a person never indicates they need help when you inquire about their progress, it means either that they don't trust you enough to be honest with you or that you haven't sufficiently challenged them to grow. If it is the latter, you need to look harder for projects you can put in front of your people that will develop them. People who aren't progressively increasing their capabilities have a shepherd who's stunting their growth. You need to wield the rod of inspection to make sure that doesn't happen."[239] Though difficult, your people will notice your interest and care over time.

---

[236] Ibid, 17.

[237] Ibid, 36.

[238] *Way of the Shepherd*, 93.

[239] Ibid, 93-4.

Will this be difficult? Will it cost you personally? Of course. Nothing worthwhile is easy and without sacrifice. "The cost. This approach to leadership comes with a high price tag for the leader…your time, your commitment, your personal energy and involvement. It will cost you yourself. You aren't learning a set of management techniques but an outlook. More than anything, the Way of the Shepherd is a lifestyle of leadership that places great value on the worth of the flock."[240] Being a true leader who develops the next generation goes to the core of Jesus' own words about laying down his life for others. Forming others to be leaders goes to the core of what it means to serve and not seek to be served. It will often push you to your limits and ask you every drop blood, sweat, and tears. It is, however, worth it. It is fruitfulness that is the crowning jewel of your calling to leadership.

I would not be surprised if part of you shakes with fear and trepidation contemplating this aspect of leadership. This is normal when you grasp the enormity of your responsibility and the demands of your office as a leader of influence. "Admittedly, being a leader is often like drinking from the fire hose. It's overwhelming. There are so many things to do, so many priorities. You may be tempted to delegate away the people piece as yet another task on an overly long to-do list."[241] Like Jesus, you must commit not to run away from this responsibility. The leader cannot completely delegate the formation of the next generation to others. Even if you were in a position to delegate to competent and well trained leaders to oversee this, you nonetheless need to stay involved. They need to see you leading by example and not off in some ivory tower. The younger generation can easily tell when they are simply an afterthought.

I would like to give you a time-tested principle for developing the leadership of the next generation. It is very important to give the younger generation a challenging responsibility that helps them take ownership of their cause or mission. In Communist circles, "this will take the form of being sent out to stand at the side of the street or in some public space…this is something very significant indeed. He is making a public witness for the cause which he is now making his own…The significance of all this is that, humble as the task may appear, to engage in it requires for many people a certain degree of moral courage."[242] In a corporate environment, this principle could be applied by giving new hires the experience of going on a sales call and being asked to represent the company with a well established client who understands this part of the training process. In the Church, it might mean sending out high school and college students to give copies of the Bible or rosaries to those they meet. Whatever means you choose, it should put the younger generations in a position where they need to give public witness to their mission. It needs to be someplace where they will likely encounter some opposition. Training the future generations must include scenarios where they make the mission

---

[240] Ibid, 99-100.

[241] Kraemer, Harry, From Values to Action: The Four Principles of Values-Based Leadership, 97.

[242] Hyde, Douglas, *Dedication and Leadership*, 43.

their own, which often implies some failure. Their idealism will often propel them to seek training and greater knowledge so they can better represent the mission.

The final test for a leader is whether he developed the next generation or not. Did you train the future generations or not? It is not something others can do for you. It is tangible and **measurable**. Influential US political commentator Walter Lippmann once wrote that "the final test of a leader is that he leaves behind him in other men the conviction and the will to carry on. ... The genius of a good leader is to leave behind him a situation which common sense, without the grace of genius, can deal with successfully."[243]   Pope Francis also spoke strongly on this theme. "A leader is a good leader if he or she is able to generate other leaders among the young. If he only wants to be the sole leader, he is a tyrant... If they do not sow leadership in others, they are of no use, they are dictators."[244]   So where do you stand on this theme? Are you convinced and committed to develop the next generation?

In this chapter, we have covered a Christian leadership model. This model is built upon the cornerstone of Jesus Christ the Good Shepherd and his loving heart. Four leadership behaviors flow from this foundation. The following two chapters will further explain the other parts of the leadership model: holistic virtue development and leadership decision making criteria. Let us continue the journey confident that this is our calling.

Questions for Personal Reflection and Group Discussion

1. What insights helped you in this chapter?
2. What did the Christian Leadership Model add to your previous conception of leadership?
3. How does the Good Shepherd Heart of Jesus Christ ground this leadership model? How does it enrich the Servant Leadership Model presented in Chapter 2?
4. Which leadership behavior caught your attention? Why? How can you incorporate this in your leadership?
5. As a leader, why is a clear identity important? How can you transmit identity to others?
6. What is the importance of virtue?
7. What struck you about being dedicated to a mission? Are you dedicated to something? What? How dedicated are you?
8. Why is developing future generations of leaders important? What (if anything) are you currently doing to live this leadership behavior?

---

[243] Walter Lippmann, in "Roosevelt Has Gone" in The New York Herald Tribune (14 April 1945)

[244] Pope Francis, Video Conference by CNN, 17th September 2015

PART IV
LEADERSHIP IN PRACTICE

CHAPTER 8
HOLISTIC VIRTUE DEVELOPMENT

Character in many ways is everything in leadership. It is made up of many things, but I would say character is really integrity. When you delegate something to a subordinate, for example, it is absolutely your responsibility, and he must understand this. You as a leader must take complete responsibility for what the subordinate does. I once said, as a sort of wisecrack, that leadership consists of nothing but taking responsibility for everything that goes wrong and giving your subordinates credit for everything that goes well.[245]

To become a Christian is to undergo a harrowing process of transformation and rebirth. When the Lord Jesus enters our human existence, he brings with him the whole dynamism of his Paschal mystery, which will surely expose the deepest flaws of our person before it can transform them into vehicles of grace. To survive this process takes enormous trust and tight clinging for life to the person at the Savior because it requires that we leave behind the self-centered, presumptuous, and logical selves we have always been.[246]

---

[245] Dwight D. Eisenhower, as quoted in Nineteen Stars : a Study in Military Character and Leadership(1971) by Edgar F. Puryear Jr.

[246] Merikakis, Fire of Mercy IV, 205

The Source and Summit of Leadership

The title of this book speaks of a summit. If you have ever climbed a mountain, you know the journey requires planning, assembling your gear and making the climb. In this book, we have spoken about the leadership needs of our day and painted a picture of true leadership founded on the shepherd heart of Jesus Christ. Holistic virtue development is the topic of this chapter. The following two chapters will detail leadership decision-making principles based on a Judeo-Christian worldview as well as apply these principles of leadership to various spheres of society. My invitation is to read these three chapters reflecting on your own leadership and how to apply them in your life.

Speaking with a fellow priest of the Legionaries of Christ, this friend reminded me not all are called to our 12-year training program. 'We undertake a serious, time-intensive formation covering classical humanities, philosophy, theology, and leadership. This is not for everyone.' I agree with my brother priest. Our extensive training program is not for everyone. On the other hand, all (you included) are called to develop their talents, influence, and gifts for the good of others. This is a mission you cannot abdicate, it is not only for priests. It is certainly not just for business leaders. Growth and formation are for all of us.

What are your core values? This is a frequent topic in business circles as well as society. I was sitting with Bob a few years ago. Like many other business leaders, he was struggling to focus and find a path forward in his leadership. "Let me see your business card," I asked. He gave me the card and what did I see but 12 core values. You could probably guess some of them: integrity, kindness, compassion, stewardship, respect, et cetera. When I pressed him, it was clear he was not enthusiastic about most of these. To make matters worse, he could not describe how he was working to personally grow in them. Integrity is one of your core values? So what does that look like? How will you *personally* grow this over the next six months? What does that look like in your spiritual life? With your family? At work? No plan, no progress.

Holistic virtue development is critical to the future of your leadership. As Aristotle described, virtue is the foundation for and path to the happy life. Happiness is much less a feeling than a state of living. It is to have all possible virtues active in you. Leadership coaches abound. They help many men and women tackle themes of leadership growth, but few are trained and able to guide you on the royal road of virtue development. If you do not understand virtue, how can you guide others to acquire it?

According to the Catechism of the Catholic Church, "a virtue is a habitual and firm disposition to do the good. It allows the person not only to perform good acts, but to give the best of himself. The virtuous person tends toward the good with all his sensory and spiritual powers; he pursues the good and chooses it in concrete actions. The goal of a virtuous life is to become like God."[247] Specific virtues abound. The cardinal (meaning 'hinge' to indicate it is upon these that many others depend) virtues are four in number: prudence, fortitude, justice and self-mastery.

---

[247] Catechism of the Catholic Church, 1803.

Holistic Virtue Development

The theological virtues (those that help us know God as he is and live as he asks) are three: faith, hope, and love. Many others flow from these seven such as loyalty, magnanimity, confidence, integrity, prayer, and many more.

When speaking of good leaders, many use the word 'character'. Character is the total sum of your virtues and vices. Successful World War II general Lucian Truscott said "character is what you are. Reputation is what others think you are. The reason that some fail to climb the ladder of success, or of leadership if you want to call it that, is that there is a difference between reputation and character. The two do not always coincide. A man may be considered to have sterling character. Opportunity might come to that man; but if he has the reputation for something he is not, he may fail that opportunity. I think character is the foundation of successful leadership."[248] It is easy to speak about someone having a good character, but does he or she? What concrete virtues does the person possess? One thing is for sure, you do not magically acquire good character the day you take on a leadership role. Character predicts most of your decisions. Think of political elections and the character of the men and women running for office. We should not be surprised that their decision-making pattern for certain issue does not change once they get into office despite their campaigning promising the contrary.

Entire books have been written about character and virtue. Based on my 20 years of experience working with and helping develop leaders, I can best serve the reader by highlighting the critical virtues for your personal development that are most needed in this time of history. Then, I will discuss how to develop each one of these. Virtues are easy to talk about but many do not understand how to forge them or create a road map to grow in them. Emperor Haile Selassie I reminds us "this whole-hearted acceptance of the demands imposed by even higher standards is the basis of all human progress. A love of higher quality, we must remember, is essential in a leader."[249] Each of us is called to seek higher quality and excellence in all parts of our life. It would be hypocrisy to claim we are true leaders if we are stagnant in our virtue development.

The following pages will cover 8 critical virtues: humility, prayer, prudence, self-mastery, perseverance, integrity, influence, and magnanimity. If you work on these 8, you are guaranteed to progress in your leadership towards the source and summit. Let's get started.

---

[248] Lucian Truscott, as quoted in Air Force Journal of Logistics, March 22, 2005, Notable quotes

[249] Haile Selassie I, Speech on Leadership in Speeches Delivered on Various Occasions, May 1957- December 1959 (1960), p. 138

HUMILITY

"When all the boasting is over, what is any man but just another man? Even when honor in this life is merited, it has no lasting value. It is smoke that weighs nothing."[250]   Humility is one of those words we throw around all the time. To some, it means weakness. To others, it is to walk around with your head down and continually say you are terrible. This is not a Christian understanding of humility. According to Saint Theresa of Avila, humility is to live in the truth of who God is, who others are, and who you are. This profound statement merits deep reflection. Do I live in the truth? In other words, do I live in reality? Objective reality is the place to begin, especially when we talk about virtue.

Even for non-Christian philosophers like Aristotle, humility has long been considered the foundation for virtue. Imagine building a skyscraper without a solid foundation. It would not take much for that structure to crumble. The same is true for a person whose life is not built on the strong foundation of humility. Without humility, it is no surprise that your leadership is often weak, twisted, and deviant. How humble were people like Hitler, Stalin, Mao Chavez, and Castro? Do their lives and words are witness to humility or pride? It is no surprise that their leadership led to disastrous results for people. "Leadership does not mean domination. The world is always well supplied with people who wish to rule and dominate others. The true leader is a different sort; he seeks effective activity which has a truly beneficent purpose. He inspires others to follow in his wake, and holding aloft the torch of wisdom, leads the way for society to realize its genuinely great aspirations."[251] Humility is the foundation so we must get it right. Without humility, the other virtues can be built on a bad foundation and, therefore, won't lead to one's personal flourishing or the flourishing of those affected by your leadership.

You and I know that humility is not easy. It is a beautiful idea and we are powerfully struck by those who authentically live it, but in practice it is a major part of the summit of leadership. Being humble sometimes feels like trying to scale a cliff-face. Leadership guru and executive coach, Pat Lencioni, speaks from experience when he says "it is very, very difficult for any leader, even the most humble of them, to avoid letting constant approval and admiration create a warped and inaccurate self-image. This is why it is so important for leaders to surround themselves with people who will be honest with them."[252]   Leaders are not immune from developing a 'God complex' and getting the impression that they are the center of the world. This is not humility.

---

[250] St Augustine, *City of God*, 5.17

[251] Haile Selassie I, Speech on Leadership in Speeches Delivered on Various Occasions, May 1957-December 1959 (1960), p. 138

[252] Lencioni, Pat, *The Motive*, 166

Humility is being aware that your position or influence does not make you any better than other people. Others are also created in the image and likeness of God and deserve just as much respect and love as you do. "Genuine humility helps you recognize that you are neither better nor worse than anyone else, that you ought to respect everyone equally and not treat anyone differently just because of a job title. When you embrace genuine humility, your leadership thrives: your team members are willing to work with you to accomplish the mission and will respect your decisions because they know you value their contributions, no matter their roles."[253] This aspect of humility harmonizes relationships, makes you an effective team builder and grounds you in the need to be close to your sheep.

A third aspect of humility is to admit your mistakes. This is a hard one to swallow. How often do you see famous businessmen, politicians, entertainers or educators own their mistakes and come clean? What you usually see is final admission of guilt once they are convicted by public court. Even then, we see the sad example of some who denied to the grave that they did something wrong whether it was stealing, sexual abuse, or indiscriminate use of power. American comedian and politician Al Franken said "mistakes are a part of being human. Appreciate your mistakes for what they are: precious life lessons that can only be learned the hard way. Unless it is a fatal mistake, which, at least, others can learn from."[254] Contrary to that internal, gut-twisting feeling when we think about admitting our mistakes, it is actually quite freeing to own up to them. Humility brings us peace of mind. Admitting our mistakes is part of the accountability process; we take public ownership for what we have done. It may not always be pleasant, but it is the right thing for a leader to do.

Saint Mother Teresa was known for many famous phrases. One of her most popular and impactful was to do the small things with great love. Focusing on doing small things every day is a great way to grow in humility. It is not easy for leaders to embrace the little things in our daily life. We can easily develop an attitude of always wanting to be in the limelight, of doing things that draw attention to ourselves. This is the opposite of humility. Humble leaders "know that giving speeches and being in the spotlight is a very small part of their work and that the daily grind of keeping the organization moving in the right direction is their real job."[255] Do you appreciate the small things? Are you content with seeing the organization, team, or family you lead progress? Or are you fixated on getting attention and adulation from others?

Pride. It is your enemy if you want to be humble. It is the antithesis of a humble leader who wants to be like Jesus the Good Shepherd. Pride makes you think you are the center of the world. You know best. You deserve the best. You are always right. People should reference you for insights and the green light to act. In other words, you have a deep-seated attitude of

---

[253] Kraemer, Harry, *From Values to Action*, 6.

[254] Al Franken, Oh, the Things I Know (2003).

[255] Lencioni, Pat, The Motive, 139.

wanting to be like God who, alone, is the center of the universe. "We all know people who have established impressive careers on the basis of raw ambition...Lacking genuine humility, they're the ones who get swelled heads and who actually believe that they are better than anyone else. They forget who they are and where they came from."[256]   We all have proud moments. The temptation to be proud grows exponentially with influence and wealth. If we're not careful, it can become an abiding attitude and a lens through which you see the world and others. The proud leader has little hope unless this cancer is excised from his mind and heart.

Pride is not simply a problem in business, politics, and academia. It also rears its jaws in religion and church organizations. In the name of God, men and women can do horrible and inhumane things. On a doctrinal level, they can quickly assume the place of God and those whom God has divinely appointed to represent him. Think of Aaron and Miriam in the Old Testament when they stir up the Israelites against Moses, thinking they know what God wants best . They are sternly corrected and punished by God for their pride and disobedience. The history of Christianity also shows us how men and women can let pride move them to go off course. We could ask each of them: 'how do you know your doctrine is divine?' 'Who made you a reference point for how to interpret the teachings of Jesus which had been given and passed down from saints and masters of the faith before you came along?' I would be much more inclined to trust 2nd century St Ignatius of Antioch or St Justin Martyr who both preached the teachings of Jesus in the Catholic faith and died at the hands of persecutors for defending the Catholic Christian faith. Those in religious circles need to be well-grounded not just in tradition but also through contact and dialogue with masters of the faith who both preceded them, as well as those who are contemporaries.

The path of humility walks through the door of obedience and submission. The humble leader is not a pushover, but, at the same time, he knows his place in the universe and the proper time and role to abide to authority greater than himself. Without this, you cannot be a true leader. As I mentioned in my book *The Future of Leadership*,

> **At the center of this dying to self which is required to experience true leadership, a leader faces the age-old enemy of pride. This vice and wound of man's heart always lurk nearby and shows itself in various forms. For leaders, it is not uncommon to want to be the best or first. This is even the case among Jesus' apostles. The Gospels recount the apostles arguing among themselves as to who is the greatest. In response to them and all people, Jesus says, "Let the greatest among you become as the youngest, and the leader as one who serves. For which is the greater, the one who sits at table, or the one who serves? Is it not the one who sits at table? But I am among you as one who serves." This is the 'door' to live the sacrificial dimension of love and leadership. Without passing through it, a**

---

[256] Kraemer, Harry, *From Values to Action*, 62.

leader finds it impossible to imitate the oblation of Jesus Christ in laying down his life for others.[257]

How do you relate to authority? Do you have a hard time obeying? How do you handle areas of disagreement with those regarded as authorities in your family, work, and other areas of social interaction?

A best practice in this area is to ask for clarification instead of exclaiming that someone else is wrong or that you will not obey. True leaders seek good at all times. It is natural for us to find ourselves in circumstances where we think we understand the good to be achieved and those in authority see it differently. A humble leader both listens to others' concerns as well as looks for clarification from higher ups. There is a time to lead and a time to follow. The humble leader recognizes this.

What are some other best practices of humility? How else can we grow it? Several quick thoughts:

- Recognize your team's (spouse's) accomplishments in front of others
- Refer praise given to you to God
- Meditate on the humble heart of Jesus Christ and ask him to grant you humility. Two meditations in particular can be helpful. The first is Jesus on the cross offering his life for you in abject humility. The second is to meditate on Jesus humbly offering himself in his Body, Blood, Soul and Divinity in Holy Communion which is reserved in the tabernacle in every Catholic church (look for the telltale sanctuary lamp which is always lit signifying his Presence).
- Listen four times as much as you speak
- Ask and support what family and friends like to do (such as choice of food to eat or activities to do together)
- Accept and offer up to God the inconveniences and sufferings of life
- Recognize you are a work in progress. You are not a failure or useless. You are also not perfect or an angel.
- Go to confession. Ask God for forgiveness for your failures in loving him, others and yourself.
- Admit your mistakes to others (especially your spouse and children)
- Find a trustworthy spiritual director (as well as therapist when needed to deal with traumas and patterns of unhealthy behavior)

These and other such actions can take you a great distance in acquiring the virtue of humility.

---

[257] Haslam, Nathaniel, The Future of Leadership, 44

As we conclude our reflection on humility, remember what we say here applies to the other virtues as well. You need two or more months to develop a virtue with intentionality every day. It is good to pick two or three practical means to live the virtue and focus on it day-after-day. Yes, you need a plan if you want to grow. It is not going to happen automatically. Think about the detailed plans that architects and construction workers use when building a house or skyscraper. The foundation itself has very detailed plans and specifications. These need to be closely followed and done with patience day after day until it is complete. Only then can the rest of the edifice be built. I encourage you to make a concrete plan for growing in humility or on any of the following virtues as you embrace holistic virtue development. Please do not get discouraged when pride rears up and wins a battle. Look to God for strength. "The triumph of humility and piety over pride and insurrection can be ours, if we but put on the mind and heart of Christ."[258]

PRAYER

Sitting at a restaurant and enjoying a chicken caesar salad with a couple in 2011, the husband and wife both reiterated how busy they were; they had no time for prayer or each other. It was amazing to see their capacity for activity both in terms of work life and family obligations. The husband was working 60 hours a week at the office and the mom spent much of her week shuttling her four children back-and-forth from school and extracurricular activities. They did not have time for a date night or even a few minutes a day to listen to one another. He wondered how much longer they could sustain such rhythm and frenetic activity. Sound familiar?

Whether you are a societal leader, stay at home parent, young professional, or college student, it is hard to make quality time for what really matters. From what we have already said in this book, you are probably not surprised that the next virtue we need to discuss is prayer. How can you be a leader without making time for God? For quiet introspection? A habit in short supply these days is prayer.

Prayer, in the Christian sense, is not simply an absence of noise, ignoring all desire, a sense of being one with yourself and the universe, or calm breathing exercises. Prayer is an encounter and communication with God, who loves and cares about you. It is a meeting with someone who is greatly interested in you. It is also a habit you can develop

It is beyond the scope of this book to give a detailed treatise on prayer. For resources on this theme, I would suggest books such as *Time for God* and *Thirsting for Prayer* by Fr Jacques Philippe. Since this book is about helping you form the virtue needed as a leader, I want to share a few thoughts about prayer that will serve you in your pursuit of this important habit in your life.

---

[258] Merikakis, *Fire of Mercy: Heart of the Word*, Vol 1, 149-50.

First, you need to work on how you see prayer. Many people (including Christians) think of prayer as reflection or introspection. If they believe in God, their prayer is often directed to a being who they see as far off and perhaps disinterested. Christian prayer, however, is meant to be a personal encounter with a living God. It is not distant or removed. The saints all speak of God as a close friend, someone they know and interact with each day. Prayer should be part of everyday, woven into the fabric of your life. You can pray when resting or exercising. You can pray when driving or working. You can pray when playing sports or sipping coffee. God is always with you and is interested in the now of your life. Prayer is a critical part of your life. Only you can pray. No one can do it for you.

Next, begin every day with prayer. We make time for what is important. Many business leaders tell me they say a quick prayer in bed before going to sleep at night. This is a good start, but leaders need to start the day with prayer. Why? Leaders fill their mind and heart at the beginning of the day with what will help them in the hours to come. They often exercise, eat a good meal, and have their cup of coffee. They also often read the Wall Street Journal or check other news outlet to be up to date headlines. Their assistants remind them of their daily appointments. So what about prayer? How can we have our 'spiritual north' and moral compass in good order if we do not start with prayer? Trust me, morning prayer changes your day; it changes you.

In the practice of daily prayer, I suggest a dedicated prayer time as well as short moments of prayer sprinkled throughout the day. As just mentioned, morning prayer is critical. I would suggest you make this the major, dedicated prayer time. Take 5, 10, 15 or more minutes. Get up early if that is what it takes to make sure you get this time. Avoid doing this in the car or on the treadmill. Multitasking does not exist. You are either fully attentive to God or not. Give space to the Lord. What to do in this time? For those getting started, I suggest using the Mass readings of the day. Slowly read the Gospel once and then again. Ask the Holy Spirit to speak a word or phrase to you. Ask him to show you how these words apply to your life. What do you want of me O'Lord? What is your will for me? How can I serve you? How are you asking me to be more like Christ the Good Shepherd?

Also, take moments during the day for exchanges with God. Think of the difference between scuba diving and snorkeling. Scuba diving is an extended time deep under water exploring and experiencing the beauty of the ocean. A dive lasts 15-45 minutes depending on depth. This is like our daily, dedicated prayer time. Snorkeling is different. It is a short period to look under water, staying at the surface and not going down deep. These are like the brief glances with the Lord when you take a few seconds for a spontaneous prayer, a 'glance' at God or a few moments, for reading Scripture or another spiritual book. " You learn to pray by praying. The single most important factor in your life of prayer is the decision to make prayer an integral part of your life. If God matters to me, I will make time for prayer if he doesn't, I won't."[259] Taking time out of your day for prayer is the best investment you can make.

How do we make or find the optimal conditions for prayer? Spiritual director and retreat master, Father Jacques Philippe, reminds us "we are not pure spirit but creatures of spirit and body so we need to learn how to use space and time in the service of the spirit."[260] We've already stressed the importance of starting the day with prayer since that prioritizes and orients our life and all the tasks of the day to God. Just as most men start the day with a good shower and shave, it is also important to start the day preparing and cleaning the soul. Where should we pray? "The best place of all, when feasible, is a Chapel with the Blessed Sacrament so that we can benefit from the grace of our Lord's Real Presence. If mental prayer is done at home, it is a good idea to make a sort of prayer-corner to suit ourselves, with icons, a candle, a little altar, or whatever else helps. We need material things and outward signs."[261] And what about our physical position during prayer? Father Philippe comments "in first place, the position chosen should be one that can be held comfortably, so that we can be still, remain recollected, breathe easily and so forth…At the same time, the physical attitude should not be too relaxed either. Sometimes, when we are tempted to be lazy, a physical attitude such as kneeling for instance, will enable us to focus on God."[262] The key to all this is God, who should be the center of our attention and worship.

In addition to daily prayer, I recommend that leaders make time for a yearly retreat. I'm not referring to a typical corporate retreat where there is team building, discussions, and perhaps some time for silent reflection. A good spiritual retreat is a time focused on giving you an extended quiet prayer and reflection time. It is a going out into the deep with God, an extended rest with the Lord to listen and chat with him. "In addition to my daily practice, every year in early December I attend a silent retreat…When we stop talking and remove ourselves from conversation, we can engage in listening on a deeper level. For me, the retreat provides a few precious days without phones and other outside distractions. The silence allows me to delve into the key questions of who I am, what my values are, and what difference I want to make during the short time I am on earth."[263] For busy people, this is not an easy sell. I challenge you, however, to make time for at least one retreat day during the year. I have never met anyone who has dedicated a day or more to retreat and has not come out more at peace, more dedicated and centered on their family and a better professional. There are many retreat options

---

[259] Handbook of the Lumen Institute, 65.

[260] Philippe, Jacques, Time for God, Scepter Press, 82.

[261] Ibid, 85.

[262] Ibid, 85-86.

[263] Kraemer, Harry, *From Values to Action: The Four Principles of Values-Based Leadership*, 23-4.

available. I would recommend the silent, preached Ignatian style retreats offered by the Jesuits, the Legionaries of Christ, the Oblates and other organizations in particular.

Prayer is to the soul as air is to the lungs. It is necessary to live. Without it, we cannot truly live as human beings. Leaders must be men and women of prayer. The quality and depth of your leadership hinges on your prayer life. Ultimately, a strong prayer life will identify you with Jesus Christ the Good Shepherd. Daily prayer will enable you to discern the will of God for you and be the conduit for the strength and grace needed to embrace it with love. Leadership is not easy and prayer is your sure support to be the leader you are called to be.

PRUDENCE

From antiquity, prudence has been extolled as a leadership virtue. Philosophers used the image of a charioteer guiding the horses for an image of prudence. The horses represented other virtues that could get out of hand and go in the wrong direction unless the guide of prudence reigned them in, and oriented them in a unified direction toward the proper goal. The modern age recommends acting on impulse and emotion. Think of the typical commercial advertising buying food, drinks, cars, iPhones and other material goods. These advertisements use images and words that excite your passions and feelings It is a time when 'on demand' is an expectation. This virtue is rare and certainly not taught in our high schools and colleges. In reality, it is a bedrock virtue for any leader. If you interview the most well respected leaders of teams, you often find this virtue present.

What is prudence? According to the Lumen Institute for business and cultural leaders (www.lumeninstitute.org), "prudence is sound judgment in determining actions."[264] When creating strategic plans for a battle, a general studies maps, assess climate conditions, evaluate their troops as well as the enemies before making decisions. Professional sports teams' coaches have their own version of this process. Politicians and business leaders have their version as well. Behind these processes, there is a desire to do the right thing at the right time, in the right way, and in the right measure. This is the heart of prudential decision making.

As we've already discussed, you need to practice a virtue. You need to practice acting prudently to become a prudent person. So how do we do this in practice? What are some time tested ways to become a prudent person?

The first thing to practice is to remember your destination and purpose every day. Without this, you are like a weather vane that is constantly shifting directional focus based on circumstances and feelings. Techniques and self help strategies do not work. You need to ground yourself in what is solid."all decisions should be made in light of life's ultimate purpose: eternal happiness

---

[264] Handbook of the Lumen Institute, 32.

through communion with God."[265] Some best practices to live this include: discuss this every morning with God in prayer, have it flash across your phone or iPad as a daily reminder, put a sticky note on your desk at home or in the office with this reminder, make it a theme of conversation at least once a week with your spouse and children (or a good friend).

A second way to build the virtue of prudence is to form the habit of mature deliberation. Do you stop and think before making decisions? I was very impressed by successful Houston business leader, Terry Looper, who regularly speaks about his 24 hour rule. He does not say yes or no to a request or a business decision for at least 24 hours to give proper time to prayer and reflection. "When you have choices to make, take time to examine your motives, reflect on the different options and their consequences, and see how each of them will help you (or not) attain the goals and goods you have set for yourself. In this stage, gather sufficient information using your conscience, the criteria of the Church and the Bible and sound advice from objective and well-informed experts."[266] I challenge you to humbly assess yourself on this point. Do you take rash decisions? Do you do a pros and cons assessment? Do you have several people you trust and can talk to when you are going to make an important decision?

A third way to work on being prudent is decisiveness. We live in a time when making a firm and committed decision is not easy or common. "Once you have intelligently and seriously weighed your options, choose whichever one seems best and go forward with care and determination. Don't second guess, don't hesitate, don't delay and don't give in to undo pressure from others around you. You cannot always know 100% if your choice was perfect, but if you've done your homework and performed due diligence, God will honor that."[267] Leaders must not be hasty to make important decisions, but once they have prudently come to a decision, they should be decisive to act upon it.

I wish to warn you about two enemies of prudence. The first is to back down when others deride your well discerned and prudent decision. American philosopher, poet and atheist Ralph Waldo Emerson reminds us "You will hear every day the maxims of a low prudence. You will hear, that the first duty is to get land and money, place and name. "What is this Truth you seek? What is this Beauty?" men will ask, with derision."[268] Do not back down. Prudent decision-making is often questioned because it runs contrary to expedient, emotional, and shooting from the hip reactions. Do not worry. Prudent decision making guarantees your character, sound mind, and conscience.

---

[265] Ibid, 32.

[266] Ibid, 33.

[267] Ibid, 33.

[268] Ralph Waldo Emerson in "Literary Ethics" an address to the Literary Societes of Dartmouth College (24 July 1838).

A second enemy of prudence is to not watch your tongue. 'Loose lips sink ships'. Leaders who cannot hold their tongue are a disaster waiting to happen. "A prudent and discreet silence will be sometimes more to thy advantage, than the most witty expression, or even the best contrived sincerity. A man often repents that he has spoken, but seldom that he has held his tongue."[269] The art of speaking well and with charity is a subject all its own. For the reader in this moment, I am simply drawing your attention to a concrete way you can assess your prudence and guard it. You need to work on listening more and being slow to speak. When you do speak, try to say what is necessary and nothing more. When you are entrusted with information, only share it with those who need to know. If you see someone living as they should not, avoid going around gossiping about them. Imprudence in your speech is often a reflection of imprudence in your decision-making. I recommend you keep a close eye on this very concrete and measurable aspect of prudence

I would like to highlight the best practice of getting input and advice from others. We take this for granted when we consider training for a marathon, seeking to become an Olympic athlete, or making an investment. Do I do this habitually and holistically? Do I have a friendly 'board' of friends and experts that I consult about important decisions in my life? "Leaders who pursue balance realize that their perspective is just that: theirs. By purposefully seeking input from others, especially those who have opposing opinions, you gain a global perspective that enables you to make choices that align with your priorities."[270] Consulting others in your decision making is a sure fast track to grow in prudence. We can all be like the car driver who does not see the blind spots. It is not always easy to share and consult, but our decisions and lives are better because of it. Who can you invite to be part of your consultation team and friendly board?

SELF-MASTERY

There is perhaps a no more under-appreciated virtue in the modern era than self-mastery. For many centuries, this virtue (also known by the names moderation or temperance) was a fundamental virtue. The stoics greatly promoted this virtue as the basis for a happy and harmonious life.

What is self-mastery? Self-mastery is the virtue by which we are able to control and moderate our passions amid personal drive and success. Leaders who want to live virtuously must recognize the deep yearning for pleasure that bubbles up from within and can easily overwhelm and control your will. What kind of pleasures most appeal to you? Those from food and drink? Sexual intimacy? Possessions or physical comfort? Having power over others? Being publicly recognized?

---

[269] Thomas Fuller, Introductio ad prudentiam: Part II, 2593 (1727).

[270] Kraemer, Harry, *From Values to Action: The Four Principles of Values-Based Leadership*, 5.

There is nothing wrong with pleasure in itself, but we need to remember that pleasure is simply a means to an end. It is part of the human experience, but not meant to be a goal in itself. As you and I both know from experience, pleasure is fleeting. If you become addicted to pleasure, you will be on a hamster wheel endlessly seeking more. I promise you that lasting and fulfilling pleasure is only possible in eternal life seeing God face to face.

For our purposes as leaders and those who hope to be better leaders, self-mastery is an important moral muscle to help us regulate (and at times say no) pleasures and desires for them. We continually hear messages of 'just do it' ,'just experience it' and 'just indulge in it'. When lasting, moral goods (like fidelity, family, friendship, justice, fairness) get crowded out by passing, pleasurable goods, we need to say no. You need to have a moral backbone that can weather the storms and tsunami's of impulse to pleasure. Self mastery is the virtue that stands at the center of this critical component of your life.

Historically, leaders who were self-indulgent hurt the people they influenced. Many notable figures spoke out against these types of leaders and exhorted humanity to filter those who were allowed to enter into a leadership based on the virtue of self-mastery. Civil War general Robert E. Lee said "I cannot consent to place in the control of others one who cannot control himself."[271] Famous Greek author and historian, Xenophon, spoke in a similar line saying "if we were at war and wanted to choose a leader most capable of helping us to save ourselves and conquer the enemy, should we choose one whom we knew to be the slave of the belly, or of wine, or lust, or sleep?"[272] We know an out-of-control leader is a danger. It is easy to point fingers, but do we point the finger at ourself? Are you so sure you are a leader who has a mature and well developed self-mastery?

How do we form the virtue of self-mastery? Once again, I would like to offer three thoughts. The first is to be convinced of your own identity. If you do not have this, you will be swayed to and fro by the passions. For a Christian, "a life of prayer, a growing knowledge of Christ's teachings and a healthy sacramental life will arm you to resist temptations. They will remind you where your true happiness lies, not in the perfumed cesspool of sin, but in the clear, fresh air of virtue."[273] Many leaders are weak in the area of their personal identity. *The Handbook for Teaching Leadership* stresses the need to form a clear and abiding identity. We've already spoken in the chapter on a leadership model about this theme. It is important to reiterate that a strong self-identity paves the way for flexing the muscle of self-mastery.

---

[271] Robert E. Lee, in a comment regarding officers who became inebriated, as quoted in Personal Reminiscences, Anecdotes, and Letters of Gen. Robert E. Lee (1874) by John William Jones, p. 170

[272] Xenophon, Socrates in Memorabilia, 1.5.1

[273] Handbook of the Lumen Institute, 53.

Holistic Virtue Development

A second pathway to develop the virtue of self-mastery is to form habits of self-denial. Many modern psychologists tell us that self denial is not healthy. Unfortunately, their education and training is not grounded in millenia of experience, which tells us that moderated self-denial forges character, restrains the passions, and leads to a healthy psyche. "if you develop your willpower by making voluntary acts of seemingly insignificant self-denial (taking the stairs instead of the elevator; praying for a couple of minutes when you get in the car instead of turning on the news right away; keeping your drawers in your closet organized), it will soon be easier to resist invitations to dangerous self-indulgence."[274]   Seminary instructors encouraged us to make a small sacrifice at each meal. Taking less of what you would like or giving up something like salt or pepper reinforces this muscle of self-mastery. It does not take heroic, public acts to become a person of self-mastery. In fact, many small and hidden acts of self-mastery create this. Once you have it, you are ready to exercise self-mastery in heroic moments.

A third practical way to grow in self-mastery is to know yourself. You are unique. Different passions sway you in ways that do not completely match others. "Examine yourself to find out which pleasures have the most mastery over you. Be honest, understand yourself deeply, and then develop a strategy to regain self mastery in that area. Check up on yourself regularly, adjusting the strategy as necessary."[275] It may also help to consult a spiritual coach and even a good therapist as needed (especially if some passion has had a long and deep hold on you and influences your behavior).

Self-reflection is a habit we need to do this. Most leadership and self help books touch the theme of self-reflection. For the purposes of our conversation, I would refer you to business leader Harry Kraemer's book *From Values to Action* that discusses four principles of values-based leadership. Self-reflection is the first theme he covers in the book.

Why is self reflection so important? Kraemer responds saying:

> **Self-reflection is the key to identifying what you stand for, what your values are, and what matters most. Through self-reflection, you are able to step back, filtering out the noise and distractions. As your view becomes clearer, you can prioritize how and where to invest your time, efforts, and energy. Self-reflection allows you to gain clarity on issues, both personal and professional, because you have taken the time to think more deeply about them. The more self-reflective you are, the easier it is to make choices that are in line with your values, with awareness of the full impact of your decisions.**[276]

---

[274] Ibid, 53.

[275] Ibid, 53.

[276] Kraemer, Harry, *From Values to Action: The Four Principles of Values-Based Leadership*, 13.

I think we can all recognize these benefits as important. Who would not like greater clarity and making better decisions about their life? The real question to ponder is whether we are firmly convinced if this is a necessity for our lives as leaders. We can all be like window shoppers, bystanders at a sporting event, or visitors to a museum who look at exhibits but go home, living life as before. The real question at hand is weather you are practicing good self reflection or not. If not, what are you going to do to change?

The consequences of not developing a habit of self reflection are far reaching. "Without self-reflection, you'll find it difficult to know what matters most, and how to stay focused on it. Your leadership will be less effective. Here's a simple way to think about the connection between self-reflection and leadership: if you are not self-reflective, how can you truly know yourself? If you do not know yourself, how can you lead yourself? And if you cannot lead yourself, how can you possibly lead others?"[277] This is a healthy reminder that all the virtues are connected like tissues and ligaments in your body. Every part affects the others. Lack of self reflection will inhibit your growth in other virtues. It will certainly have destructive impact on the way you influence and deal with others around you. The person who does not have self reflection and leads others is like a blind bus driver behind the wheel with students on the bus. I think neither one of us wants to be on that bus.

Self reflection impacts all aspects of your life. "Whether you are trying to set priorities about time spent with your children or with your team members, self-reflection helps you pause and look at things holistically."[278] It helps us identify and ponder challenging moments and circumstances such as the impact of trauma upon us, difficulties in relationships, struggles with addiction, labels, and lies that we have accepted ('you are not loveable' ,'you will never change' ,'you are a failure' ,'you are not beautiful' ,'you cannot be forgiven', et cetera) as well as possible decisions facing us. Self-reflection is always a good investment on yourself and the quality of your leadership.

How can you practice self reflection? What are some ideas to grow in it? "There is no right or wrong way to engage in self-reflection. The key is to find time when you can be silent and really focus on what matters most. Some people are able to do this when they are jogging or walking, others while they are commuting by train or car. For some, it is when they pray or meditate. You focus on the inner voice, rather than the outside noise."[279] I agree with Harry about the importance of making time. This is the number one difficulty for people in our day and perhaps throughout history. Making time and space for reflection is critical and irreplaceable. You either do it or you don't. This same point applies to prayer.

---

[277] Ibid, 5.

[278] Ibid, 17.

[279] Ibid, 23.

During your time of self reflection, it can be very helpful to ask yourself a series of questions. Good questions help you arrive to the treasure of self knowledge and deeper understanding of reality. *"What did I say I was going to do today, and what did I actually do? If what I did was different than what I planned, what were the reasons? What went well, and what did not? How did I treat people? Am I proud of the way I lived this day? If I had the day to live over again, what would I do differently?* And finally, *What did I learn today that will have an impact on how I live the next day, the next week, and going forward?"*[280] I would highly suggest you pick several questions like these and begin asking them during your time of self reflection. It might help to write these down on a notepad, sticky note, or as recurring appointment in your online calendar. Like anything else, this is a habit that takes time to build, and keeping reminders in front of you is often a help. 'Out of sight, out of mind' applies to virtue development as well.

How else could we describe self-mastery in practice? Self-mastery is getting out of bed on time. It is eating a balanced diet. Following a regular schedule is a sign of this virtue. Self-mastery avoids wasting time with excessive entertainment including the use of social media. It means drinking alcohol with moderation or not at all. Self-mastery avoids pornography, flirting if you are married, and anything that stimulates your sexual desires outside the context of marriage. This virtue also helps you control your temper. The person with self-mastery does not complain, spend the day snacking, turn hobbies into obsessions, flaunt wealth, or waste things.

In business, the person with self-mastery treats colleagues and employees with respect. He or she organizes and prioritizes responsibilities in the short, middle, and long term. Self-mastery keeps track and honestly reports their expenses. It implies dressing respectfully so as not to attract attention. It does not tolerate substance abuse at the workplace, cutting corners on anything, or encourage off color jokes.

I highly encourage you not to underestimate the power of self-mastery. In the 21st century, this is perhaps the most needed virtue, especially for those getting started on their leadership journey. "Self-mastery is the inner strength that enables you to keep your natural desires for pleasure in their place. It keeps the garden of virtue from being overrun by the wild beasts of your passions. It ensures that the fruits of virtue — peace of mind, meaning and purpose, lasting happiness, wisdom — all ripen for the harvest."[281] It is clearly countercultural so be brave, to put your hand in the plough, and don't look back when people criticize you or laugh at you for not joining them in their self-indulgence.

---

[280] Ibid, 23.

[281] Ibid, 56.

INTEGRITY

You've heard this one before. It's often the first core value on company business cards. What does it mean? Do you have a plan for becoming a person of greater integrity? This is where we go from giving lip service to something to being the real deal.

According to the Lumen Institute for business and cultural leaders, integrity is "consistency between what one professes to be and how one lives."[282] This consistency is where we run into problems. This is where we distinguish between true virtue and virtue signaling. Fools gold looks like the real thing, but it is a fake. "People long to follow a leader who is a person of integrity, authenticity, and compassion. That person will have the loyal following and trust of his people."[283] As sheep can distinguish their shepherd from pretenders, people can see through the mirage of false integrity. They want to follow people who back up their words with action. They want leaders who go from 'integrity' as a word on their business card to one who embodies this important virtue.

We can understand integrity by thinking of a bridge. Civil engineers and architects use the word integrity to describe the consistency and solidity of the structure. It describes a structure that is sound, complete, and safe. "Moral integrity means moral solidity. A person with integrity is someone who sticks it by what he believes: someone with consistency, someone you can count on, someone you who doesn't say 'yes' with words and 'no' with his actions, either to God, to himself, or to others. Like the sturdy bridge, this person will earn the confidence of others, and wherever he goes they will be disposed to follow."[284] No wonder most businesses claim integrity as a core value. They (like all of us) want to be thought of as ones acting with integrity.

So how can we live integrity? The first thing is to believe in integrity. Recognize its importance and be convinced of the need to possess it. Self indulgence is an easy, slippery slope to walk upon and quickly find ourselves spinning out of control. "To develop and deepen integrity, therefore, involves strengthening your conviction that integrity matters. Studying the Bible is a good place to start, as is reading biographies of great sinners and great saints. Visiting criminals in prison can help as well."[285] Reflecting and praying on this topic is very important.

A second practical way to grow in your integrity is to live by clear, reasoned principles. In today's world, it's fashionable to live in chaos and instability, which is the result of a relativistic mindset. Some people actually think it is mature to live without principles other than satisfying their own

---

[282] Ibid, 90.

[283] The Way of the Shepherd, 49.

[284] Handbook of the Lumen Institute,

[285] Ibid,

pleasures and passions. Hopefully by this point in the book, you would agree with me to say this is a delusion; the majority of societal leaders with whom I have spoken attest to the fact that they have lived their lives with clear principles. "Without criteria to guide your decisions in accordance with who you want to be, integrity is impossible. If you don't profess (at least yourself) to be one way, your actions can't be either consistent or inconsistent. You end up being like a jellyfish: filled with passing waves of fashionable behavior and changing moral shape when the waves change. For a Christian, this step is easy: Christ is your criteria. Know him better and better and follow in his footsteps."[286] Do you have clear criteria and principles? What are they? Take a few moments to reflect an write them down. You will know very quickly if you actually have any or not. A good next step would be to think about what criteria and principles would be good for your life. With those defined, you can actually begin crafting a plan to live your life going forward.

A third and final way to grow in integrity is to form and follow your conscience. "Your conscience is where God tells you whether a particular decision or action measures up to the principles of natural law and of Christian behavior. It's the integrity "homing device" that never runs out of batteries. The more faithful you are to your conscience, the clear it's voice becomes, and the easier it is to follow. Studying and knowing the church's teachings helps inform your conscience and keeps it from absorbing corrupt principles from the secular world. Examining your conscience each night keeps it strong and uncluttered."[287] We all know from experience that it is not always easy to follow our conscience. Do this good and avoid that evil. This is what we hear deep inside. Unfortunately, we do not always follow that inspiration to choose the good. How do we form our conscience? Besides following those nudges to choose this or that good, it also helps to read the Bible, consult official church teaching, and ask advice from those with experience on the subject under consideration. For readers who are not Christian or may not be comfortable at this moment reading the Bible or another holy book, I recommend at least reading something by a person well recognized for their personal living the virtue of integrity.

How does integrity look in practice? We've already mentioned it follows its conscience including in small things. The person of integrity is quick to admit his or her faults as well as apologize when appropriate. Integrity implies keeping promises, correcting mistakes, thinking before acting, and discerning decisions according to established principles and criteria. On the flip side, integrity does not flee responsibility or pass the buck. It doesn't criticize others to take attention off your own failings, much less telling lies or gossip about people. A good rule of thumb is to ask yourself "would I say this about that person if they were right here with us?" integrity does not cover up mistakes, stretch the truth beyond recognition, ignore the tug of conscience, or do one thing in public but a completely different one in private. This also includes the theme of living your faith at work. Being of a person of integrity means living with consistency of your faith in your 'private life' as well as in the public sphere.

---

[286] Ibid,

[287] Ibid,

Integrity is truly a necessity for leaders. It is hard fight to attain it, and almost impossible to reclaim if lost. "A man can sell his integrity for a nickel, but all the money in the world won't buy it back again."[288] As leaders, expert Pat Lencioni also recommends that we quickly address failings of integrity in our teams and organizations sooner rather than later. "Failing to confront people quickly about small issues is a guarantee that they will become big issues."[289] Let us commit to a life of integrity despite the challenges that are therein.

PERSEVERANCE

Leaders persevere. Name someone who excels in their field and you can count on many stories of perseverance behind that person's life. Look at your own life. You persevered to this point (including reading this book to this page.). For millenia, perseverance (also known as fortitude) is a hinge or critical virtue upon which many other virtues rise or fall. For those in positions of societal influence, perseverance is expected as part of the moral fiber of the officeholder.

We can define perseverance as a strong commitment to overcome all obstacles. Take, for example, the commitment to gardening. This is a painstaking activity that requires vigilance and hard work over the long haul. In her book *Forming Intentional Disciples*, Sherry Weddell mentions it took her almost seven years to create a thriving garden in what was formerly a very desolate landscape near her home in Colorado. "If you don't keep watering the plants, fertilizing them, yanking out the weeds, and killing off the pests, your plants may survive, but they won't bear the fruit they are meant to. Analogously, to enjoy the incomparable fruit of virtue, you have to persevere in the exercise of virtue, to the end."[290] The word perseverance comes from Latin, It indicates following through despite severe difficulties. This virtue is intricately linked to the other virtues—they all require persevering in repetitive, habitual action.

How do we acquire the virtue of perseverance? Once again, I will share 3 areas for your reflection and application in your own life. The first is to know yourself and recognize where laziness and fear have a hold on you. These are the enemies of perseverance. We all get lazy when faced with things we do not like to do. Fears? We have those as well. "Fear of failure, fear being rejected, fear of discomfort, fear of humiliation, fear of ridicule, fear of displeasing others, fear of suffering, fear of having to give up your own opinion, plan, or idea, fear of not being able to do things your own way."[291] Take a serious look at your life right now. In what areas am I lazy? In what areas does fear exert a strong hold over you? Until you recognize these, evil be

---

[288] The Way of the Shepherd, 47.

[289] Lencioni, Pat, The Motive, 150.

[290] Handbook of the Lumen Institute, 38.

[291] Ibid, 39.

like the bird tide down by a little string. The string may look so tiny and insignificant, but it will not let you fly. If you do not address these areas of your life, perseverance will be a good intention but just a fantasy that often does not come to fruition.

A second means to grow in perseverance is to accept yourself. I'm not talking about some pop psychology catch phrase or self esteem building exercise. Accepting yourself means to recognize where you are at in objective reality. You and I both have our weak areas. Recognizing and accepting them brings great freedom and peace. It also helps us begin working on ways to compensate for them and build stronger habits to overcome them. "This will save you from making false excuses to justify giving up worthwhile goals, breaking worthy resolutions, and relaxing necessary effort."[292]

A third and final practical way to grow in perseverance is to deepen your convictions. The first two steps above prepare you for this action. Many of the important fruits of perseverance are not tangible, like money and power. "Perseverance in virtue yields intangible results such as peace of soul, harmony infidelity in relationships, wisdom, family joy and tranquility and a clean conscience."[293] We need deeper convictions about the importance and value of virtue if we're going to persevere. You can dip in and reinvigorate your convictions through prayer, Bible studies, and church teaching, as well as frequent and fruitful reception of the sacraments.

What does perseverance look like? In family, it looks like daily appreciation to your spouse and consistent, positive standards to discipline your children. It also implies frequent forgiving your family members as well as asking pardon to begin again. It means staying faithful even when apparent reasons to remain faithful seem to disappear. It does not give up correcting your own faults or abandon a family member when their faults don't go away. We can also include finishing family projects and not forsaking promises you made to your spouse or children. "In business, perseverance finds solutions to problems and ways around obstacles, stays on task even when the task becomes repulsive, keeps its commitments, sticks to its policies and has courage to change when needed. Perseverance does not make frequent changes to vision, mission or the plan. It does not give up after the first "no". It does not give up because of bad moods, initial struggles or slow development."[294] Perseverance for the things we want may be present in our lives, but we really need to ask ourselves as leaders if our perseverance is selective and not present in the various areas listed above.

There are several specific areas worth highlighting for a moment. For example, the great Roman philosopher, orator and politician, Cicero, reminds us that "persistence in a single view

---

[292] Ibid, 39.

[293] Ibid, 39.

[294] Ibid, 41.

has never been regarded as a merit in political leaders."[295] We see single minded persistence running rampant in 21st century society. As leaders, each one of us needs to work on being more open minded and persevere in listening to the perspectives of others. This does not mean buying into a relativistic mentality, but it does mean being open enough that we are not in an echo chamber and at least hear what others are saying so we can better understand their perspective. We need to learn to wade into uncomfortable conversations. "You will need to reset your expectations about how "comfortable" your job is supposed to be and find courage to start entering into dangerous conversations until it becomes natural."[296] In a day and age when we tiptoe around people, afraid to make them uncomfortable, we need to recognize that crucial conversations and confrontations are part of leadership. We do a disservice to one another and lack the shepherd heart of Jesus Christ when we do not enter into these important discussions.

Another area for perseverance is in habitually communicating important messages to those we influence. In an age of rapid and diverse forms of communication, where information comes at us from all directions, we need to be clear and repetitive in sharing important messages. "I've read studies that say employees have to hear a message seven times before they believe executives are serious about it. Until then, they discount it as corporate speak or internal propaganda."[297] Ever wonder why people do not listen to you? Sometimes feel like your spouse, child, friend, or a coworker does not hear you? It is not likely due to ill will or because you are not a modern day Demosthenes level public speaker. Your message is competing with the other ideas, emotions and distractions which fill the mind and heart of your audience. For these things, form the habit of perseverance in your communication.

Lastly, I would also like to draw your attention to the importance of perseverance in your spiritual life.please remember that perseverance is required in your daily prayer life. Working with hundreds of business and cultural leaders over the past ten years, I promise you persevering in prayer is a difficult thing to do. Programs and scheduling can help you, but ultimately we need to call upon the help of God in order to become men and women of habitual prayer. I recommend asking God for this gift every day. We cannot give ourselves a strong prayer life; it is a gift we have to ask for and be open to receive from the hands of our loving God.

INFLUENCE

Leadership is influence. We have previously discussed this theme, but now is a good moment to delve a bit deeper. Former U.S. President John Adams was quoted saying "if your actions

---

[295] Marcus Tullius Cicero in Epistulae ad Familiares, I, 9, 21

[296] Lencioni, Pat, The Motive, 153.

[297] Ibid, 158.

inspire others to dream more, learn more, do more and become more, you are a leader."[298] Influencing others' thoughts, attitudes, convictions and behaviors is part of leadership. The ideal, role model, source, and summit of leadership, Jesus Christ himself, exhorted us to learn from him, follow him as well as influence others to know and love him.

In an age when people easily fall into conformity and want to avoid perturbing others, it is easy to forget that leadership does include helping move others toward goals and behaviors that are not often the norm. Famous pastor and civil rights leaders, Martin Luther King said "ultimately a genuine leader is not a searcher for consensus, but a molder of consensus."[299] You need to remember that your influence should remain at the service of others, while ensuring this service is helping them achieve objective goods for themselves and society. Good leaders do this without resorting to frenetic activity or micromanaging. Ancient philosopher Laozi wrote "Superior leaders get things done with very little motion. They impart instruction not through many words, but through a few deeds. They keep informed about everything but interfere hardly at all. They are catalysts, and though things would not get done as well if they were not there, when they succeed they take no credit. And, because they take no credit, credit never leaves them."[300]

The Lumen institute for business and cultural leaders defines influence as "moving others to think and act uprightly through conscientious effort."[301] Being an effective leader implies increasing your influence on two levels: quantitative influence and qualitative influence. Quantitatively, we influence a certain number of people. This number can increase and decrease. This is the aspect of leadership and influence most think about and pay attention to changing in their lives. The other aspect is, however, more important. Qualitative influence refers to objectively helping others and advancing toward the goal at hand. "if the influence moves people toward virtue and happiness, its quality is good; If it moves people toward selfishness and vice, its quality is bad."[302] I have previously given examples of good and bad leadership, but I would like to reiterate and challenge you to look inside yourself and ask two questions. How is my qualitative influence? How is my quantitative influence? It would be a good exercise to journal this and write down specifics so you can assess the reality of your situation.

---

[298] John Quincy Adams, attributed, The Paradox of Power

[299] Martin Luther King, Jr., In an address at the Episcopal National Cathedral, Washington D.C. (31 March 1968)

[300] Laozi, as quoted in Growing the Distance: Timeless Principles for Personal, Career, and Family Success (1999) by Jim Clemmer, p. 137

[301] Handbook of the Lumen Institute, 102.

[302] Ibid, 102.

Influence occurs in different spheres based on different sets of relationships. It is also linked to your God given talents. "Some people exercise influence because their personality is naturally magnetic. Others, like actors or athletes, occupy social positions that give them influence. Politicians, executives, and intellectuals exercise influence both because of their position and their expertise. Parents influence their children by the natural bonds of family. All these cases deal with leadership, because they deal with influence."[303] No matter your reality, you can also grow your influence. How do we do that?

The path to increase your influence is not lots of networking or getting an advanced degree. These things can be helpful but they are not the most important. This entire chapter is dedicated to the importance of virtue development and formation. As you grow in any virtue, your quantitative and qualitative influence grows. "Join to that a sincere desire to make an everlasting difference in the world, and God will take care of the rest."[304] You will probably not be surprised that I am convinced the most powerful influence available to us is the love of God. There is nothing more powerful and attractive to others as unconditional and sacrificial love that Jesus Christ offers to pour into your heart when you turn your life over to him with trust and abandonment. If you want your influence both qualitatively and quantitatively to skyrocket, I highly encourage you to invite Christ into your heart and to work through you.

As with the other virtues, it can help to describe what it looks like in practice. Influence "takes responsibility for its actions, it realizes that actions and decisions including small ones have real consequences both for oneself and for others. It engages in frequent and demanding self examination in order to keep things on track and continue growing. Influence keeps the big picture in mind and remembers that people are what matter most. It learns from mistakes as well as constantly seeks to increase its perimeter and depth."[305] It goes without saying that influence makes an effort to work together with others to be more effective. Jesus Christ reminds us that sincere respect is a powerful form of influence.

Looking at great leaders throughout history, we notice they often devote large quantities of time to influence person-by-person. It is not so much about large numbers of people but influence over a few that greatly multiplies the leaders' effectiveness. Look at Jesus for example. He spent much of his time with 12 chosen apostles who he developed and sent out to spread his message of salvation to the world. From a human influence perspective, he has touched many billions of lives and is still rated as the most influential person in human history on most Google searches. "You can lead from afar, or you can do it up close and personal. You can impress from afar, but to influence, to really leave your mark, you're going to have to do it personally.

---

[303] Ibid, 102.

[304] Ibid, 103.

[305] Ibid, 103.

Remember, for great leaders, leadership isn't just professional; it's personal."[306] Is this how you approach your leadership with others? Do you hide behind titles and say it is someone else's job to be up close with team members? Is your default to resort to text messages and emails instead of having regular conversations about life and the mission at hand with those you influence? We each should take stock of our mode of influencing and assess if we're really working to give person-to-person attention.

Leadership consultant Pat Lencioni reminds us of two final areas of influence that deserve special attention. The first is to give first place to influence the members of your team. This could include your family members, staff at work, those involved in ministry with you, or some other team including sports. "If people on a leadership team don't believe that the leaders sees team development as one of his or her most critical roles, they're not going to take it seriously, and it's not going to be effective. The leader simply must take personal responsibility for, and participate actively in, the task of building his or her team."[307] I can tell you from experience that this labor of love is not easy. It should be your first line area of attention. Identify your team(s). How are you going to help them develop? What do they need from you? How are you going to prioritize influencing your team(s) in the coming six months?

The second and final point on influence is something I have addressed in other places but it bears repeating. A leader must influence by leaning into difficult conversations and confrontations. "One of the main responsibilities of a leader is to confront the difficult, awkward issues quickly and with clarity, charity, and resolve. What kind of issues am I talking about? Everything from a team member's annoying mannerisms to poisonous interpersonal dynamics and politics. There isn't a leader out there who hasn't balked at a moment when they should have "entered the danger" and had a difficult conversation about these things. Almost no chief executive likes to do this. Most loathe it. And yet, when leaders dodge these situations, they jeopardize the success of the team and the organization as a whole."[308] You and I both know this is not easy. This is why there are not many *great* leaders. We so often try to coexist and contain uncomfortable situations and relationships. Instead of inviting the other person(s) to speak and work through tough situations together, we run and hide from them. Where and with whom do you act this way? I challenge you to point out the one or two people with whom you need a serious conversation in order to move your team and organization forward. This might be a subordinate, an equal on the team, or a superior. I invite you to be bold and ,at the same time, humble and loving as you address issues in the truth.

---

[306] The Way of the Shepherd, 51.

[307] Lencioni, Pat, *The Motive*, 142.

[308] Ibid, 148.

MAGNANIMITY

This is the final virtue that we will consider in this book. If humility is the foundation for all virtue and leadership, this one is the crowning jewel. When virtue is properly cultivated and developed, it will overflow in a magnanimous heart. This is the essence of the Good Shepherd's heart of Jesus Christ who is the source and summit of leadership. Famous leadership coach Marshall Goldsmith tells us "successful people become great leaders when they learn to shift the focus from themselves to others."[309] I have already shared many thoughts with you about leadership being other centered, but now we can better describe what this virtue entails and demands in practice. I will also give you some tips on how to develop it in yourself.

What is magnanimity? "It is the commitment to serve by putting others needs first."[310] The word comes from Latin meaning great soul. This word speaks to us of greatness. It brings to mind images of initiative, big works, going out of the way to help others, striving above and beyond, the Call of Duty and always looking to do more for others. Saint Mother Teresa of Calcutta may come to mind, for example, when saying these things. She constantly sought to help more and more of society's most neglected and unwanted.

There are so many men and women throughout history who took initiative for the good of their fellow men and women. "They saw a great need and strode forth to meet it; they saw a great opportunity and they ventured out to seize it. America's Founding Fathers built a country from scratch, creating a brand new form of government to redress the injustices of those that already existed. Henry Dunant, the Swiss founder of the Red Cross, didn't agonize over the human carnage churned out by the bloody battles he witnessed as a young man. Instead, he founded an organization that would prepare in times of peace to help those wounded did in times of war. That is what great souledness is it all about."[311] Would you characterize yourself as a person of initiative? Would others say that about you? Have you ever asked God to help spark the fire of an initiating spirit within you?

The magnanimous leader takes initiative and tries to do things better than they have seen it done before. How do we grow in magnanimity? Once again, I offer you three suggestions. The first is to start with little things. Leaders and leadership often called to mind images of giving the big speech before a crowd, influencing many teams of people, doing what others thought as impossible, and being in the public limelight to celebrate your accomplishments. This, however, is not the day-to-day reality for leaders. Every leader has many moments of doing the small things with love and excellence. "Form the habit of thinking in terms of others' needs and desires by doing one small act of charity or kindness for a family member every day. Do it in a

---

[309] Marshall Goldsmith (2010), *What Got You Here Won't Get You There.* p. 72

[310] Handbook of the Lumen Institute, 96.

[311] Ibid, 96.

hidden way, without drawing attention to yourself. Soon this one little act will open your soul and blossom into a steady flow of ingenious charity that spreads happiness into everyone in your life."[312] The same could be said about paying attention to a coworker or someone at a function who is not popular, ignored, or who looks like they need support. Pursuing great and large scale accomplishments is important for leaders, but these can only happen when one has the habit of doing the small and seemingly hidden things with love.

A second means to grow in magnanimity is to do good to people you don't like. This one is hard. We all recoil a bit when faced with serving and loving those who rub us the wrong way, have drastically different personalities or outright have hurt and wounded did us. "The colleague or acquaintance or employee that naturally rubs you the wrong way is the perfect target for acts of charity and kindness, if you want to expand the reach of your soul. Magnanimity, to be authentic and have a real impact, has to spring from the depths of your heart, but you can't get down that deep unless you peel off your protective covering of selfishness and self-righteousness. This is the only way to do so."[313] History reveals noble souls who embodied this. The standard an example of this is of course the Lord Jesus himself who freely gave his life to redeem each one of us and open the doors of paradise for our eternal joy and celebration. How can any of us forget and not be moved hearing his words during the horrifying moment of his physical crucifixion? "Father, forgive them. They know not what they do."[314] By the grace and power of God, we too can join Jesus to not only serve, but also to forgive those who hurt us. Who in your life has hurt you? Who has let you down? Who do you not get along with? Serving and forgiving these individuals is part of the road you must travel to become a true leader.

A final suggestion for growing in magnanimity is praying for this type of heart. I suggest you go beyond a generic concept of magnanimity and pray for specific growth. Ask others where you can grow and be attentive when others give you feedback. It could help you to write these down in a list and bring them to prayer. You will notice a difference when talking to God about specific points of growth.

How would I describe the magnanimous person or the one who is not magnanimous? Those who are magnanimous "think big, invest resources to get maximum return, pay sincere attention to and take sincere interest in the needs, problems, and points of view of everyone else, from the smallest child to the eldest grandparent, checks in on a sick employee, finds solutions for those in financial difficulty as well as does the unexpected such as visiting a ruthless criminal being vilified in all the news reports."[315] On the other hand, the person who is not magnanimous

---

[312] Ibid, 97.

[313] Ibid, 97.

[314] Luke, 23:34.

[315] Handbook of the Lumen Institute, 99.

ignores the needs of those around him, will often say 'that is their problem, not mine', looks to others to figure things out, verbally complain about the inconvenience of doing more, broadcasts its good deeds out of vanity, pass judgment on others as well as impose its viewpoint.

Magnanimity is the currency of human satisfaction and happiness. I have never been at the bedside of someone who is dying and complained they hadn't made more money or had more vacations. They usually speak about the times they wish they had loved and done more to help family, friends, coworkers, and strangers. We were not born to make money, but to love and give our lives in service to one another. Jesus Christ reminds us that true reward and treasure is found in magnanimous love for others. Money, property, and influence evaporate the moment we pass from this life to eternity. Am I living with the illusion that the material things are the priority in my life? Do I not realize the overarching and superior value of a life lived with magnanimity? The person living the virtue of magnanimity most significantly contributes to the progress of humanity and society. As society becomes more magnanimous, this virtuous cycle naturally influences other people to choose to be magnanimous in their own lives.

This theme forces us to clarify our motives for leadership. Why am I really doing this? Is it to serve others? Is it to serve my own ego and self interest deep down? "I want to be the CEO… because I see my job as a responsibility and a sacrifice…I used to think that being a CEO was a reward for a lifetime of hard work, which meant it was about getting to do what I wanted because I had earned the right to do so…but it never works for the people or the organization you're supposed to be leading."[316] Every single one of us can be those selfless leaders. God invites us to answer this calling. Zeid Ra'ad Al Hussein, the Perry World House Professor of the Practice of Law and Human Rights at the University of Pennsylvania, says "My hope lies in… the leaders of communities and social movements, big and small, who are willing to forfeit everything—including their lives—in defence of human rights. Their valour is unalloyed; it is selfless. There is no discretion or weakness here. They represent the best of us... There are grassroots leaders of movements against discrimination and inequalities in every region… the real store of moral courage and leadership among us…"[317]

I would like to finish this section on magnanimity as well as this chapter reminding all men and women of faith (Christians in particular) that virtue development is absolutely necessary to be a leader. Without virtue, you can call yourself a leader but you are not. We need to call things by their name and there is such a thing as pseudo leadership that is like fool's gold. It might shine like gold but it is a fake. You either have virtue or you do not. The beating heart of the virtuous person is magnanimity and this will require you to suffer at times. As Spiderman Peter Parker was famously told, 'with great power comes great responsibility.' We can add with leadership comes great sacrifice. "The practice of leadership for the Christian is sacrificial in character. The

---

[316] Lencioni, Pat, *The Motive*, 104.

[317] Zeid Ra'ad Al Hussein in Grassroots leaders provide the best hope to a troubled world, The Economist, (30 August 2018)

Holistic Virtue Development

quality of commitment implied in faithful presence invariably imposes costs. To enact a vision of human flourishing based in the qualities of life that Jesus modeled will invariably challenge the given structures of the social order. In this light, there is no true leadership without putting at risk your time, wealth, reputation, and position."[318] Are you willing to make the sacrifice? Are you willing to go the distance to fulfill the role of leadership? Do you want to be the real deal as a leader? If so, then answer the call of Jesus who said to each one of us "deny yourself, take up your cross each day and follow me."[319]

Questions for Personal Reflection and Group Discussion

1. What leadership insights were mentioned in this chapter? What did you learn?
2. Which leadership virtue struck you most? Why?
3. What is humility? Why is it so important in leadership? How can you live this virtue?
4. What is prayer? "   "   "   "
5. What is perseverance?   "   "   "
6. What is prudence? "   "   "   "
7. What is self-mastery? "   "   "   "
8. What is integrity? "   "   "   "
9. What is influence? "   "   "   "
10. " magnanimity? "   "   "

---

[318] Hunter, James, *To Change the World*, 259.

[319] Luke 9:23.

CHAPTER 9

LEADERSHIP DECISION-MAKING PRINCIPLES

"What should I do?" I looked up from my plate of chicken ravioli. As CEO of his company, my friend was facing a difficult business decision. He was approached by the adult entertainment industry asking if his company could produce a certain product line. It was a lucrative opportunity and several board members indicated they thought the company should sign a contract. My friend, however, was conflicted. His values told him this was not an industry they should support, yet it would be financially profitable for his business and would also create more local jobs.

Another friend recently came to me asking what she should do. She found herself chairing a national level non-profit board representing stakeholders from different sectors of society. Representatives of an ideological platform approached her and asked that the board publicly support their cause. She found herself in a tug-of-war between her position of not allowing their organization to become a platform for ideological issues, and public pressure to lend their support.

We live in a confusing world. Each generation probably felt this way to some degree. The 21st century, however, is a time of disorientation, mass information and relativism. Those with influence leverage these to their advantage. This is nothing new in many respects, but it creates the perennial challenge of how to make decisions in difficult situations. What are some of those

Leadership decision-making principles

situations today? Look at what is in the news each day: political parties vying for power, immigration issues, vaccine mandates, privacy, abortion rights, universal health care, jobs and the economy. There is no shortage of issues to discuss and debate, but is there a lens or set of principles that can best help us evaluate leadership solutions to these issues? Is there a time-tested path for leaders who need to discern the path forward in these areas?

Just over 10 years ago, I had the blessing of assisting in the coordination of the Vatican Executive Summit. This historic event was an opportunity for 75 global business and political leaders to discuss the global economic crisis and search for a common set of ethical principles by which men and women of different faiths and goodwill could help their countries chart a course forward. It was amazing to see the attendees (Christians, Jews, Muslims, Hindus, as well as atheist of goodwill) align on several principles that are at the forefront of the Catholic social teaching. These principles are perennial, time tested, and robust criteria and building blocks for holistic and equitable leadership decisions. "Bringing a simple solution to a complex and resistant problem almost never works. Nevertheless, people bet on single-source influence strategies all the time."[320] Instead of making decisions based on opinion, emotion or one dimension of a problem, these allow us to create a robust solution which also meet the demands of right reason and divinely revealed truth. Leaders need principles for decision-making. They require a lens to see the world and through which they assess reality. With such principles, they can evaluate and propose solutions to simple as well as complex situations and problems.

The following sections will summarize the different criteria and principles that I propose you include in your leadership decision making. Together, they form a lens to more clearly see the situation at hand and provide a decision-making matrix to create robust solutions. As a reference where these principles can be described at length, I will be quoting from the *Compendium of the Social Doctrine of the Church* which is the Catholic Church's official interpretation of what the Bible says about family life, business, politics, economics and the environment.

> **These principles, the expression of the whole truth about man known by reason and faith, are born of "the encounter of the Gospel message and of its demands summarized in the supreme commandment of love of God and neighbor in justice with the problems emanating from the life of society".[343] In the course of history and with the light of the Spirit, the Church has wisely reflected within her own tradition of faith and has been able to provide an ever more accurate foundation and shape to these principles, progressively explaining them in the attempt to respond coherently to the demands of the times and to the continuous developments of social life.[321]**

---

[320] Patterson, *Influencer: The Power to Change Anything*, 75.

[321] Compendium of the Social Doctrine of the Church, 160.

Leadership decision-making principles

The church sees these principles as and valuable and important for all times and places. They are not limited to certain cultures or periods of history. "These are principles of a general and fundamental character, since they concern the reality of society in its entirety: from close and immediate relationships to those mediated by politics, economics and law; from relationships among communities and groups to relations between peoples and nations. Because of their permanence in time and their universality of meaning, the Church presents them as the primary and fundamental parameters of reference for interpreting and evaluating social phenomena, which is the necessary source for working out the criteria for the discernment and orientation of social interactions in every area."[322] I encourage you to go online or buy a physical copy so you can read and reference this important text for your own use.

What are the leadership decision-making principles? They are: human dignity, the common good, solidarity, and subsidiarity. You can probably list other important decision-making criteria, but I would suggest they are either synonymous with the above ones or they derive from these.

HUMAN DIGNITY

Famous army general George Patton once said, "we herd sheep, we drive cattle, we lead people."[323] Leadership is about people. When we speak about making tough decisions and evaluating challenging problems, the central focus is always people. This is why human dignity is always the first and most important criteria and principle for evaluating situations and deliberating about solutions. What does human dignity mean? It means every human person is infinitely valuable, irreplaceable, deserving of love and respect. No person can be exploited, used as a means, abused, neglected or tortured. The ultimate foundation for human dignity is being created in the image and likeness of God, loved and redeemed by Jesus Christ on the cross and destined for eternal glory in Heaven.

How do I see people? Do I see their dignity? Or do I evaluate and judge them based on appearance, intelligence or physical and professional abilities? "How you view your people determines how you lead them. If you don't have a heart for your people, you'll see them as expenses and interruptions, and you'll never invest yourself in them like a shepherd would. You may talk a good game, even play a good game for a while, but...you'll eventually count the cost as too high, focus on nothing but the work, and leave your people to fend for themselves."[324] The criteria of human dignity forces us to evaluate what we see in people. As a leader, we must always start with their dignity. Each person is a gift and mystery. No matter who they are, they deserve love and respect. If we do not start there, our leadership decision making is already off

---

[322] Ibid, 161.

[323] George S. Patton, as quoted in Pocket Patriot : Quotes from American Heroes (2005) edited by Kelly Nickell, p. 157

[324] The Way of the Shepherd, 102.

to a bad start and likely headed for problems. Human dignity is the foundation for good decision making and solutions. Far too often, however, it is a secondary consideration for leaders who put their own selfish priorities or what is easiest at the forefront of decision making.

Human dignity is at the center of God's revelation and permeates both the Bible and is present in other religious traditions. "*The fundamental message of Sacred Scripture proclaims that the human person is a creature of God* (cf. Ps139:14-18), and sees in his being in the image of God the element that characterizes and distinguishes him...Therefore, being in the image of God the human individual possesses the dignity of a person, who is not just something, but someone. He is capable of self-knowledge, of self-possession and of freely giving himself and entering into communion with other persons. Further, he is called by grace to a covenant with his Creator, to offer him a response of faith and love that no other creature can give in his stead."[325] At a time when we celebrate the progress of science, we perhaps forget that God created men and women. It is easy to think that humankind is something that is produced and at our disposal to manipulate. This is not the case and the criteria of human dignity reminds us of this fact.

The 21st century has continued to see progress in appreciation for and defense of both men and women. Compared to previous centuries that had, at times, less appreciation for the gift of women and their femininity, various cultures are recognizing and defending their strengths and contributions to the human race. "Man and woman have the same dignity and are of equal value[211], not only because they are both, in their differences, created in the image of God, but even more profoundly because the dynamic of reciprocity that gives life to the "we" in the human couple, is an image of God[212]. In a relationship of mutual communion, man and woman fulfill themselves in a profound way, rediscovering themselves as persons through the sincere gift of themselves."[326] Human dignity reminds us that men and women are equal yet not the same. This is something to celebrate as well as respect in leadership decision making. A best practice that highlights this is the inclusion of qualified women in leadership positions in the different sectors of influence.

We need to recognize the perennial temptation to reduce the human person to less than he or she is. This is so often at the heart of ideologies that claim to and be at the service of mankind but really are selfish, self centered, and trample upon the dignity of men and women. We saw this on center stage with Nazism and Communism. "Prizing highly the marvelous biblical message, the Church's social doctrine stops to dwell above all on the principal and indispensable dimensions of the human person. Thus it is able to grasp the most significant facets of the mystery and dignity of human beings. In the past there has been no lack of various reductionist conceptions of the human person, many of which are still dramatically present on the stage of modern history. These are ideological in character or are simply the result of widespread forms of custom or thought concerning mankind, human life and human destiny.

---

[325] Compendium of the Social Doctrine of the Church, 108.

[326] Ibid, 51.

The common denominator among these is the attempt to make the image of man unclear by emphasizing only one of his characteristics at the expense of all the others."[327] Leaders need to defend human dignity and be on the watch for the temptation to reduce men and women to less than they are. We need to always begin and end focused on the grander and ineffable dignity of each human person from the womb to the tomb.

Most societies would readily agree that the ideal is to seek, promote, and achieve a just and peaceful civilization. Unfortunately, most leaders do not understand the absolute and fundamental importance of human dignity as the first building block to this goal. "A just society can become a reality only when it is based on the respect of the transcendent dignity of the human person. The person represents the ultimate end of society, by which it is ordered to the person: Hence, the social order and its development must invariably work to the benefit of the human person, since the order of things is to be subordinate to the order of persons, and not the other way around. Respect for human dignity can in no way be separated from obedience to this principle. It is necessary to consider every neighbor without exception as another self, taking into account first of all his life and the means necessary for living it with dignity. Every political, economic, social, scientific and cultural program must be inspired by the awareness of the primacy of each human being over society."[328] As we will see when discussing the common good, the human person cannot be considered in isolation from others an absolutized therein. We are each linked to one another and so leadership decisions must consider this facet of reality as well.

Human dignity implies we can never use or abuse a human person no matter their age, physical or economic status, race, gender or intelligence. "The person cannot be a means for carrying out economic, social or political projects imposed by some authority, even in the name of an alleged progress of the civil community as a whole or of other persons, either in the present or the future. It is therefore necessary that public authorities keep careful watch so that restrictions placed on freedom or any onus placed on personal activity will never become harmful to personal dignity, thus guaranteeing the effective practicability of human rights. All this, once more, is based on the vision of man as a person, that is to say, as an active and responsible subject of his own growth process, together with the community to which he belongs."[329] This implies we cannot and should never use or kill human beings in their most vulnerable stages such as when they are developing in the womb or later in life during stages of physical weakness. Human experimentation is never illicit. Leaders are complicit in evil when they turn a blind eye and say 'those people are someone else's problem'.

---

[327] Ibid, 124.

[328] Ibid, 132.

[329] Ibid, 133.

I suggest you make a serious examination of conscience asking yourself if you truly appreciate the dignity of each human person. Secondly, is this your first criteria of evaluation and decision making? Many people say this is important to them, but it is not the first in the scale of priorities in the way they evaluate and make decisions. "Since something of the glory of God shines on the face of every person, the dignity of every person before God is the basis of the dignity of man before other men. Moreover, this is the ultimate foundation of the radical equality and brotherhood among all people, regardless of their race, nation, sex, origin, culture, or class."[330] Let us recommit to make this the first building block of our leadership decision making. Your family, teams, coworkers, and all those in your circle of influence depend upon this.

THE COMMON GOOD

The second leadership decision making criteria in principle is the common good. What does it mean? What does it imply for you as a leader? Presidents of nations use this term when addressing the nation. Scientists reference it when Speaking of human progress. Teams refer to it when exhorting players to work together. Once again, the Catholic Church offers an abundance of reflection on this theme through its experience building and contributing to society over the last 2000 years. "The principle of the common good, to which every aspect of social life must be related if it is to attain its fullest meaning, stems from the dignity, unity and equality of all people. According to its primary and broadly accepted sense, the common good indicates the sum total of social conditions which allow people, either as groups or as individuals, to reach their fulfillment more fully and more easily."[331] This last sentence is critical. Notice the emphasis on people and groups on the individual level. The common good is not a generic buzz word or phrase talking about something abstract. It reminds us that the good of the whole must always be oriented towards the existencial fulfillment and maturity of each individual.

The purpose and mission of exercising authority is moderated and oriented through this lens of the common good. Whether you are a parent, business or sports team leader, state governor or someone entrusted with a punctual task at the service of a larger group, the common good demands you to help those you influence towards their fulfillment. Keeping healthy order in society is an important dimension to achieve the common good. This is where we see critical problems and errors when some leaders speak of a society without any police or group in charge of maintaining law and order. While not neglecting abuses, which clearly happened when we look at history, we nonetheless need healthy enforcement of law and order in order to promote the peace and security required for the development of human persons and to safeguard their dignity.

---

[330] Ibid, 144.

[331] Ibid, 164.

While the principle of human dignity is first and foremost, it is incomplete without the common good. "A society that wishes and intends to remain at the service of the human being at every level is a society that has the common good — the good of all people and of the whole person — as its primary goal. The human person cannot find fulfillment in himself, that is, apart from the fact that he exists "with" others and "for" others. This truth does not simply require that he live with others at various levels of social life, but that he seek unceasingly — in actual practice and not merely at the level of ideas — the good, that is, the meaning and truth, found in existing forms of social life."[332] Realities such as smartphones and the Internet only reinforced the point that we can claim to be connected to one another, but in reality trend towards separating and isolating ourselves. When looking at difficult situations and societal problems, we need to consider the common good. Should a drug like marijuana be legalized? Is abortion a natural woman's right? Should someone be allowed to pursue sex reassignment surgery? These are all questions which have a very personal and individual component, but they cannot be considered in isolation to the entire body of humanity. Decisions made on such issues affect us in the way we think and interact. You cannot make decisions simply based on what people want and call love and respect.

The common good touches all levels of society and puts limits on individual rights. "The demands of the common good are dependent on the social conditions of each historical period and are strictly connected to respect for and the integral promotion of the person and his fundamental rights. These demands concern above all the commitment to peace, the organization of the State's powers, a sound juridical system, the protection of the environment, and the provision of essential services to all, some of which are at the same time human rights: food, housing, work, education and access to culture, transportation, basic health care, the freedom of communication and expression, and the protection of religious freedom."[333] When you think about it, it quickly becomes apparent how challenging it is to make wise and magnanimous decisions. This is why leaders should be chosen carefully. Key influence roles, at every level in society, should be safeguarded against those who are either insufficiently trained to carry out the office or who have demonstrated by their life decisions that the common good is not their criteria.

As I've shared throughout this book, leadership is a common responsibility. It is not for a few special people. Every one of us has influence. God wants each one of us to develop that influence and deploy it at the service of others. This is all part of the story of living the common good. Each one of us needs to take on this mindset. "The common good therefore involves all members of society, no one is exempt from cooperating, according to each one's possibilities, in attaining it and developing it. The common good must be served in its fullness, not according to reductionist visions that are subordinated by certain people to their advantages; own rather it is

---

[332] Ibid, 165.

[333] Ibid, 166.

to be based on a logic that leads to the assumption of greater responsibility."[334] As a leader, people will follow you. "Great leaders instill a sense of meaning and belonging in their followers by putting the personal imprint of who they are and what they stand for on their people. That imprint becomes the common ground where the people collectively meet and identify with their leader. A leader's personal mark, in other words, becomes the common denominator of gathering organization."[335] As a leader, commit not just to promote individual human dignity but also the overall common good of society and the specific organization you serve. While it might not be easy, this will ensure solutions and impact that achieves the overall good of individuals and society.

SOLIDARITY

This is the third leadership decision making criteria in principle. It directly follows from human dignity and the common good. Do you remember the story of Cain and Abel from the Old Testament? You might recall that Cain killed his brother out of jealousy. When God came and asked Cain about his brother, he famously replied "am I my brothers keeper?"[336] God replies in the affirmative. We are responsible for both our relatives as well as those around us in our society. We are all connected by the fabric of our common creation by God, and the command to love one another just as we have been loved by God.

As mentioned in the section on the common good, we live in a time of unprecedented connectivity and awareness of different cultures around the world. "Solidarity highlights in a particular way the intrinsic social nature of the human person, the equality of all in dignity and rights and the common path of individuals and peoples towards an ever more committed unity. Never before has there been such a widespread awareness of the bond of interdependence between individuals and peoples, which is found at every level."[337] Despite this, we can easily be disconnected and indifferent from a person suffering in our family, at our workplace, or who we pass on a street corner. Leadership decision making requires this principle and criteria by which we take responsibility for injustice, suffering, and those in need of assistance. True leaders do not turn a blind eye to those who suffer. The solidarity God shows us by taking our humanity in Jesus Christ implies and demands our solidarity with him who is present and suffers in each person around us.

Although globalization and the Internet have connected us all the more, there are stark inequality's and struggles. Solidarity implies we give special attention to these places and these

---

[334] Ibid, 167.

[335] *The Way of the Shepherd*, 46.

[336] Genesis 4:9.

[337] Compendium of the Social Doctrine of the Church, 192.

people. "In the presence of the phenomenon of interdependence and its constant expansion, however, there persist in every part of the world stark inequalities between developed and developing countries, inequalities stoked also by various forms of exploitation, oppression and corruption that have a negative influence on the internal and international life of many States. The acceleration of interdependence between persons and peoples needs to be accompanied by equally intense efforts on the ethical-social plane."[338] It is true that we should not go to extremes and say globalization and capitalism have not helped many people. Evidence and data show these systems have, indeed, brought many people out of poverty and enabled them to have a dignified lifestyle. This does not deny, however, the reality of many still being left out of the system, overlooked. Solidarity implies a leader will not leave anyone behind, and will personally take the initiative to seek out those on the margins.

How do we do this in practice? The Catholic Church has spoken about structures of sin over the past century. This refers to political systems, economic structures, education institutes, media outlets, organized crime, and other centralized hubs of influence that promote a lack of solidarity. "Solidarity must be seen above all in its value as a moral virtue that determines the order of institutions. On the basis of this principle the "structures of sin" that dominate relationships between individuals and peoples must be overcome. They must be purified and transformed into structures of solidarity through the creation or appropriate modification of laws, market regulations, and juridical systems."[339] Leaders at different levels of society need to own this issue. Each one of us can cry out and demand justice and solidarity where structures and systems promote instead isolation, indifference, and favoritism of only some members of society.

Each of us should keep in mind that solidarity (like love itself) is not so much a feeling as it is an intentional action. "Solidarity is also an authentic moral virtue, not a feeling of vague compassion or shallow distress at the misfortunes of so many people, both near and far. On the contrary, it is a firm and persevering determination to commit oneself to the common good. That is to say to the good of all and of each individual, because we are all really responsible for all."[340] I'm reminded of this every time I see a homeless person on the street begging. There rises up feelings of compassion, care and pity, but also thoughts of not having time to stop or that I have important matters to attend to. I never regret having stopped to talk with someone on a street corner or who is suffering, asking their name and how they're doing, and showing them what support I can give them in a minute or two. We all should be ambassadors and apostles who bestow dignity and solidarity to those around us. This is our mission as human beings. It is certainly our mission as leaders who are called to be out front and model the way for others.

---

[338] Ibid, 192.

[339] Ibid, 193.

[340] Ibid, 193.

A final point mentioned in the *Compendium of the Social Doctrine* is our indebtedness to our predecessors as well as our responsibility to the future generations. Solidarity is like a bridge linking us to those who came before us to those who are to come. "The principle of solidarity requires that men and women of our day cultivate a greater awareness that they are debtors of the society of which they have become part. They are debtors because of those conditions that make human existence livable, and because of the indivisible and indispensable legacy constituted by culture, scientific and technical knowledge, material and immaterial goods and by all that the human condition has produced. A similar debt must be recognized in the various forms of social interaction, so that humanity's journey will not be interrupted but remain open to present and future generations, all of them called together to share the same gift in solidarity."[341] As you think about making a decision or proposing a solution to a cultural problem, ask yourself if it includes and respects your elders as well as includes the younger generations. Leadership decision making often favors one group over the other.

The most practical and common place you can practice solidarity is through teamwork. Whether it be at the family, business, or at a sports level, we all find ourselves on one type of team or another. Solidarity is critical in your teams. Famous 13 year old peace advocate and author, Mattie Stepanek, said "unity is strength... when there is teamwork and collaboration, wonderful things can be achieved."[342] In a similar way, brand futurist Simon Mainwaring, wrote "creating a better world requires teamwork, partnerships, and collaboration, as we need an entire army of companies to work together to build a better world within the next few decades. This means corporations must embrace the benefits of cooperating with one another."[343] One way or the other, we each find ourselves as part of a team. Think of the team of your family, teams at work, and of course any sports teams that you are part of. How is your solidarity on each of those teams? Do you go out of your way to pay attention and include everyone? Do you make sure not to leave anyone on the margins and left out of involvement? Your leadership will be insufficient as long as solidarity does not characterize your decision making. I believe with the help of God you can make future decisions based on solidarity with others around you.

SUBSIDIARITY

This is the 4th and final leadership decision-making principle and criteria. It is also the least known and understood. What is subsidiarity? Subsidiarity says that the higher level government, organization, or authority should not do for the lower level what it can do for itself. For example, the federal government should not legislate or intervene at the state or city level

---

[341] Ibid, 195.

[342] Mattie Stepanek in: John Chen 50 Digital Team-Building Games:, John Wiley & Sons, 4 April 2012, p. 125

[343] Simon Mainwaring in: We First: How Brands and Consumers Use Social Media to Build a Better World, Macmillan, 7 June 2011, p. 125

when those two levels can handle things for themselves. When living through hurricane Harvey in Houston, the people needed state and federal government support due to the level of devastation. On a day to day and year to year level, however, this type of intervention and support is not needed. Think about the executives at a company. They should not interfere or micromanage those under them or on specific teams when they can handle things on their own. We could say the same in religious circles in regards to the operations at the local level.

Why is this the case? Subsidiarity protects and promotes the individual development, maturity, and takes responsibility of those closest to the situation. When a higher level authority or organization steps in and does this for you when you can do it yourself, it stunts your growth, makes you dependent and does not give you a chance to take responsibility for your life and maturity. "Just as it is gravely wrong to take from individuals what they can accomplish by their own initiative and industry and give it to the community, so also it is an injustice and at the same time a grave evil and disturbance of right order to assign to a greater and higher association what lesser and subordinate organizations can do. For every social activity ought of its very nature to furnish help to the members of the body social, and never destroy and absorb them."[344] As we have already seen in our assessment of perennial and contemporary trends, human beings can easily tend towards complacency and laziness. Unnecessary intervention from higher level authority and organization feeds and promotes mediocrity and under development of those at the lower level.

The role of leaders includes promoting and insisting that men and women develop to their full maturity and potential. Leaders should never promote mediocrity or behaviors that will stagnate those under their influence. Brigadier General Samuel Lyman Atwood Marshall, also known as Slam, was a military journalist and historian. He served with the American Expeditionary Forces in World War I, before leaving to work as a journalist, specializing in military affairs. He taught "the art of leading, in operations large or small, is the art of dealing with humanity, of working diligently on behalf of men, of being sympathetic with them, but equally, of insisting that they make a square facing toward their own problems."[345] The modern era is rife with entitlement mentality and expecting handouts. As a leader, you are called to row against this current and encourage decisions and solutions which respect subsidiarity.

A final thought on subsidiarity is a practical one. As a rule of thumb, it is so easy to tell people what to do. If they don't know how to fish, you show them. When they get a new phone, you set it up for them. When they are having technical issues with an appliance, you fix it. It is easy to step in and do things for others when you had the experience. Although I'm not advocating to never do this, I would encourage you to take on a mindset of helping others to learn to do things for themselves and mature. The idea of 'Big Brother' (big government) doing everything for you does not lead to human maturity. Leaning on a dearth of experience, General Patton counseled

---

[344] *Compendium of the Social Doctrine of the Church*, 186.

[345] S. L. A. Marshall in *Men Against Fire : The Problem of Battle Command in Future War* (1954), p. 160

"never tell people how to do things. Tell them what to do, and they will surprise you with their ingenuity."[346] Try to learn to be a coach and human development pro more than a boss or a leader who insists people do things as you would. I think you will be pleasantly surprised by people's capacity to develop and the joy it brings you to see them flourish and come into their own maturity.

Conclusion

Human dignity, the common good, solidarity, and subsidiarity. These four leadership principles and decision-making criteria provide a robust and powerful framework for holistic and effective decision making. Trust me, your average leader would be hard pressed to articulate a thoughtful, organized, and well reasoned set of principles for making holistic decisions on tough issues. In the different sectors of society, principles like these are not being applied on a regular basis. I would boldly wager that our society would be a much different and better place if we each took time to internalize and apply these four decision-making principles. It starts by doing it in our own lives and in the situations closest to us. This will then have ripple effects and influences citywide, state wide, and in national decision making.

The next chapter is dedicated to applying what we have seen in this book to the different sectors of leadership. In particular, the above 4 leadership decision-making principles can be used and applied in each sector. I invite you to approach the next chapter thinking about how you can transform the sector in which you find yourself the most. God has allowed you to be there and wants you to be like leaven in dough. His loving shepherd heart wants to influence others through you in the places where you find yourself the most.

Questions for Personal Reflection and Discussion

1. What struck you in this chapter?
2. Why do you need clear decision-making principles?
3. What is human dignity? What are 2-3 implications? How can you live this better?
4. " the common good? "   "   "   "
5. " solidarity?   "   "   "   "
6. " subsidiarity?   "   "   "   "
7. What do you see as the most pressing issue of the day? What does human dignity say about it? The common good? Solidarity? Subsidiarity?

---

[346] George S. Patton, in War As I Knew It (1947) "Reflections and Suggestions"

CHAPTER 10

LEADERSHIP IN THE DIFFERENT SECTORS OF SOCIETY

We lack Leadership capable of striking out on new paths and meeting the needs of the present with concern for all and without prejudice towards coming generations.[347]

If he has grown up in Christian circles he will know that Christianity demands the whole man and that Christians were intended, and are expected, to change the world. That they should be active; that membership in a church is not like membership of a club. That in theory, at least, the Christian should be relating his Christianity to his whole life and to the world about him, all the time, everywhere.[348]

"What do you make of all this mess? Where do we go from here?" These are common questions I get over coffee, meals, in one to one spiritual guidance sessions, as well as from parishioners when chatting after Sunday Mass. People recognize that the world and so many lives are adrift like a ship in a stormy sea without a rudder and compass. My hope is you better understand the lay of the land after reading the previous chapters. You should have a much clearer vision of leadership and what is required in your life. Now we have one more step to

---

[347] Pope Francis, On Care For Our Common Home, 2015, 53

[348] Hyde, Douglas, Dedication and Leadership, 37

travel together. We need to reflect and ponder on how to apply leadership in the various sectors of influence. Whether it is at the family level or in sectors like business, politics and entertainment, the previous chapters should help us chart a course for current and future leaders. One way or the other, this involves you.

Society and your fellow men and women need the best from you. God himself trusts you very much and hopes that you will take up your call to leadership. I would be letting you down if I did not challenge you in this regards. "The Communists make far bigger demands upon their people than the average Christian organization would ever dare to make. They believe that if you make big demands upon people you will get a big response."[349] There are many peoples' lives attached to yours like links in a chain. Your "yes" to leadership will greatly influence and positively effect many others. "If anyone is going to change the world for the better, it may be argued, it ought to be the Christians, not the Communists. For myself, I would say that if we started applying our Christianity to the society in which we live, then it would be we, indeed, who would change the world. Christians, too, have a world to change and a world to win. Had the early Christians gone in for slogans these might well have been theirs."[350] Whether you are a Christian or someone of goodwill, your times demand the best from you. All your talents need to be deployed for the service of your fellow men and women. Giving from your 'surplus' of time, talent, and treasure is not enough. Living up to the potential of your leadership demands giving everything at the service of others.

The leadership we are called to live is not a private thing. It is not a conformity to what makes other people feel comfortable an unchallenged. Living in the midst of a culture that embraces mediocrity, doing whatever you want, entitlement, and conformity embrace fringe ideological groups, leaders must boldly step forward to herald and announce a paradigm consistent with right human reason and the revelation of the loving shepherd heart of Jesus Christ. The *Evengelium* ('Good News') referred to paradigm shifting and world defining proclamations in ancient times by the Roman emperor. This was supplanted and elevated by Christians who proclaimed Jesus Christ as the good news who defines reality and brings true joy and peace to human beings. He, alone, can provide the 'revolution of heart' needed that can create a Society of justice, peace, and love. The world once more needs to hear the 'Good News' through you.

A 'revolution of heart' always starts in the individual, but we need to remember it should overflow to permeate and transform culture. This needs to include institutions that are a primary element in the formation and transmission of culture. "Without a fundamental restructuring of the institutions of culture formation and transmission in our society—the market, government-sponsored cultural institutions, education at all levels, advertising, entertainment, publishing, and the news media, not to mention church—revival would have a negligible long-term effect on

---

[349] Ibid, 27

[350] Ibid, 32

the reconstitution of the culture."[351] What are the institutions you are called to influence? Have you thought about this? Have you ever asked God where he wants to send you to influence? The institution of your family? Institution of your workplace? The institution where you attend classes (or your alma mater)?

Author and professor Dr. James Hunter strongly recommends faithful presence as the critical path to lead towards positive culture transformation. What is faithful presence? It means to live like leaven in the dough. Living your life with excellence and intentionality as a witness to truth, justice, and love. You cannot control others, but you can control the way you live and this necessarily influences others. "Faithful presence in the world means that Christians are fully present and committed in their spheres of social influence, whatever they may be: their families, neighborhoods, voluntary activities, and places of work. As I argued in Essay II, power is a given of social life. Christians will wield it in relationships and in the institutions and organizations of which they are a part. The question we face is how will we use whatever power we have. Needless to say, it is critically important that power not be exercised thoughtlessly, in passive conformity to the ways of the world."[352] This idea of faithful presence in your sectors of influence can be both a guide and a grounding, especially in times when you think you are insignificant and that the road of leadership is too difficult. Faithful presence is not out of your league, it is a game plan you can follow.

As we already seen and proposed, faithful presence is rooted in Jesus Christ and his loving shepherd heart. "Where power is exercised, therefore, it must conform to the way of Jesus: rooted in intimacy with the Father, rejecting the privileges of status, oriented by a self-giving compassion for the needs of others, and not only non-coercive toward those outside of the community of faith, but committed indiscriminately to the good of all."[353] Inspire Dan grounded in the heart of Jesus Christ, we can each be proactive and discern where we are called to make a difference in the lives of others. This might be in close and ongoing relationships such as family members and coworkers or in sporadic contact with strangers such as those who are homeless, sick or in other forms of difficulty. "Faithful presence means a constructive resistance that seeks new patterns of social organization that challenge, undermine, and otherwise diminish oppression, injustice, enmity, and corruption and, in turn, encourage harmony, fruitfulness and abundance, wholeness, beauty, joy, security, and well-being."[354] Have you ever thought of yourself and your leadership in terms of faithful presence?

---

[351] Hunter, James, To Change the World, 46

[352] Ibid, 247

[353] Ibid, 247.

[354] Ibid, 247.

Before delving into specific sectors of society which may help you go deeper in your own understanding and commitment to influence for the good, I would like to highlight and reflect on the importance of you intentionally influencing those entrusted with leadership in society. As we spoke about earlier in this book, it is a perennial complaint that leaders are often ineffective and sometimes outright despicable. Unfortunately, most of us are content and complacent in our complaining instead of rolling up our sleeves and getting to work in helping these individuals entrusted with great leadership and influence. Pause and think about it for a minute. Who do you know that has influence over a number of other people? A popular socialite? A mom or dad who exercises great influence at your child's school? A teacher? Your boss at work? A coach? A journalist? An author? A bishop, priest, nun, minister or rabbi? Now take that list and ask yourself a very hard and telling question: what am I doing to positively influence each of these people? Am I doing anything? Am I intentionally reaching out to at least one of them? I think we could all do much more to intentionally serve and influence these individuals. To a large degree, it is due to our negligence and complacence that our world and culture are in their current state.

I want to be clear about two things when speaking of those occupying existing roles and positions of influence in the different sectors of society. First, they are children of God just like everyone else. God loves them and wants them to flourish and thrive. He has a plan for them and wants them to live it to the full. Second, societal leaders and influencers have the greatest, most effective impact on culture change. This is part of their stewardship and it is a great responsibility for which one day God will hold them accountable. Dr Hunter writes that "change in a culture or civilization simply does not occur when there is change in the beliefs and values in the hearts and minds of ordinary people or in the creation of mere artifacts...The beliefs and values of ordinary people, then, are not irrelevant to the story of change. Yet in none of the instances recounted here was change dependent on the popular appeal and acceptance of the alternative culture proposed. The beliefs and values of ordinary people have a place in the unfolding drama; but it is neither the central nor the decisive place in the instigation and direction of change itself."[355] Through many historical examples, he affirms that it is primarily through societal leaders (and networks of these leaders working together) in the different sectors (the arts, education, business, politics, entertainment, sports, et cetera) that culture changes.

Given this backdrop and our desire to be servant leaders in the decades to come, I would like to take a quick walk with you through different societal sectors. Drawing from insights from the *Compendium of the Social Doctrine of the Church*, I believe we can apply the previously mentioned four leadership decision-making principles and and chart a path forward in each sector. Please read these next sections thinking about your reality. How does this apply to me? How am I called to lead here? What difference am I called to make?

FAMILY LIFE

---

[355] Ibid, 77.

Family is the most basic cell of society. We take it for granted, but leaders need to understand that the world goes as the family goes. The family is fundamental, the starting place to develop your leadership. Leaders should be quick to recognize and defend the role of the family and not allow it to be subverted by different ideological groups. "Enlightened by the radiance of the biblical message, the Church considers the family as the first natural society, with underived rights that are proper to it, and places it at the centre of social life. Relegating the family to a subordinate or secondary role, excluding it from its rightful position in society, would be to inflict grave harm on the authentic growth of society as a whole."[356] We historically see this subordination through different influences such as education and politics.

Throughout history and in most cultures, family begins with the exclusive commitment of a man and woman. "The family, in fact, is born of the intimate communion of life and love founded on the marriage between one man and one woman. It possesses its own specific and original social dimension, in that it is the principal place of interpersonal relationships, the first and vital cell of society. The family is a divine institution that stands at the foundation of life of the human person as the prototype of every social order."[357] A point of data for any leader should be the fact that all major world religions through history stress that marriage is between one man and one woman. Even secular societies through history align on this point. Leaders should not take for granted the stability, order, and fruitfulness for future generations that are inherent and intrinsic to marriage between one man and one woman. Are we dismissing the idea of marriage being between one man and one woman as something old and of the past? Is this being done based on solid scientific, psychological, and sociological evidence? How many of our leaders and decision-makers have studied the historical, psychological, sociological, philosophical, and theological groundings for marriage before deliberating and deciding on courses of action? When making decisions, are they consistent with the intersection of human dignity, the common good, solidarity and subsidiarity? Or, are decision-makers only offering a solution through the lens of 'dignity' or 'common good'? Proposed solutions must include all four principles to be robust and offer a solution with the best chances of creating a flourishing society.

family is like an anchor that stabilizes and orients society. "A society built on a family scale is the best guarantee against drifting off course into individualism or collectivism, because within the family the person is always at the centre of attention as an end and never as a means. It is patently clear that the good of persons and the proper functioning of society are closely connected with the healthy state of conjugal and family life."[358] Extreme individualism as well as nationalism and socialism continue to be challenges in our day. Strong family life cuts through

---

[356] Compendium of the Social Doctrine of the Church, 211

[357] Ibid, 211.

[358] Ibid, 213.

and exposes the aberrations in these. Strong family life helps each member with a healthy balance and perspective.

The family unit has always been (and will always be) more important and superior to the state. This runs completely contrary to socialist, communist, and totalitarian regimes, which think that they are the reference point for society. "The priority of the family over society and over the State must be affirmed. The family in fact, at least in its procreative function, is the condition itself for their existence. With regard to other functions that benefit each of its members, it proceeds in importance and value the functions that society and the State are called to perform. The family possesses inviolable rights and finds its legitimization in human nature and not in being recognized by the State. The family, then, does not exist for society or the State, but society and the State exist for the family."[359] This last sentence might make some politicians and social leaders shudder, but it is the truth. Humanity needs to take a good dose of the truth and be oriented by it. Family is the reference point for society and culture.

Marriage and family life require great sacrifice and commitment. Leaders should stand up and defend the dignity and excellence of married life. It is a failure of duty and good shepherding when leaders in different strata of society (including religious leaders) do not stand up and defend the demands of marriage. We see many act as if it were a contract that can be easily entered into and just as easily be left aside. "The characteristic traits of marriage are: totality, by which the spouses give themselves to each other mutually in every aspect of their person, physical and spiritual; unity which makes them "one flesh"; indissolubility and fidelity which the definitive mutual giving of self requires; the fruitfulness to which this naturally opens itself. …A radical denial of God's original plan is found in polygamy, "because it is contrary to the equal personal dignity of men and women who in matrimony give themselves with a love that is total and therefore unique and exclusive."[360] These are the traits of true marriage and they should be crystal clear to each leader. One of your first leadership duties and responsibilities is to stand up for the beauty and excellence of marriage and all that it entails.

A 21st century challenge for society and marriage is the proposal of gender fluidity. Like any proposal, leaders should ask, 'where is the proof for claims of gender fluidity?' Watching a 2022 TV program, it was striking to see a list of 100+ personal pronouns being proposed as if it was something normal and cutting-edge. We should ask who is confused. Those who are having a hard time accepting these ideas or those proposing them?

The Church has centuries of experience defending and promoting true humanity and dignity. What is the Church's view of gender fluidity? What has Pope Francis taught on this theme? During his visit to Poland in 2016, he called gender fluidity an ideology. "In Europe, America, Latin America, Africa, and in some countries of Asia, there are genuine forms of ideological

---

[359] Ibid, 214.

[360] Ibid, 217.

colonization taking place. And one of these — I will call it clearly by its name — is [the ideology of] 'gender.' Today, children — children! — are taught in school that everyone can choose his or her sex. Why are they teaching this? Because the books are provided by the persons and institutions that give you money. These forms of ideological colonization are also supported by influential countries. And this is terrible!"[361] In a similar vein, the Holy Father identified gender ideology as a threat to marriage. "You, Irina, mentioned a great enemy to marriage today: the theory of gender. Today there is a world war to destroy marriage. Today there are ideological colonizations which destroy, not with weapons, but with ideas. Therefore, there is a need to defend ourselves from ideological colonizations."[362] As leaders, the pope invites us to understand ideas have consequences on society. As leaders, you need to treat all people with love and respect; this includes helping each person embrace the unity of their gender and sexual identity.

Another issue affecting the family is divorce. Whether it is among those who claim religious or non-religious affiliation, we see 21st century divorce rates around 50% for first marriages. This is staggering and a telltale sign there is much work to do. We should also be clear that this is a modern phenomenon. "The introduction of divorce into civil legislation has fueled a relativistic vision of the marriage bond and is broadly manifested as it becomes 'truly a plague on society'."[363] Leaders need to distinguish between real life, challenging circumstances that lead to separation, yet also hold firm to the conviction that marriage is meant to last a lifetime. Do we see commitment as a good for society? Do we think rampant divorce strengthens or weakens society? Strong preparation by the couple in advance of marriage is critical. Marriage is a mission and a commitment for life which will require much sacrifice and willingness to grow together over a lifetime.

Alternate forms of marriage are another family challenge. Are any and all family configurations of equal value and validity? Should polygamy be allowed? Should 'open marriages' be promoted (ie allowing the other partner to have sexual relationships with another person)? Should one be allowed to legally marry their pet (dog, cat, horse, bird, et cetera)? What is to stop redefining marriage to any and all configurations? Is public opinion the criteria for such important decisions? As someone interested in leadership, I assume you will answer with a clear 'no'. Culture changing decisions of this magnitude require clear, well-reasoned thinking based on science, psychology, historical evidence, and theological understanding. The four leadership decision-making principles should be front-and-center when talking about such ideas. Do proposals past the test of these filters? Yes or no? If not, they should not be accepted.

---

[361] Pope Francis, Address to Polish Bishops, July 27, 2016.

[362] Pope Francis, Apostolic Journey to Georgia and Azerbaijan, October 1, 2016.

[363] Compendium of the Social Doctrine of the Church, 225.

Another area of attention is male presence and proactive leadership. Let us be clear. A strong marriage and family life requires the presence of both husband and wife; they both play an important role. The absence of either one is a tremendous loss. Whereas in past centuries the role of the man and father was perhaps overstressed and the wife and mother marginalized, the opposite is often true in our day. Husbands and fathers are often absent, missing, and even derelict in their responsibilities. Psychological studies show the immense damage done when a husband is unfaithful and leaves his wife. Other studies clearly show the traumatic impact of fathers who verbally (or physically) abuse or abandon their children.It should also be noted that children and teen belief in a loving, transcendent God is often directly linked to the belief and practice they see in their father. Leaders need to promote and encourage men to be faithful husbands and committed fathers. One of the most important areas where leaders can influence is the promotion of a society where no child grows up without a loving father.

As a final consideration on family life, I reiterate some of the points mentioned in the chapter on virtues. Family life is a gymnasium for virtue and it is your first line priority after your union and obedience to God. It is so easy to put family life on the second or third tier. Work should not be more important than family. Is it for you? Do you give the best of your time too your family or to the office? Social and community activities should not be more important than family. Do you dedicate more time, energy and enthusiasm (of course in the name of doing good) to these lesser priorities than to your family? Family is the first place where we should pray, work, socialize, and strive to do good. You would be a pseudo-leader if you claimed to be doing much good in your professional life and social impact, but were neglectful at home to what is supposed to be your first priority. This each recommit to give our best leadership and impact to those entrusted as closest to us in our family.

BUSINESS

Business and leadership are often synonymous. Getting ahead. Leading teams. Accomplishing goals. Creating vision. These and so many other aspects of leadership are taught in business schools and are the bread and butter of many businesses. Although the business sector does not have a monopoly on leadership, it is certainly a sector of society which emphasizes leadership more than many other sectors. For those of you reading this book and find yourselves in roles of business leadership, are young professionals or planning a future career, How are you called to apply what has been discussed in this book? What does true leadership in the business sector look like?

In February 2011, the Vatican published a 30-page document called '*The Vocation of the Business Leader*'. This landmark document is intended for entrepreneurs as well as business leaders. It highlights the important role of the vocation for the entrepreneur in the context of the current globalized economy. We can glean many insights from this document which applies the principles described in the last chapter. As we previously saw, "good business decisions are those rooted in principles at the foundational level, such as respect for human dignity and

Leadership in the different sectors of society

service to the common good, and a vision of a business as a community of persons."[364] Our challenge is to apply them to the concrete aspects of business.

As an example, I was impressed by a Fortune 100 global leader who highlighted the distinction between a company ethos based on 'let's avoid breaking the law' versus 'let's strive for excellence" .'Some companies talk a good game and have plaques on the wall stating their mission and values, but their day-to-day actions tell a different story."[365] How do we make sure we are living business with excellence instead of a half-hearted effort to stay out of jail while making the most money possible?

First, it is important to start with your identity and the noble calling you have received from God. Business is not some arbitrary choice that you found. It is not something you are simply good at or like. Business is a human good and it is a field of mission and dedication. "In the Gospel, Jesus tells us: "From everyone who has been given much, much will be demanded; and from the one who has been entrusted with much, much more will be asked" (Lk 12:48). Businesspeople have been given great resources and the Lord asks them to do great things. This is your vocation."[366] God has given you great talents and this particularly applies to those in existing roles of business influence. Do I see my role in business as a calling? As a mission? As a way to contribute and change the world for the better? As a way to serve people? As a path to serve God, be holy and become more like Jesus Christ the Good Shepherd?

Second, recognize that business is never simply about you. It is not about you accomplishing or getting what you want. At its core, it is always and most importantly something at the service of others. This is why business properly understood is always about the common good both at the level of society as well as at the level of the business itself. "Business leaders can put aspiration into practice when they pursue their vocation, motivated by much more than financial success. When they integrate the gifts of the spiritual life, the virtues and ethical social principles into their life and work, they may overcome the divided life, and receive the grace to foster the integral development of all business stakeholders. The Church calls upon the business leader to receive—humbly acknowledging what God has done for him or her —and to give—entering into communion with others to make the world a better place."[367] What is your current motivation for doing business?

Third, every generation of businessmen and women face the temptation towards absolutizing wealth and profit. "Business leaders increasingly focus on maximizing wealth, employees

---

[364] The Vocation of the Business Leader, 3.

[365] Kraemer, Harry, *From Values to Action: The Four Principles of Values-Based Leadership*, 92.

[366] The Vocation of the Business Leader, 4.

[367] Ibid, 3.

develop attitudes of entitlement, and consumers demand instant gratification at the lowest possible price. As values have become relative and rights more important than duties, the goal of serving the common good is often lost."[368] I understand this from experience. Pursuing profit by all possible means can become an obsession. Stealing? I have done it. Cutting corners? I did that too. Maneuvering and positioning yourself to best and leap-frog over coworkers for personal advantage? Of course, I have done that as well. Sound familiar to you? Have you done such things? You would be an exception in this day and age if you have not. Even if you have not gone to these lengths, accumulation of physical wealth is an insidious passion which can easily become part of your life 'operating system'. It would be good to run a good diagnostic (a thorough examination of your conscience) to see how ingrained this mentality is in you.

Fourth, watch out for living a divided life. "Obstacles to serving the common good come in many forms —lack of rule of law, corruption, tendencies towards greed, poor stewardship of resources —but the most significant for a business leader on a personal level is leading a "divided" life. This split between faith and daily business practice can lead to imbalances and misplaced devotion to worldly success."[369] The previous point was about pursuit of profit. Here I want to stress how imbalance and lack of virtue can lead the business person to a schizophrenic existence. They are one person at home and another at the office. It is never healthy to live a divided life. We are meant to be holistic people. The person at home or church should also be the one who shows up at the office. This is an important area for a personal prayer as well as getting feedback from family and friends. This lack of consistency and integrity of life is often a blind spot and hard to detect. Openness to God and others helps us detect divisions in our life.

A fifth point of examination for the business person (especially those in leadership roles) is to avoid reducing workers to a means to an end. This gets things backwards. As previously indicated, the dignity of each human person demands we put them at the center and not profit, prestige or power. "Any form of materialism or economic tenet that tries to reduce the worker to being a mere instrument of production, a simple labour force with an exclusively material value, would end up hopelessly distorting the essence of work and stripping it of its most noble and basic human finality. The human person is the measure of the dignity of work."[370] This abuse of workers occurs in every nation and I would speculate in most businesses that exist. This is not to say that business is evil, but that human pride and vanity easily creeps into the human heart and influences those in leadership roles. If you run a business, a division or manage a team, how do you see those under your charge? Are they just a means to reach your personal goals? It means to reach corporate goals? Or is your focus on helping them flourish and in so doing you together produce products and services that help others? This in turn includes financial profit for company stakeholders as well as the employees doing the work.

---

[368] Ibid, 3.

[369] Ibid, 2.

[370] Compendium of the Social Doctrine of the Church, 271.

Leadership in the different sectors of society

This is a pivotal and critical topic that every business person should keep front and centered. The moment we take for granted the challenge of running an employee centered business, we easily drift into using people for personal or corporate gain. "The challenge is simply to recognize that employees and customers have a greater intrinsic value than their tangible contribution as economic actors. In this light, the challenge is to conceptualize the relationship of employer to employee or the relationship between business and customer in terms that go beyond mere contract to covenant."[371] I would challenge business owners, senior executives, and all levels of management to incorporate a monthly assessment on the level of employee-centered decision making present in their leadership. This should be an ongoing and critical criteria for companies which is seen at all levels of authority.

Business leaders and management staff could start by asking "what do employers owe to their employees besides a payment for services? What do businesses owe customers besides a product or service for a fee? Such a reconceptualization would fundamentally change the established terms of market relations and, in turn, profoundly humanize the work environment."[372] Contrary to the Marxist, socialist and communist viewpoint an ideology, business leaders and employees are not diametrically opposed or enemies. This is a paradigm which is unscientific and has led to vast destruction and human animosity as mentioned earlier in this book. A Judeo-Christian worldview is much more balanced and consistent with the evidence of history and sociology when it proposes a working relationship of respect and reciprocity between employer and employee. "In considering the relationship between labour and capital, above all with regard to the impressive transformations of our modern times, we must maintain that the "principal resource" and the "decisive factor" at man's disposal is man himself, and that "the integral development of the human person through work does not impede but rather promotes the greater productivity and efficiency of work itself."[373]

Sixth, business and religion should not be opposed. It is amazing to see in the 21st century how every group and ideology is allowed to promote itself, but religious thought and expression is frowned upon. This is an incredible form of hypocrisy and discrimination. Leaders in every form of company (Private, ESOP, Publicly traded, et cetera) should foster and allow public displays of religious expression. Companies permit culture and racial expressiveness so why not religious belief? Even more, some companies and employers do not give their employees a chance to attend worship services. "Public authorities have the duty to ensure that, for reasons of economic productivity, citizens are not denied time for rest and divine worship. Employers have an analogous obligation regarding their employees...Every Christian should avoid making

---

[371] Hunter, James. *To Change the World*, 264.

[372] Ibid, 265.

[373] Compendium of the Social Doctrine of the Church, 278.

unnecessary demands on others that would hinder them from observing the Lord's Day."[374] Whether it is taking the approach of companies such as Chick-fil-A, which are closed on Sunday or simply give a more flexible work schedules to allow for for worship, employers have the responsibility to help their employees flourish. This includes allowing employees space and time for prayer and worship every week.

I invite you to take the four principles in the last chapter (Human dignity, common good, solidarity and subsidiarity) and begin practicing applying them to all aspects of your work decisions. This might be difficult at the beginning since it requires a habitual change of thought. He will come up, however, gradually see your mindset and decision making process adjust. You will begin to see business and the people you work with in a different light. You will also be empowered to deal with difficult decision making topics with a much more robust and holistic tool kit. I challenge business leaders and professionals at all levels to propose another framework for decision making which offers as much depth and holistic life consideration as these four principles. It will not be easy to follow through on this decision making analysis or embracing the conclusions found therein, but you will be rewarded with leadership decisions which are people-centered and highly impactful.

POLITICS

"I will tell you whatever you want to hear to get myself elected." This is what a certain politician told a friend of mine when he went to a fundraiser for this person's campaign. The previous day, my friend heard this politician give a certain message to a crowd, but now he was saying the exact opposite thing. When questioned about this discrepancy and contradiction, the politician came up into my friend's face, cursed at him a few times and then said the above.

Politics is a noble profession and a high calling to service. Whether you are a politician, thinking about running in the future or simply trying to understand how politicians can live up to this mission, the following reflections will help on the journey. During an interview, Pope Francis commented "I say that politics is the most important of the civil activities and has its own field of action, which is not religion. Political institutions are secular by definition and operate in independent spheres. All my predecessors have said the same thing, for many years at least, albeit with different accents. I believe that Catholics involved in politics carry the values of their religion within them, but have the mature awareness and expertise to implement them. The Church will never go beyond its task of expressing and disseminating its values, at least as long as I'm here."[375] Once again, the Catholic Church has 20 centuries of wisdom and insight on politics. She has lived through and worked with political regimes and politicians of all types: kings, queens and nobles; presidents and prime ministers; war mongers and peace lovers;

---

[374] Ibid, 286.

[375] Pope Francis, interviewed in "How the Church will change" by Eugenio Scalfari in La Repubblica(1 October 2013), as translated from Italian to English by Kathryn Wallace

Leadership in the different sectors of society

Democrats, Republicans, Libertarians, Marxists and Nazis. In our day, we can all learn something about the role of politics and politicians. Given the polarization of different sectors of society through a political lens, it is urgent and necessary to purify our vision of politics and so put it in its proper place in the leadership spectrum.

First, leaders need to be clear about the nature of politics. Everything starts with your vision and understanding of a thing. "The human person is the foundation and purpose of political life... The political community originates in the nature of persons, whose conscience reveals to them and enjoins them to obey...This order must be gradually discovered and developed by humanity. The political community, a reality inherent in mankind, exists to achieve an end otherwise unobtainable: the full growth of each of its members, called to cooperate steadfastly for the attainment of the common good, under the impulse of their natural inclinations towards what is true and good."[376] When was the last time you heard that the human person was the center of politics? How often do you see that being lived out in practice? Are politicians truly focused on and basing their decisions around the good of the people they represent? This is where the discussion and purification of politics and politicians starts.

Seeing the evils done by politicians, we might be tempted to say that politics is not necessary, forever flawed and contrary to the will of God. The same flawed logic is often applied when seeing bad examples of priests and ministers as well as those in different professions. In reality, "God made men social by nature, and since no society can hold together unless some one be over all, directing all to strive earnestly for the common good, every civilized community must have a ruling authority, and this authority, no less than society itself, has its source in nature, and has, consequently, God for its author."[377] God has willed the need for leaders to guide society and this includes politicians.

Since God has wanted political authority and ordained it to serve humanity, politicians are mandated to uphold and help provide for the basic needs of people. "The rights and duties of the person contain a concise summary of the principal moral and juridical requirements that must preside over the construction of the political community. These requirements constitute an objective norm on which positive law is based and which cannot be ignored by the political community, because both in existential being and in final purpose the human person precedes the political community. Positive law must guarantee that fundamental human needs are met."[378] Let me say it again: politicians are completely at the service of each person in their jurisdiction. They should respect and protect their dignity by ensuring they have access to food, water, education, housing, and medical care. These are fundamental for each person.

---

[376] Compendium of the Social Doctrine of the Church, 384.

[377] Ibid, 393.

[378] Ibid, 388.

Politicians should also protect religious liberty and defend those who are most vulnerable in society (the poor, outcast, unborn, and elderly).

How should we see civil disobedience? Is it something good, bad or indifferent? According to the mind of the Church, leaders need to know how to walk a fine line on this theme. "Whoever refuses to obey an authority that is acting in accordance with the moral order "resists what God has appointed" (Rom 13:2). Analogously, whenever public authority — which has its foundation in human nature and belongs to the order pre-ordained by God — fails to seek the common good, it abandons its proper purpose and so delegitimizes itself."[379] Civil disobedience is legitimate when the governing authority does not uphold the common good. This is no justification for violence. Civil disobedience should be carried out through peaceful protests and respectful non-compliance where human rights and natural law are violated.

Leaders should have crystal clear the need to personally resist unjust and evil laws. They should embrace their responsibility to encourage those under their influence to do the same. "It is a grave duty of conscience not to cooperate, not even formally, in practices which, although permitted by civil legislation, are contrary to the Law of God. Such cooperation in fact can never be justified, not by invoking respect for the freedom of others nor by appealing to the fact that it is foreseen and required by civil law. No one can escape the moral responsibility for actions taken, and all will be judged by God himself based on this responsibility (cf. Rom 2:6; 14:12)."[380] This reality requires all politicians to not only refrain from enacting unjust laws, but also to resist them from within the government despite pressure from within and outside the government. This is a matter of defending the common good and it would be a sin of omission and mediocre leadership to do otherwise.

As we saw at the beginning of the book, relativism is a perennial as well as a contemporary danger to humanity. Instead of being rooted in principles based on natural law as well as divine revelation, politicians who subscribe to relativism are like boats without an anchor or sail during a violent storm at sea. They are blown along by public opinion and personal passions for success, popularity and power. Politicians who base their lives and career on the truth, however, meet with opposition. "Those who are convinced that they know the truth and firmly adhere to it are considered unreliable from a democratic point of view, since they do not accept that truth is determined by the majority, or that it is subject to variation according to different political trends. It must be observed in this regard that if there is no ultimate truth to guide and direct political action, then ideas and convictions can easily be manipulated for reasons of power. As history demonstrates, a democracy without values easily turns into open or thinly disguised totalitarianism."[381] Those aspiring to serve in politics need to be ready to sacrifice

---

[379] Ibid, 398.

[380] Ibid, 399.

[381] Ibid, 407.

themselves holding to the true and good that can be discerned using the four decision-making principles. The good politician is not the one who manages to get elected and hold onto office for the longest time. This would be a life of manipulation and self serving. True politicians put their lives (even to the point of death) on the line to help those they serve flourish according to the truth which includes living a life of virtue.

The 21st century and globalization has raised awareness of the common human family despite different races and cultures. A challenge facing politicians is how to balance promoting and respecting minorities while, at the same time, challenging them to embrace their responsibility towards the common good of the nation. "Minorities have the right to maintain their culture, including their language, and to maintain their religious beliefs, including worship services. In the legitimate quest to have their rights respected, minorities may be driven to seek greater autonomy or even independence; in such delicate circumstances, dialogue and negotiation are the path for attaining peace. In every case, recourse to terrorism is unjustifiable and damages the cause that is being sought. Minorities are also bound by duties, among which, above all, is working for the common good of the State in which they live."[382] As we learned in the last chapter, leaders will need to act in solidarity with minorities and also challenge them to roll up their sleeves and work for the good of society.

Leaders, by definition, are willing to do what it requires to solve problems and change the world. Yes, the majority of us are not directly involved in politics per say, but we can nonetheless make a difference in the world. Voting and personal action are two sides of the coin that must take shape in each one of our lives. "Christians are urged to vote and become involved in politics as an expression of their civic duty and public responsibility. This is a credible argument and good advice up to a point. Yet in our day, given the size of the state and the expectations that people place on it to solve so many problems, politics can also be a way of saying, in effect, that the problems should be solved by others besides myself and by institutions other than the church."[383] This is a healthy reminder that we have a double duty. The duty to vote and the duty to work in personal ways for the common good and serving the Kingdom of God. Each of you as leaders needs to transmit this to those you influence. Do you encourage other people to vote? Do you challenge them to do so? Do you go further by challenging them to get involved in making a difference in the world? Have you ever invited coworkers and friends to join you in some form of action serving at say a soup kitchen, an elderly care facility, in a program that mentors young people or other such initiatives? We need to watch out and avoid becoming complainers and back seat quarterbacks. Let us each embrace our responsibility to positively contribute to the common good by getting involved and encouraging others to do the same.

I would advise everyone to purify their attitude of politicizing everything. Marriage gets political. Sports becomes political. Entertainment becomes a political platform. Schools and even

---

[382] Ibid, 387.

[383] Hunter, James, To Change the World, 172.

churches are becoming polarized by politics. As leaders, let me remind you to be crystal clear about the nature of politics. Politics is a noble, yet limited field. It should not be guiding other sectors of society especially education, science and religion. These are out of its spectrum and expertise. Politics and the state are by their nature meant to be at the service of family life, religion, education, business and medical care. I encourage you to stand up and and against letting politics take over these other dimensions of your life. If you do this, politics will become more authentic and true to itself: a simple, humble servant of humanity.

MEDIA

We see it all the time. Whether on planes, in restaurants, or even with the family together in the living room, people are constantly on their phones and using social media. YouTube. Instagram. Facebook. These and so many more are used across the world hour-after-hour. Ever take a moment in a public place to just stop and watch people? I find it fascinating and a bit disturbing to look around and see so many people in close proximity and so little person to person communication. Couples at a meal and both on their phone. Parents and children together yet on their phones. Friends hanging out together although constantly looking at some app or video.

You may not be surprised to learn that many people are spending hour after hour on TV and social media. The World Health Organization in 2021 estimates that the average person over their lifetime will have used social media for about 3,500,000 minutes. "In other words, that is nearly 6 years and 8 months...Since the trend over the past decade has been for people to spend more and more time on social media, humans are on track to spend a decade or more on social media during a lifetime."[384] This does not include traditional TV watch time so we can estimate adding a few years to that time dedicated to entertainment.

As leaders, we need the principles to evaluate what it means to have a balanced and moderate approach to the use of TV and media use. In this book, you've heard me speak about virtues such as reflection, prayer, and self control. You are probably not surprised when I say that a leader need to set healthy boundaries and avoid spending large chunks of time on their phone or in front of the TV each day. At the same time, I would be the first one to advocate for using technology and the media for good purposes such as communication with family, friends, and coworkers as well as for periodic learning and rest. Just like anything else in life, a leader needs to know how to put things in the proper order and put something aside when it is not conducive and helpful to flourishing. I think we both deep down know that spending a decade of your life on social media and on the TV is not a healthy way to live.

As mentioned in the chapter about a Judeo-Christian worldview, we cannot fully understand society and human relationships unless we grasp the inherent brokenness of the human heart and our tendency towards selfishness and being self centered. This manifests in every aspect of

---

[384] https://www.broadbandsearch.net/blog/average-daily-time-on-social-media

social life including the type of programming that appeals to our fallen heart. Author Patrick Hurley write "The media are slavishly subservient to the entertainment desires of their audience."[385] It also rears its ugly head in leaders who control media outlets, who support and intentionally advance programming contrary to the flourishing of those who listen and watch. This includes outright manipulation of truth and facts. "The media have long operated as agents of moral indignation in their own right : even if they are not self-consciously engaged in crusading or muck-raking, their very reporting of certain facts can be sufficient to generate anxiety, indignation or panic."[386] This is completely contrary to what leaders with the Shepherd Heart of Jesus Christ do or seek when working in the media.

As previously mentioned, the *Compendium of the Social Doctrine of the Church* speaks on many facets of social life. There are several gold nuggets on the theme of media therein. In the first place, the media and technology in general should be created, governed, and used at the service of the dignity of the human person. When was the last time you heard that? Think that is currently how things are being done? "The essential question is whether the current information system is contributing to the betterment of the human person; that is, does it make people more spiritually mature, more aware of the dignity of their humanity, more responsible or more open to others, in particular to the neediest and the weakest. A further aspect of great importance is the requisite that new technologies respect legitimate cultural differences."[387] Leaders need to be attentive and careful to avoid accepting and applying the standard of 'if it is possible to do it then it is fine and good'. The standard in principle we should and must promote is to examine if something is for the overall good and flourishing of the human person or not. This is what should guide us in our leadership decision making.

Also, in accord with what was discussed in the last chapter, the media should be subservient to the common good. It is never meant to be autonomous and cut off from what is good and noble for society. It should also not exacerbate individualism and relativism and contribute to it becoming rampant in society. "The media must be used to build up and sustain the human community in its different sectors: economic, political, cultural, educational and religious. The information provided by the media is at the service of the common good. Society has a right to information based on truth, freedom, justice and solidarity."[388] If you are working in a media-related company and business, is this how you see things? Are you contributing to the common good or hurting it? Do you see it as your mission to imbue truth in the social media? To foster a balanced use of the media instead of addiction?

---

[385] Patrick J. Hurley, A Concise Introduction to Logic (2000 [Seventh edition], Wadsworth, ISBN 0-534-52006-5), p. 595

[386] Cohen S., Folk Devils and Moral Panics, London, Routledge, 2002, p. 7; as qtd. in Julian Petley, ""Are We Insane ?". The "Video Nasty" Moral Panic", Paniques et croisades morales, 43-1, 2012, pp. 35-57.

[387] Compendium of the Social Doctrine of the Church, 415.

[388] Ibid, 415.

There are many leadership issues involved with the media. "In the world of the media the intrinsic difficulties of communications are often exacerbated by ideology, the desire for profit and political control, rivalry and conflicts between groups, and other social evils. Moral values and principles apply also to the media. The ethical dimension relates not just to the content of communication (the message) and the process of communication (how the communicating is done) but to fundamental structural and systemic issues, often involving large questions of policy bearing upon the distribution of sophisticated technology and product (who shall be information rich and who shall be information poor?)."[389] For this reason, leaders in the media should do their best to make sure the content of media is objective, true and fact based. They should also protect the media (TV programs, movies, content uploaded to social media including photos, et cetera) from being hijacked by ideological groups or become a platform for distribution of immoral and denigrating content. This will require media leaders and staff to be counter-cultural and perhaps risk losing their jobs as they live by their convictions.

The media is one facet of social life that can easily be controlled by a select few elites and influencers. Leaders in the media and those who want to lead in the future must set their sights on garnering greater participation and guidance from those who use this important means of information and communication. "It is necessary that citizens participate in the decision-making process concerning media policies. This participation, which is to be public, has to be genuinely representative and not skewed in favor of special interest groups when the media are a money-making venture."[390] When was the last time you heard of citizens like yourself being invited to participate in decision making policies about how the media is governed and the content that is produced? The reality is this does not happen. It is up to people like you to insistently voice the need for this and to work for it. If you are working in the media in some capacity, this mission falls on you in a more direct way since you better understand this sector of influence and have connections within it. What are you going to do? What is God asking you to do?

I would like to close this section by inviting all Christians in those of goodwill to take s their commitment to use the media with moderation and purity seriously as well as use it for the spreading of the Kingdom of God and the building of a civilization of justice, peace, and love. "It is, therefore, an inherent right of the Church to have at its disposal and to employ any of these media insofar as they are necessary or useful for the instruction of Christians and all its efforts for the welfare of souls. It is the duty of Pastors to instruct and guide the faithful so that they, with the help of these same media, may further the salvation and perfection of themselves and of the entire human family. In addition, the laity especially must strive to instill a human and Christian spirit into these media, so that they may fully measure up to the great expectations of

---

[389] Ibid, 416.

[390] Ibid, 416.

mankind and to God's design."[391] As a Christian or person of good will, I challenge you to take ownership of the way you use the media and to live it as if all humanity were watching and following your example.

JOURNALISM

"I cannot stand the news." Without joking, I would estimate that about 50% of my one-on-one conversations with men and women include a comment like this. Does that resonate with you? Whatever news outlet you follow, be it in printed media, on TV, or a social media feed, my guess is that you are less than satisfied with the tone of what you hear, the lack of balance towards what is being reported, and the negative attitudes which often come across. How should we see this important and noble profession? How should you carry out your work as a journalist?

I think we can gain great insight from a recent speech given by Pope Francis in Rome to a group of journalists. There are several ideas that communicate both esteem for this profession as well as key performance indicators for doing a good job. "The Pope cares about you, follows you, esteems you and considers you precious. Journalism does not come about by choosing a profession, but by embarking on a mission, a little like a doctor, who studies and works so that the evil in the world may be healed. Your mission is to explain the world, to make it less obscure, to make those who live in it less afraid of it and look at others with greater awareness, and also with more confidence. It is not an easy mission. It is complicated to think, to meditate, to study more deeply, to stop and collect ideas and to study the contexts and precedents of a piece of news. The risk, as you well know, is to be overwhelmed by the news instead of being able to make sense of it. This is why I encourage you to preserve and cultivate that sense of mission that is at the origin of your choice. And I will do so with three verbs that I believe characterize good journalism: listen, investigate and report."[392] As we touch on these three verbs, I would invite you too keep the four social and leadership criteria of the last chapter in mind (human dignity, common good, solidarity, subsidiarity).

There is so much information flying around us that it is hard to authentically listen. Even more troubling is we often have a 'listening filter'. This filter screens information for what we want to hear (taking it in) and for what we do not want to hear (rejecting it). While this can apply in every relationship and sector of life, here we are concretely speaking about the importance of the journalist to truly listen without filters. "For a journalist, listening means having the patience to meet face to face with the people to be interviewed, the protagonists of the stories being told, the sources from which to receive news. Listening always goes hand in hand with seeing, with being present: certain nuances, sensations, and well-rounded descriptions can only be conveyed to readers, listeners and spectators if the journalist has listened and seen for him- or

---

[391] Decree on the Media of Social Communications, *INTER MIRIFICA*, St POPE PAUL VI, DECEMBER 4, 1963, 3.

[392] Address of Pope Francis to Journalists, November 11, 2021.

herself. This means escaping - and I know how difficult this is in your work – escaping from the tyranny of always being online, on social networks, on the web. The journalism of listening and seeing well requires time. Not everything can be told through email, the telephone, or a screen. As I recalled in this year's Message for Communications Day, we need journalists who are willing to "wear out the soles of their shoes", to get out of the newsroom, to walk around the city, to meet people, to assess the situations in which we live in our time. Listening is the first word that came to my mind."[393] This is the first necessary characteristic of a good journalist who truly leads in their field: listen.

Secondly, a good and leading journalist investigates. It is not simply a 'getting to the bottom' of an event or issue, but also helping the reader-viewer process the information based on objective criteria. "At a time when millions of pieces of information are available on the web, and when many people obtain their information and form their opinions on social media, where unfortunately the logic of simplification and opposition sometimes prevails, the most important contribution that good journalism can make is in-depth analysis. Indeed, what more can you offer to those who read or listen to you than what they already find on the web? You can offer the context, the precedents, the keys to interpretation that help to collocate the fact that has happened. You know very well that, even when it comes to information about the Holy See, not everything said is always "new" or "revolutionary"."[394] As highlighted in the beginning of this book as well as the chapter on worldviews, it is not surprising that journalists bring an agenda and lens by which they see and interpret reality. Unfortunately, many news outlets leaders (and hence the journalists who report to them) are focused on delivering 'shock and awe' news stories. They often operate on the fallen human tendency to seek the debased, scandalous, and negative instead of the good, true, beautiful, and inspiring. It is important for journalists to remember their calling, to base their reporting on facts, and communicate in a way that leads the reader-listener towards living a good life. This is hard to do if you condition your reporting to suit a political or ideological agenda that you (and your news firm) want to advance.

This leads us to a third aspect of good journalism: reporting. "Reporting means not putting oneself in the foreground, nor setting oneself up as a judge, but allowing oneself to be struck and sometimes wounded by the stories we encounter, in order to be able to tell them with humility to our readers. Reality is a great antidote to many "ailments". Reality - what happens, the lives and testimonies of people - deserves to be told…Today we are in great need of journalists and communicators who are passionate about reality, capable of finding the treasures often hidden in the folds of our society and recounting them, allowing us to be impressed, to learn, to broaden our minds, to grasp aspects that we did not know before. I am grateful to you for your effort to recount reality. The diversity of approaches, of style, of points of view linked to different cultures or religious affiliations is also a wealth of information. I also thank you for what you tell us about what goes wrong in the Church, for helping us not to sweep

---

[393] Ibid.

[394] Ibid.

it under the carpet, and for the voice you have given to the victims of abuse: thank you for this."[395] When reporting something (whether in print, TV, social media, as well as in day-to-day conversations), ask yourself 'is this based in reality?' In other words, am I saying something because I want to paint a narrative and justify my point of view? Am I filtering the facts (accepting some and ignoring others) to accommodate and tell a story that meets the approval of a certain audience and agenda? This would not be good reporting and journalism.

As leaders and future leaders, we each should demand nobility from journalism. In the 21st century, you rarely here of people lauding news programs or newspapers. Why? We should seriously consider if it is because we have abandoned true reporting for agenda based stories and focusing on the negative, debased and shock-and-awe stories. Leaders in our day need to reimagine a world where reporters and journalists tell the facts but bring to bear a worldview based on human dignity, the common good, solidarity, and subsidiarity. Where there is will and commitment, this is a possible future.

THE ARTS

Think of a moment when you were surprised by beauty. Was it a sunset? Majestic mountains or a tranquil beach? A powerful symphony, an amazing sculpture or a luminous painting? Beauty always influences us and touches the most transcendent and spiritual level of our being. The arts are a critical sector of influence and leadership which deserves our attention. This sector can influence us towards the good or draw us towards the debased. There are many commentaries on the arts who we could reference, but in this short section I will primarily share insights and conclusions offered by Pope Saint John Paul II. His letter to artists in 1999 is a treasure trove of inspiration and I recommend reading it.

First, the arts share a participation in and likeness to God's creating action. Only God creates something out of nothing, but through reason, skill, and free will we are able to communicate the beauty, thoughts, and feelings we contemplate through different mediums such as the pen, chisel, musical note, or a painter's brush. "None can sense more deeply than you artists, ingenious creators of beauty that you are, something of the pathos with which God at the dawn of creation looked upon the work of his hands. A glimmer of that feeling has shone so often in your eyes when—like the artists of every age—captivated by the hidden power of sounds and words, colors and shapes, you have admired the work of your inspiration, sensing in it some echo of the mystery of creation with which God, the sole creator of all things, has wished in some way to associate you."[396] This is a noble and dignified calling and activity. If you practice art in some form, have you thought in this way? Do you see this aspect of your life (and the role of the arts in society in general) as from God for the good of you and humanity?

---

[395] Ibid.

[396] Pope St John Paul II, Letter to Artists, 1999, 1.

Second, the arts should be windows to and reminders of each person as a work of art. Indeed, each life is an 'in progress' work of art. "Not all are called to be artists in the specific sense of the term. Yet, as Genesis has it, all men and women are entrusted with the task of crafting their own life: in a certain sense, they are to make of it a work of art, a masterpiece. It is important to recognize the distinction, but also the connection, between these two aspects of human activity. The distinction is clear. It is one thing for human beings to be the authors of their own acts, with responsibility for their moral value; it is another to be an artist, able, that is, to respond to the demands of art and faithfully to accept art's specific dictates."[397] This reminds us as leaders that the arts should influence mankind towards morally upright and noble acts. They should inspire us to live the virtues such as those discussed earlier in this book. When we do not live a life of virtue, we are an incomplete, corrupted work of art.

Third, we should always promote the arts and encourage men and women with passion and talents for this. Recent centuries show an increasing focus and appreciation for the scientific and technical professions as well as a decreasing interest in the arts (especially painting and sculpture). "Society needs artists, just as it needs scientists, technicians, workers, professional people, witnesses of the faith, teachers, fathers and mothers, who ensure the growth of the person and the development of the community by means of that supreme art form which is "the art of education". Within the vast cultural panorama of every nation, artists have their unique place. Obedient to their inspiration in creating works both worthwhile and beautiful, they not only enrich the cultural heritage of each nation and of all humanity, but they also render an exceptional social service in favor of the common good."[398] The world is dying for lack of beauty. We need artists more than ever. I encourage leaders to foster and support the arts in their countries and local areas. Please do not think I am supporting every self-proclaimed artist. The world needs men and women who emulate reality, transmit the true, good, and beautiful in their art. True art is not simply transmitting your feelings or experiences, but also inspiring and helping others live according to the true, good, and beautiful (ie. a virtuous life).

This brings us to the fourth insight from St John Paul II: artists have a responsibility to the world and those who partake of their art. The artist is not in a vacuum. They (like all of us) are moral agents and responsible for what they do and create. They will be held accountable by God for how they invested their artistic talent. "The particular vocation of individual artists decides the arena in which they serve and points as well to the tasks they must assume, the hard work they must endure and the responsibility they must accept. Artists who are conscious of all this know too that they must labour without allowing themselves to be driven by the search for empty glory or the craving for cheap popularity, and still less by the calculation of some possible profit for themselves. There is therefore an ethic, even a "spirituality" of artistic service, which contributes

---

[397] Ibid, 2.

[398] Ibid, 4.

in its way to the life and renewal of a people."[399] The vane seeking of applause and popularity is a temptation knocking at the door of every artist's heart. Artists must base their labors in the virtues of humility and magnanimous service to others. As leaders, we should remind artists we know of this important duty and help them stay grounded in what matters. We should affirm them in their value and encourage them to be artists focused on helping others through their creations.

More than any other world religion, Christianity promotes and favors the arts in its different expressions. Proof of this is easily seen over the previous 2,000 of artistic creation (paintings, murals, frescos, sculptures, untold number of books, plays, songs as well as presence in radio, television, and the movies). This should not be a surprise given the belief in the all beautiful one, God himself, becoming man like us in all things but sin. This is what we celebrate at Christmas each year. This joyful truth and love so magnanimous has been celebrated for all ages through the arts. "This prime epiphany of "God who is Mystery" is both an encouragement and a challenge to Christians, also at the level of artistic creativity. From it has come a flowering of beauty that has drawn its sap precisely from the mystery of the Incarnation. In becoming man, the Son of God has introduced into human history all the evangelical wealth of the true and the good, and with this he has also unveiled a new dimension of beauty, of which the Gospel message is filled to the brim."[400] This is why the arts are important to Christianity. Properly speaking, the arts are concerned with the presentation and transmission of the true, good, and beautiful. This is why all true art is linked to Jesus Christ and somehow speaks to who God is, his love for us and his plan for our eternal glorification in Heaven.

True art is never simply about the artist and surface level experiences and feelings. Real art is much deeper and springs from touching the mystery of God, creation, and our own lives. "Every genuine artistic intuition goes beyond what the senses perceive and, reaching beneath reality's surface, strives to interpret its hidden mystery. The intuition itself springs from the depths of the human soul, where the desire to give meaning to one's own life is joined by the fleeting vision of beauty and of the mysterious unity of things. All artists experience the unbridgeable gap which lies between the work of their hands, however successful it may be, and the dazzling perfection of the beauty glimpsed in the ardor of the creative moment: what they manage to express in their painting, their sculpting, their creating is no more than a glimmer of the splendor which flared for a moment before the eyes of their spirit."[401] As in previous centuries, artists face the danger of using their art to simply vent, express their feelings, or influence the masses by appealing to our lower passions (such as using sounds and imagery to provoke sexual desire). Leaders and those who sponsor the arts should ensure that artists are reminded and guided towards creating art that inspires admiration, pursuit of the good and self-control.

---

[399] Ibid, 4.

[400] Ibid, 5.

[401] Ibid, 6.

Given continued modern trends towards building utopian societies without God (always a fruitless and disastrous endeavor), leaders should be mindful of the systematic attempt to divorce God from the arts. 'Separation of Church and State' is today often translated into 'separation of God and the arts" ."It is true nevertheless that, in the modern era, alongside this Christian humanism which has continued to produce important works of culture and art, another kind of humanism, marked by the absence of God and often by opposition to God, has gradually asserted itself. Such an atmosphere has sometimes led to a separation of the world of art and the world of faith, at least in the sense that many artists have a diminished interest in religious themes."[402] This is a sad reality since God is the foundation for true art. It is like sawing the branch you sit upon. As St John Paul II famously said, when you eclipse God in society, man's identity is lost. We can translate this to saying when God is eclipsed, true art is lost.

The arts needs the Church just as the Church needs the arts. They are connected and cannot be separated. "The Church therefore needs art. But can it also be said that art needs the Church? The question may seem like a provocation. Yet, rightly understood, it is both legitimate and profound. Artists are constantly in search of the hidden meaning of things, and their torment is to succeed in expressing the world of the ineffable. How then can we fail to see what a great source of inspiration is offered by that kind of homeland of the soul that is religion? Is it not perhaps within the realm of religion that the most vital personal questions are posed, and answers both concrete and definitive are sought?"[403] I see a great panorama where the Church is proactively supporting artists. This is not done simply through sermons or as financial benefactors. The Church can support artists through study and discussion groups that bring together men and women of the arts. A vast sphere of action is also available to spiritual guidance and accompaniment of artists. How many arts students, professional artists, and those leading institutions of the arts are meeting with a spiritual guide to discuss their life, challenges, progress in their artistic field and helping them be accountable to their art being grounded in the true, good, and beautiful? There is much more Christians can do to support the arts.

Finally, I instruct all artists to see their art as a personal mission from God. So many of us have never been told that we have been entrusted with a divine mission. No one has told us that God created us out of love and sent us to Earth with unique talents to deploy in a mission for him and others. People come alive and discover unknown depths to life, reality, and their work when their mission becomes clear. "On the threshold of the Third Millennium, my hope for all of you who are artists is that you will have an especially intense experience of creative inspiration. May the beauty which you pass on to generations still to come be such that it will stir them to wonder. Faced with the sacredness of life and of the human person, and before the marvels of the

---

[402] Ibid, 10.

[403] Ibid, 13.

universe, wonder is the only appropriate attitude."[404] As leaders who interact with those in the arts, I encourage you to intentionally seek to share this sense of mission with others. They need to know their mission. this is a critical leadership trait and behavior.

MEDICINE AND HEALTH CARE

This sector is important to us all. Health care and medicine. We all want it. We each need it. Many of us take for granted the ability to buy medicine at a grocery store, CVS, or Walgreens pharmacy. Medical care is readily available in first world nations. As a leader, do I see this as a right for all? Do not all people deserve good and timely medical care? Should only those in wealthy nations have medical care upon demand? Based on the leadership decision-making principles of human dignity, the common good and solidarity, the answer is a resounding no.

We should start by recognizing the great dignity of each person as well as the dignity of suffering. Suffering is not something we should ignore or to which we should turn a blind eye. No, suffering is the lot of each person; suffering was the lot chosen by Christ the Redeemer. Suffering is part of our mission. Speaking to those who suffer, St John Paul II said "yours is a mission of most lofty value for both the Church and society. You that bear the weight of suffering occupy the first places among those whom God loves. As with all those He met along the roads of Palestine, Jesus directs a gaze full of tenderness at you; his love will never be lacking."[405] The reality of the suffering person must always be met by love, compassion, and respect.

Health care workers live a noble life and service to humanity. We can easily take them for granted. "You are the unsung heroes of this pandemic. How many of you have given your lives to be close to the sick! Thanks for the closeness, thanks for the tenderness, thanks for the professionalism with which you take care of the sick."[406] The Coronavirus pandemic has reminded us of the immense value and service provided by health care staff. You would be hard-pressed to identify people who have served and sacrificed as much as these men and women over the past two years of the pandemic. We should celebrate the dedication, care and concern shown by hundreds of thousands of health care workers in recent times.

It is a good moment in history to recall that the health care 'industry' is not meant to be a business *per se*. While many doctors, administrative staff, nurses, technicians, pharmacists, and

---

[404] Ibid, 16.

[405] Pope John Paul II, Address to the Sick and Suffering, Tours, September 21, 1996, 2, in L'Osservatore Romano, September 23-24, 1996, p.4

[406] Pope Francis message, November 21, 2020

specialists are employed in the health care sector, this should never be primarily about 'my job'. Health care is primarily oriented towards the service of others. Each employee has the right to a good wage, but things are out of control when doctors and others staff demand exaggerated salaries that drive up service prices and limit access to the average patient. Those in the medical field act like center-stage sports stars or famous CEOs when they play hardball to make higher-and-higher wages. Medical staff should daily remind themselves of their servant role. They are at the service of their patients.

Health care and medical leaders should regulate this sector according to defined ethics and morality. Science is not absolute and free to do as it pleases; science is always in function of the good of the human person and must be steered in that direction. This goes for medical research, biotechnology and different forms of intervention (including DNA manipulation). "Human interventions that damage living beings or the natural environment deserve condemnation, while those that improve them are praiseworthy. The acceptability of the use of biological and biogenetic techniques is only one part of the ethical problem: as with every human behavior, it is also necessary to evaluate accurately the real benefits as well as the possible consequences in terms of risks. In the realm of technological-scientific interventions that have forceful and widespread impact on living organisms, with the possibility of significant long-term repercussions, it is unacceptable to act lightly or irresponsibly."[407]

Health care workers have all heard of the Hippocratic Oath to treat the ill to the best of their abilities and to do no harm. Harm (not health care) is done when human beings are destroyed through abortion, manufactured, manipulated, or frozen through *in vitro* fertilization as well as in attempts to clone human persons. It goes without saying that harvesting organs from living persons as well as sex 'reassignment' surgery are never licit and always an abuse of human dignity. I would also recommend leaders in the medical field to be cautious before accepting new technologies and procedures. They should be in regular dialogue and consultation with bioethicists as well as religious experts who can provide a counter-balance to the temptation of expediency. Just because something is legal and scientifically possible does not mean it will be for the good and progress of mankind.

A final thought is the need for international cooperation and solidarity in medical research and technology. "In a spirit of international solidarity, various measures can be taken in relation to the use of new biotechnologies. In the first place, equitable commercial exchange, without the burden of unjust stipulations, is to be facilitated. Promoting the development of the most disadvantaged peoples, however, will not be authentic or effective if it is reduced to the simple exchange of products. It is indispensable to foster the development of a necessary scientific and technological autonomy on the part of these same peoples, promoting the exchange of scientific and technological knowledge and the transfer of technologies to developing countries."[408] Once

---

[407] *Compendium of the Social Doctrine of the Church*, 473

[408] Ibid, 475.

again, medicine is not a business; it is defined by and at the service of humanity. As new medical technologies are developed, a first-line leadership conversation must be how to make these advances available to the greatest number of people possible including those in third world nations.

EDUCATION

Education is a dimension of social life touching all of us. Have you attended school as a child? As a teenager? University or technical school? Graduate level classes? Ongoing education sessions? We easily remember our times at school. I think back to the early years at Catholic kindergarten and elementary school. Those were times of exploration and discovery with knowledge of the world opening before me. God was someone presented as part of life yet not forced on us. Public high school was a different experience: advanced classes, puberty, sports, and deepening friendships. Attending Rensselaer for engineering studies offered the opportunity to deepen your identity, seek greater purpose and mission as well as having a greater sense of ownership for my faith and life as a whole. What were your experiences of education and schooling?

This sector of leadership challenges both those who work in schools (leaders, administration staff and especially teachers) as well as parents (those primarily responsible for the education of their children) to clearly understand the mission of education and to put themselves at the service of this mission. "For a true education aims at the formation of the human person in the pursuit of his ultimate end and of the good of the societies of which, as man, he is a member, and in whose obligations, as an adult, he will share."[409] As with other sectors of leadership, we need to be crystal clear about the final end to which true education is oriented and then order educational goals, processes, programs and staff toward that end. If we do not do this, we allow education to fall short of its proper excellence which damages (or at the very least gives an imbalanced experience) those who partake of it.

Education does indeed involve the transmission of subject knowledge. Math, science, languages, history, and much more. This, however, is only part of what true education entails. Indeed, leaders interested to unpack and offer true education must grapple with the call to educate the entire person. "Children and young people must be helped, with the aid of the latest advances in psychology and the arts and science of teaching, to develop harmoniously their physical, moral and intellectual endowments so that they may gradually acquire a mature sense of responsibility in striving endlessly to form their own lives properly and in pursuing true

---

[409] St Paul VI, *Gravissimum Educationis*, 1965, 1

freedom as they surmount the vicissitudes of life with courage and constancy."[410] When was the last time you heard about education and schooling offering learning in morality and character? Yes, those are first and foremost a responsibility of their parents to pass on, but much of our lives is spent at school. Educational institutions must provide guidance and reinforcement in these areas. Think of the previous chapter on holistic virtue formation. Why not design classes and educational benchmarks which include growth in virtues such as the ones covered in this book? Imagine physical education classes that included exercises on self-control. Why not include exercises in self-reflection during certain classes as well as pausing the day for a time of silent prayer and meditation? It is a shame that many Christian schools (who should lead the way in this area) do not have set times for prayer and worship in their daily and weekly schedules.

Parents own the education of their children. Contrary to Communist, Socialist, and Marxist ideology, the state does not own your children or their education. Each parent needs to take stock of their leadership role with their children and commit to stay involved at all levels of their education. In 2022, parents in the United States are sometimes labeled as 'terrorists' for putting school board members in their place by demanding accountability for school policies and class content. This is a clear example of people in leadership roles forgetting they are simply servants who should always be accountable to parents. "Since parents have given children their life, they are bound by the most serious obligation to educate their offspring and therefore must be recognized as the primary and principal educators. This role in education is so important that only with difficulty can it be supplied where it is lacking. Parents are the ones who must create a family atmosphere animated by love and respect for God and man, in which the well-rounded personal and social education of children is fostered. Hence the family is the first school of the social virtues that every society needs."[411] Parents should feel no shame to stand up and demand fair and appropriate treatment for their children. I am not saying parents should be closed to their children being at fault, underperforming and not being stellar students (this is where young people need to be held accountable). I am suggesting parents have a right to hold educators accountable for providing excellence at all levels to their children.

School choice is another hot topic. Although there is variety in different countries, many families have the option to send their children to public or private schools as well as charter schools. As we work together to improve education at all schools, we should not miss the fact that parents have the right to decide which schools to send their children. "Parents who have the primary and inalienable right and duty to educate their children must enjoy true liberty in their choice of schools. Consequently, the public power, which has the obligation to protect and defend the rights of citizens, must see to it, in its concern for distributive justice, that public subsidies are paid out in such a way that parents are truly free to choose according to their conscience the

---

[410] Ibid, 1.

[411] Ibid, 3.

schools they want for their children."[412] In an ideal world, governments should allow public funds to be distributed to private (including religious) and schools as well as public schools. There is a danger that public schools might not receive as much funding, but the competition for students and funding will certainly drive up the quality of public institutions which in turn will attract more students.

All schools and their staff serve a noble mission. In particular, Christian schools have demonstrated they play an irreplaceable part in global education. Billions of men and women have attended Christian schools over the past 50 years and received a more robust, holistic formation as compared to what is offered in most public schools. "No less than other schools does the Catholic school pursue cultural goals and the human formation of youth. But its proper function is to create for the school community a special atmosphere animated by the Gospel spirit of freedom and charity, to help youth grow according to the new creatures they were made through baptism as they develop their own personalities, and finally to order the whole of human culture to the news of salvation so that the knowledge the students gradually acquire of the world, life and man is illumined by faith."[413] This aspect should not be overlooked. Christian schools are not just called to impart book knowledge. They are also commissioned to share Christ and his Good Shepherd heart with all humanity.

Mission drift is a danger in all organizations including Christian schools. I recommend being attentive and proactive to keep educational institutions on track to fulfill their God-given mission. It is a complete contradiction to use a school for your own pet cause such as to indoctrinate students in political or ideological causes. Another failure of educational mission takes place when it purports to be a religion-based school but it sells out being consistent with this identity in the name of being 'mainstream', having a top-tier academic program or being more 'inclusive'. Schools should be proud of their identity and mission; this is what attracts parents and students.

Whether you are part of the school staff, a parent with children in school, a concerned citizen or member of the clergy, I invite you to take education seriously. This is a forum where much good can be done for the formation and development of the future generations. As stated in a previous chapter, true leaders are committed to help the future generations. We should be aware that education is also a place where evil and deformation of young people can be present. Each of us should be proactive to ensure that education institutions at all levels are places of high character and intellectual standards. This does not happen without involvement from all of us.

INTERNATIONAL RELATIONS

---

[412] Ibid, 6.

[413] Ibid, 8.

Look at the social relationships in your life: family, friends, coworkers, students, and teammates. Do you see perfect peace and serenity? Perhaps you are the one person on Earth who can say 'yes' to the above, but I have my doubts. Relationships are an essential and beautiful part of the human experience, but they are fraught with difficulty, disagreements and disasters. If this is true about your close relationships, think it is any easier on the international level?

International relations is a popular college major and subject of nightly news reports. It is also an increasingly important leadership sector. The global economy, internet, satellite communications, possibilities of international travel (despite pandemics), and study abroad experiences all touch relationships between countries. What are some leadership principles and areas for our attention? *The Compendium of the Social Doctrine of the Church* offers us several insights on this topic.

The first is a call to unity as a global people. This does not mean being one, global nation, or amalgamating all cultures and religions. No, I am proposing a unity based on our common human dignity given by God. "The Christian message offers a universal vision of the life of men and peoples on earth that makes us realize the unity of the human family. This unity is not to be built on the force of arms, terror or abuse of power; rather, it is the result of that "supreme model of unity, which is a reflection of the intimate life of God, one God in three Persons, ... what we Christians mean by the word 'communion'"; it is an achievement of the moral and cultural force of freedom."[414] If you ask the average citizen, few would say they want unity through force of arms. We know deep down that forced 'unity' is no unity at all; it would be a fake. True unity is based on love for each other and respecting the equal dignity of the other.

This common dignity reminds us that racism is never appropriate. It is beneath us to be racist towards someone in our own country or those in other countries. Are you racist towards any group of people be they in your own country or abroad? This is not to say we should be discerning about immigration policies and how they are enacted since government has a right to maintain the stability and peace of the nation under its charge. "The centrality of the human person and the natural inclination of persons and peoples to establish relationships among themselves are the fundamental elements for building a true international community, the ordering of which must aim at guaranteeing the effective universal common good.[880] Despite the widespread aspiration to build an authentic international community, the unity of the human family is not yet becoming a reality. This is due to obstacles originating in materialistic and nationalistic ideologies that contradict the values of the person integrally considered in all his various dimensions, material and spiritual, individual and community. In particular, any theory or form whatsoever of racism and racial discrimination is morally unacceptable."[415] This is not an easy scourge to eliminate. Each of us must be proactive to promote mutual respect and appreciation for different cultures.

---

[414] *The Compendium of the Social Doctrine of the Church*, 432.

[415] Ibid, 433.

International relations depends on balancing healthy national sovereignties and inter-country dependencies, alliances and unions. "National sovereignty is not, however, absolute. Nations can freely renounce the exercise of some of their rights in view of a common goal, in the awareness that they form a "family of nations" where mutual trust, support and respect must prevail. In this perspective, special attention should be given to the fact that there is still no international agreement that adequately addresses "the rights of nations",the preparation of which could profitably deal with questions concerning justice and freedom in today's world."[416] There is much room for further dialogue between world leaders to foster a commitment towards common, national rights.

Also, there is a common and shared path towards true, flourishing international relations. It is the universal moral law, which is written in each person's depth. "The universal moral law, written on the human heart, must be considered effective and indelible as the living expression of the shared conscience of humanity, a "grammar" on which to build the future of the world."[417] Without recognizing a shared moral 'law', dialogue among nations will be guided by subjective and self-serving standards instead of by love and respect. As an expression of this universal moral law, we could simply invite global leaders to speak and negotiate from the perspective of human dignity, common good, solidarity, and subsidiarity.

The use of force to create 'unity' has haunted humanity since the dawn of time. In our day, certain nations use force to impose regime rule. Others use force to conquer in the name of unity. "Not only does the Charter of the United Nations ban recourse to force, but it rejects even the threat to use force. This provision arose from the tragic experience of the Second World War."[418] We should not be naïve to think the temptation to use force is not present today or will not appear in the future. Each generation must make a firm commitment to not impose rule by force or attempt to conquer other nations. Leaders in all strata of society should be vocally opposed to manifestations of using unjustified and immoral force to rule internally or in the quest to conquer other nations.

A theme of contemporary (yet also of long-standing historical nature) discussion and attention is underdevelopment in some nations. Leaders of nations as well as all those who influence international relations should be proactive to confront underdevelopment and strive for solidarity. "It may seem that underdevelopment is impossible to eliminate, as though it were a death sentence, especially considering the fact that it is not only the result of erroneous human choices but also the consequence of economic, financial and social mechanisms and structures of sin that prevent the full development of men and peoples.These difficulties must nonetheless

---

[416] Ibid, 435.

[417] Ibid, 436.

[418] Ibid, 438.

be met with strong and resolute determination, because development is not only an aspiration but a right that, like every right, implies a duty. Collaboration in the development of the whole person and of every human being is in fact a duty of all towards all, and must be shared by the four parts of the world: East and West, North and South."[419] I agree with those who say capitalism and globalizations have helped bring many out of poverty and have given access to basics such as housing, medical care, and education. This being said, there is still a long way to go to help underdeveloped nations.

Underdevelopment is often fueled by irresponsible leaders, internal strife such as civil war and racism. Also "among the causes that greatly contribute to underdevelopment and poverty, in addition to the impossibility of acceding to the international market, mention must be made of illiteracy, lack of food security, the absence of structures and services, inadequate measures for guaranteeing basic health care, the lack of safe drinking water and sanitation, corruption, instability of institutions and of political life itself. There is a connection between poverty and, in many countries, the lack of liberty, possibilities for economic initiative and a national administration capable of setting up an adequate system of education and information."[420] We should not turn a blind eye to this reality despite progress in previous decades. What was written at the turn of the 3rd Millennium is just as valid today: "At the beginning of the New Millennium, the poverty of billions of men and women is the one issue that most challenges our human and Christian consciences.Poverty poses a dramatic problem of justice; in its various forms and with its various effects, it is characterized by an unequal growth that does not recognize the equal right of all people to take their seat 'at the table of the common banquet'."[421] It is true that most of us are not leaders on the international level, but we can all make an effort to build bridges with those we know from other countries. We can each be proactive to stand in solidarity with the poor, the homeless, and the migrant who are in our neighborhood.

THE ENVIRONMENT

Every day is a new opportunity to experience creation through the environment. Whether you live in a big city, rural country, near the beach, in a jungle or desert-like area, the environment is a constant reality. We can easily take it for granted. I try to go for a daily walk and purposefully take a few minutes to put the phone and noise aside. Trying to focus on a tree, a stream, the sky, or some other aspect of the environment, I take a few moments to ponder and appreciate the concrete environment in which we live and from which we daily benefit. It is truly a gift to steward.

---

[419] Ibid, 446.

[420] Ibid, 447.

[421] Ibid, 449.

Leadership in the different sectors of society

The Judeo-Christian view of the environment is shared by many thinkers and religious persons (though to different degrees). For those reading this book, God has made men and women as the apex of creation. The environment is ordered to mankind. We are not a stain or 'disease' on the Earth as some environmental ideologues posit. Each person was "created in God's image, received a mandate to subject to himself the earth and all that it contains, and to govern the world with justice and holiness. A mandate to relate himself and the totality of things to him who was to be acknowledged as the Lord and Creator of all. Thus, by the subjection of all things to man, the name of God would be wonderful in all the earth."[422] Each man, woman and child has been entrusted with caring for the environment and all created things. All leaders should look at the environment from this starting point. It is pointless to get into arguments about recycling, the ozone layer, cutting down trees, or using fossil fuels without first being clear on man's place on this Earth.

For this reason, human progress (including advances in technology) must be ordered and measured based on our proper place in creation. We are responsible for our decisions and the impact they have on the environment. "The triumphs of the human race are a sign of God's grace and the flowering of His own mysterious design... the fact that the greater man's power becomes, the farther his individual and community responsibility extends, and that every human activity is to correspond, according to the design and will of God, to humanity's true good."[423] Our decisions about he environment cannot be based on what is expedient for us, our families, our company, or our town. No, our decisions should always reference the common good and solidarity both with each other and with the environment (which is a patrimony of future generations).

I want to draw your attention to a serious danger and problem in the 21st century. We have already spoken about pride and how this vice makes you think you are the center of the world. This is an illusion. The world does not revolve around you and you are not the measure of what is right and correct. This translates into how we treat the environment. Do you subtlety act as if you are lord and master of the environment? Littering? Indiscriminate use of plastic bottled water? Leaving your AC on a low temperatures for an extended time including when you are not home and even when away on extended travel? You might be rolling your eyes at me on such examples, but I want to draw your attention to the pernicious attitude of 'there is no problem with doing this" .'Man, then, must never forget that his capacity to transform and in a certain sense create the world through his own work ... is always based on God's prior and original gift of the things that are. He must not make arbitrary use of the earth, subjecting it without restraint to his will, as though it did not have its own requisites and a prior God-given purpose, which man can indeed develop but must not betray. When he acts in this way, instead of carrying out his role as a co-operator with God in the work of creation, man sets himself up in place of God and thus ends up provoking a rebellion on the part of nature, which is more tyrannized than governed by

---

[422] Compendium of the Social Doctrine of the Church, 456.

[423] Ibid, 457.

him."[424] Let us be careful to stay humble and not become illusory dictators of what belongs to God and the common human family.

The malignant attitude of pride can easily lead us to exploit the environment. This is not to say we cannot use natural resources within reason, but this must always be in a balanced and moderate way. "The tendency towards an "ill-considered" exploitation of the resources of creation is the result of a long historical and cultural process. The modern era has witnessed man's growing capacity for transformative intervention. The aspect of the conquest and exploitation of resources has become predominant and invasive, and today it has even reached the point of threatening the environment's hospitable aspect: the environment as 'resource' risks threatening the environment as 'home'. Because of the powerful means of transformation offered by technological civilization, it sometimes seems that the balance between man and the environment has reached a critical point."[425] There is room for opinion on the proper balance between not using natural resources and exploiting them. Leaders therefore need to have serious and fraternal discussion about what is balanced and appropriate. Where exploitation is taking place, it must be stopped.

The environment is our common patrimony. Each of us is responsible for it. This is a clear sector of leadership and stewardship for you and me. "Care for the environment represents a challenge for all of humanity. It is a matter of a common and universal duty, respecting a common good, destined for all, by preventing anyone from using with impunity the different categories of beings, whether living or inanimate — animals, plants, the natural elements — simply as one wishes, according to one's own economic needs It is a responsibility that must mature on the basis of the global dimension of the present ecological crisis and the consequent necessity to meet it on a worldwide level, since all beings are interdependent in the universal order established by the Creator. One must take into account the nature of each being and of its mutual connection in an ordered system, which is precisely the 'cosmos'."[426] I suggest each of us take a few moments to pause and ask if we are embracing this leadership mission. Am I a steward of the environment? Do I consider that left-leaning politics? Only for 'tree-huggers'? Something contrary to Christian orthodoxy and 'important doctrine'? Let us be straight here: caring for the environment is a mission God give you and he will ask you for an accounting of your stewardship therein.

We commit to this responsibility not only because God asks us to do it for him, but also with our eye to future generations. We are like links in a chain. Many are coming after us. What will they find on Earth? A damaged environment? An attitude of using and abusing which they continue since we teach them to do this? "Responsibility for the environment, the common heritage of

---

[424] Ibid, 460.

[425] Ibid, 461.

[426] Ibid, 466.

mankind, extends not only to present needs but also to those of the future. We have inherited from past generations, and we have benefited from the work of our contemporaries: for this reason we have obligations towards all, and we cannot refuse to interest ourselves in those who will come after us, to enlarge the human family. This is a responsibility that present generations have towards those of the future, a responsibility that also concerns individual States and the international community."[427] This is a concrete application of the leadership decision-making principle and behavior of solidarity. I am my brothers keeper. True leaders commit to preserving and passing along the gift of the environment.

Energy production and use is a final point worth consideration. There continues to be much debate and heated contention on this issue. "Particular attention will have to be reserved for the complex issues surrounding energy resources. Non-renewable resources, which highly-industrialized and recently-industrialized countries draw from, must be put at the service of all humanity. From a moral perspective based on equity and intergenerational solidarity, it will also be necessary to continue, through the contribution of the scientific community, to identify new sources of energy, develop alternative sources and increase the security levels of nuclear energy. The use of energy, in the context of its relationship to development and the environment, calls for the political responsibility of States, the international community and economic actors. Such responsibility must be illuminated and guided by continual reference to the universal common good."[428] Leaders should have a balanced view of the energy issue. On one hand, all nations have a right to energy production and fossil fuels provide an easy and cost effective option for many nations including those who cannot afford renewable energies. On the other hand, alternative energy sources are needed for two prudential reasons: the possibility of diminished supplies in the decades ahead and to minimize environmental damage. The future of energy is unknown, but leaders can walk a wise path by investing in fossil fuels as well as renewable energies such as wind and solar power.

THE CHURCH

I would be remiss to not share a few thoughts about leadership in the Christian Church. We know from experience that the Church has lost much moral credibility in the 21st century. Sexual and financial scandals have shocked many, led to some leaving the Church and has stifled the evangelizing spirit of others. One author givers us an example of the cynicism often present. "The Pope could decide that all this power, all this wealth, this hierarchy of princes and bishops and archbishops and priests and monk and nuns could be sent out in the world with money and art treasures, to put them back in the countries that they once raped and violated, they could give that money away, and they could concentrate on the apparent essence of their belief, and then, I would stand here and say the Catholic Church may well be a force

---

[427] Ibid, 467.

[428] Ibid, 470.

for good in the world, but until that day, it is not."[429] This author makes several presumptions and false claims. The trouble is the Church is in a challenging place to stand its ground and call out the falsities in such statements while simultaneously acknowledging where there has been wrongdoing and publicly apologizing.

Leaders in the Church should start by recognizing their worst enemy: division and rivalry. There will always be enemies and problems outside the Church, but the followers of Christ are called to be united. They should treat each other with human dignity and pursue the common good. Jesus Christ prayed for us and commanded us to seek unity among believers. Division and rivalry within the Church is disgusting and a cancer that must be eliminated. It tears us apart and turns us against one another. "Rivalry gets people working against one another rather than with one another. There's no telling how many companies have been brought down because the people fought each other rather than the competition."[430] We in the Church need to be very carefully about letting evil into our hearts and turning clergy against laity (and vice-verse), Catholics against Protestants, diocese against religious orders and parishes against Ecclesial Movements. The number one strategy of a good general (the devil too) is divide and conquer. Church leaders need to have their radar up for division and rivalry and confront it head on and without giving quarter to preserve unity and charity.

Leaders of the Church know all too well the damage done by scandal. I have already mentioned this in the first chapter of the book, but I want to reiterate that Church leaders are called to holiness and purity of life. When a Church leader becomes a stumbling block for the faithful, the Church loses vitality and believers can become disheartened. As a Church leader, remember that people are always watching you hoping to find in you an authentic example of one following the Good Shepherd, Jesus Christ. You should also never doubt that the devil and his servants want you to fall. They are like hunters who seek a prize catch so be on the lookout for their traps and temptations which will lead you to sin and mediocrity.

Another place for Church leaders to focus is on being a faithful presence in society. In this book, I have advocated for influencing and changing the world. At the same time, I recognize that 'change' is very unpredictable at the level of culture, society and even within the Church. There are many factors beyond our control. Dr James Hunter's studies on culture and Christianity bring him to conclude we cannot likely change culture in a complete and total way, but we can influence in a positive way by living our faith joyfully and lovingly. What does this mean? "First, faithful presence means that we are to be fully present to each other within the community of faith and fully present to those who are not. Whether within the community of believers or among those outside the church, we imitate our creator and redeemer: we pursue each other, identify with each other, and direct our lives toward the flourishing of each other through

---

[429] Stephen Fry, "The Catholic church is a force for good in the world", Intelligence Squared Catholic Church Debate, (November 7th 2009).

[430] Way of the Shepherd, 59.

sacrificial love."[431] We have to start living unity and communion with other believers of whatever Christian denomination despite real doctrinal disagreements which need to be respected and openly discussed. Second, living faithful presence applies to those who do not share Christian belief and way of life. "The difficult part for most is what it means to be faithfully present to those outside the community of faith. But here scripture makes it clear that the burden is precisely the same—we are to pursue others, identify with others, and labor toward the fullness of others through sacrificial love."[432] Let all members of the Church make a serious commitment to lead forward by being faithful witnesses both to other Christians as well as to those of different beliefs.

Another area for leadership in the church is to grapple with and minimize the influence of politics within the church. "The second task is for the church and for Christian believers to decouple the "public" from the "political." Politics is always a crude simplification of public life and the common good is always more than its political expression. As we have seen, the expectations that people place on politics are unrealistic for most of the problems we face today are not resolvable through politics. That, however, is not the most serious problem. Far more grave is the way politicization has delimited the imaginative horizon through which the church and Christian believers think about engaging the world and the range of possibilities within which they actually act. Politics is just one way to engage the world and, arguably, not the highest, best, most effective, nor most humane way to do so."[433] Church leaders at every level must face the reality of the temptation to think, speak and act through a political lens. This applies to the way we see the church and each other as well as the tendency to over-invest apostolic efforts to influence politics.

In his book *To Change the World*, Dr Hunter goes on to recommend Church leaders take time off from political involvement to have a better understanding and approach to what is healthy versus unhealthy in this arena. He also opines that Christian leaders at different levels of the Church err in their approach especially when pointing the finger of blame at laity instead of themselves. "What has been missing is a leadership that comprehends the nature of these challenges and offers a vision of formation adequate to the task of discipling the church and its members for a time such as ours. By misreading the nature of the times and by focusing so much energy and resources on politics, those who have claimed the mantle of leadership have fixed attention on secondary and tertiary problems and false solutions. By admonishing Christian lay people for not, in effect, being Christian enough, they shift responsibility for their own failures onto those that they lead."[434] I understand this is a tough message to hear whether you are a bishop, priest, deacon, pastor, catechist or part of a parish administration team. As a

---

[431] Hunter, James, *To Change the World*, 244.

[432] Ibid, 244.

[433] Ibid, 185.

[434] Ibid, 225.

leader, however, you need to learn how to take feedback and constructive criticism if you will lead with the Good Shepherd heart of Jesus Christ. Good and honest feedback should be part of your daily nourishment. We can all keep learning to be better leaders.

Another area of leadership for those in the church is to be bold and stand up in defense of your faith and the people entrusted to your care. People tell me every day how much they want to hear their leaders defend the truth of the Christian faith and not be wishy-washy or cowardly before secular ideology. A friend recently told me about an experience at a Catholic Church where the priest during his homily was justifying divorce based on personal whim instead of what Jesus himself affirmed as a lifelong commitment. These and so many other examples reek of mediocrity and confusion. The Christian faithful do not want this and expect better from their leaders. As shepherds, stand up and defend the truth. "It didn't take terribly long before people in the company learned that offensive behavior directed toward someone in my flock would earn them a face-to-face encounter with me."[435] As Christ told us, vicious wolves would attach his flock. Leaders are the front-line soldiers called to defend the beloved sons and daughters of God.

Another point of work for church leaders is to get leadership training. It is all too easy to make the excuse that leadership education and development is something for business or politics. No. As a church leader, you need to develop your leadership muscles as well. Public speaking. Methods of motivation. Conflict resolution. Negotiation. Dealing with different cultural sensitivities. Apologetics. Leading small groups and teams. These and other themes are your territory as a church leader. I recommend that you get to work. There are many resources including online seminars, in person courses as well as many books to read. You might consider creating a leadership book club or starting a seminar at your parish or in your organization. The main thing, however, is to start doing something to grow your leadership.

One particular aspect of leadership is to be a good communicator. Many people tell me they are unsatisfied with the communication they receive from their pastors. They say he is either absent, ineffective or a 'bulldozer' who retorts to feedback and suggestions with 'I am the pastor'. I think two insights from leadership expert, Pat Lencioni, can help Church leaders with their communication. First, "the reason a CEO communicates to employees, at all levels, is to ensure that people are aligned with and have bought into what is going on and where they fit into the success of the enterprise."[436] Pastors should strive to be clear with their people and help them align on vision, plans, ideas and the path forward. Second, "you need to change your general attitude about communication and see it as a tool for helping others understand and internalize important ideas."[437] Your communication attitude is the key to how you relate to

---

[435] *The Way of the Shepherd*, 86.

[436] Lencioni, Pat, *The Motive,* 160.

[437] Ibid, 163.

others. I suggest you look inside and see how open you are to others. It would do all who preach (bishops, priests, deacons, Protestant pastors and ministers) good to solicit feedback on the quality of your messaging. You might be surprised how ineffective you are. By humbly asking and receiving critical feedback, you can then work to improve. Your flock will be grateful for your efforts to improve for their benefit.

My final recommendation to Church leaders hearkens back to a previous topic: form true disciples. It is easy to give lip service to this theme, but many in the church do not do this. Forming disciples is much more than encouraging church attendance and going to catechism class. "Beyond the worship of God and the proclamation of his word, the central ministry of the church is one of formation; of making disciples. Making disciples, however, is not just one more program—it is not Sunday School, a Wednesday night prayer meeting, or a new book one must read. Formation is about learning to live the alternative reality of the kingdom of God within the present world order faithfully. Formation, then, is fundamentally about changing lives. It is the church's task of teaching, admonishing, and encouraging believers over the course of their lives in order to present them "as complete in Christ," "fit for any calling.""[438] Instead of measuring mission success by only church and catechism attendance, we should add formation activities and metrics such as: Bible study groups at each age level, local evangelization and faith teaching missions for young people and entire families, priesthood and consecrated life seminars at each parish and religious school every year as well as leadership training programs at local and national levels.

As you form disciples, you send them out. The Great Commission of Jesus Christ is still as real and important as the day he gave it to the 12 Apostles. "The great commission can also be interpreted in terms of social structure. The church is to go into all realms of social life: in volunteer and paid labor—skilled and unskilled labor, the crafts, engineering, commerce, art, law, architecture, teaching, health care, and service. Indeed, the church should be sending people out in these realms—not only discipling those in these fields by providing the theological resources to form them well, but in fact mentoring and providing financial support for young adults who are gifted and called into these vocations. When the church does not send people out to these realms and when it does not provide the theologies that make sense of work and engagement in these realms, the church fails to fulfill the charge to "go into all the world."[439] The Church is called to be a faithful presence in all sectors of human life. Let us as leaders be intentional and systematic in forming and launching our people into the different strata of society. If there are parts of the world that do not know Christ and are wallowing in doubt, confusion and despair, we should look at ourselves and ask why we are not preparing and sending people to these children of God in need of the Good News. This is your responsibility. Keep your hand at the plow and push forward with confidence in the fruitfulness of your labors united to Christ the Good Shepherd.

---

[438] Hunter, James, To Change the World, 236.

[439] Ibid, 256-57.

Discipleship leads to accept being a modern day apostle of Jesus Christ. Apostles are those who accept the call of Jesus to announce him to others. They go out in his name and empowered by the Holy Spirit. How can you learn to be an apostle? In addition to parish and diocesan resources, various Ecclesial Movements help men and women become and live as apostles. Regnum Christi (www.regnumchristi.org) is one such movement. According to author Fr John Bartunek, LC, "in Regnum Christi, we focus our apostolic activity on the integral formation of new generations of apostles, Christian leaders who enthusiastically and joyfully put their natural talents and influence at the service of Christ in whatever ways the Holy Spirit leads them."[440] Movements such as *Regnum Christi* are spiritual families within the Church offering you a path to experience and grow as an apostle of the Lord.

Conclusion

The call to lead in the above-mentioned sectors of society is real and present. In which sector are you? Where are you called to intentionally influence? What means will you employ to help your leadership? Finding a group of like-minded leaders is a powerful support on the journey.
For those in established leadership positions, you could join a Christian leadership organization such as the Lumen Institute or Legatus. The Lumen Institute (www.lumeninstitute.org) was created to give highly personalized formation to Catholic business and cultural leaders so they in turn influence society with the light of Christ. Members of the institute receive frequent one-to-one spiritual coaching as well as participate in monthly member small group discussions looking at the example of Jesus Christ and his living the core values of faith, character and leadership. Legatus (www.Legatus.org) is Catholic business leaders organization which offers a monthly couples Mass and speaker dinner. These and other such organizations are powerful supports in the journey to responsibly live your God given influence.

Questions for Personal Reflection and Group Discussion

1. What leadership insights were mentioned in this chapter?
2. What sector of society interests you the most? Why?
3. How can you better influence in this sector? What would you do based on the four leadership decision-making principles?
4. Which persons of influence do you know in each of the sectors of society covered in this chapter? What can you do to share these insights with them?

---

[440] Bartunek, John, *What is Regnum Christi?*, 61.

CHAPTER 11
YOUR CALL TO LEADERSHIP

The nineteenth-century American industrialist and philanthropist Andrew Carnegie once said, "The older I get, the less I listen to what people say and the more I watch what they do."[441]

Be leaders. Leaders of thought, leaders of action, leaders of joy, leaders of hope, leaders of the construction of a better world.[442]

Ever see a person's eyes light up? A child's? A teenager's? A college student's or young professional's? An older adult? It is powerful to see hope and joy kindled in others.

This is what I experience every time I sit with someone and speak about their call to leadership. "What, me? Really?" This is often how they react. They have never been told that they are called to play an a part in the history of our world. Each one of you has a mission from God. You are unique and irreplaceable in your personhood as well as the leadership contribution God wants from you. This book has hopefully affirmed you and given you plenty of food for thought, as well as opened some pathways for your leadership growth.

Before finishing, I would like to remind you of your leadership calling and challenge you to generously embrace it. As Emeritus Pope Benedict XVI wrote, "at the heart of all temptations, is

---

[441] Kraemer, *From Values to Action*, 93.

[442] Pope Francis, Video Conference by CNN, 17th September 2015

the act of pushing God aside because we perceive him as secondary; if not actually superfluous and annoying, in comparison with all the apparently far more urgent matters that fill our lives. Constructing a wold by our own lights, without reference to God, building on our own foundation; refusing to acknowledge the reality of anything beyond the political and material, while setting God aside as an illusion — that is the temptation that threatens us in many varied forms."[443] Our world needs God more than ever. Leaders and leadership studies need God. Without including him in leadership discussions and development, we are not able to live up to our personal potential and we certainly cannot build a society of justice, peace, and love.

Leadership complacency is a clear and present danger for humanity. We all (at least sometimes) want to stay out of the limelight and attention. We want to avoid risk and danger. We want to preserve our good name. We do not want to struggle and deal with the messiness of human relationships. While acknowledging these desires, we must step forward to lead with the strength that comes from the shepherd heart of Jesus Christ. This is our calling. Many concrete men, women, and children depend on the present and future impacts of your leadership. Do you see this? Do you hear them calling your name in the depths of your heart?

Complacency before the problems of the world is our enemy. We have seen at length the many challenges facing the world throughout history and in our own times. We should pause and ponder the words of Scripture commentator Erasmo Merikakis: "how can you still be sleeping and resting? Can't you see what is at stake in my life and the life of the world at this very moment? You cannot afford to remain waterlogged in unconscious passivity! How can you now live in a state of escapist inertia at the same time my enemies, those who hate the kingdom of my Father, offer their eyes no sleep and are never depleted of energy as they run about hatching plots against me and scouring the land for accomplices in my ruin?"[444] Now is not the time to be resting on your laurels. It is the time to take action and lead. The world needs you. Concrete people need you. Are you going to sit by and not be the leader you are called to be?

The call to lead knocks at your door. At the same time and consistent with what I mentioned earlier in this book, we need to have a humble, realistic vision and expectation about changing the world. It is easy to be idealistic and unrealistic to the point that we get discouraged when we do not see men and women accepting to live a life of virtue and welcoming the love of God into their lives. Culture expert, Dr James Hunter, reminds us "that the best understanding of the creation mandate is not about changing the world at all. It is certainly not about "saving Western civilization," "saving America," "winning the culture war," or anything else like it. The reason is that so much of the discussion surrounding this kind of world-changing is oriented toward the idea of controlling history. The presumption is both that one can know God's specific plans in

---

[443] Pope Benedict XVI, *Jesus of Nazareth*, 28.

[444] Erasmo Merikakis, *Fire of Mercy: Heart of the Word*, IV, 254.

human history and that one possesses the power to realize those plans in human affairs."[445] Leaders are called to live a faithful presence in the midst of the world. At times, you will see people follow and others not. Despite your best efforts to influence for good, culture may not seem to change. Keep going and do not give up.

The vision of leadership shared in this book is one of being in the trenches and close to people. In a time when we are tempted to replace people with machines and substitute virtual relationships for the real thing, leaders must renew their valiant efforts. This will not be easy. It will not always result in being popular. Let retired general, Stanley McChrystal, remind you that "leaders are not necessarily popular. For soldiers, the choice between popularity and effectiveness is ultimately no choice at all. Soldiers want to win; their survival depends on it. They will accept, and even take pride in, the quirks and shortcomings of a leader if they believe he can produce success."[446] Believe in yourself. Believe in the talents God gave you. Above all, believe that God is with you to strengthen and guide you in your leadership.

At the heart of the leadership model I shared with you, we see the invitation to sacrifice yourself for others. Jesus Christ the Good Shepherd shows us this by example and invites each one of us to do the same for one another. Bad and negligent leadership abounds, but you are called to be a good shepherd and leader for others. "The sheep didn't have a shepherd who was willing to pay the price to be who he was supposed to be. So the sheep ended up paying for his poor leadership. That's what I'm talking about. *Someone* has to pay; it's just a matter of who will pay. The thing is it's not the sheep who get to decide. That decision is made by the one who tends the flock. So every day when you go to work, *you* get to decide who's going to pay for your leadership that day — you or your people."[447] I invite you to make the decision to strive to be the leader you are called to be. Do not make others pay due to your lack of sacrificing yourself for them.

No matter where you find yourself, no matter what sector of life, you can be a leader who influences. Those who follow a cause lead in their sector. "Each Communist Party member is expected to be a leader in any field of activity into which life may take him."[448] As a person of goodwill, you are called to lead where life takes you. Christians in particular are missionary by nature; they are oriented by baptism to lead and influence society. In what sector of society are you called to lead and influence? Be shepherds, with the "odor of the sheep , make it real, as shepherds among your flock, fishers of men."[449] I invite you to see yourself as an intentional

---

[445] Hunter, James, *To Change the World*, 95.

[446] Stanley A. McChrystal, *My Share of the Task* (2013), p. 392

[447] Leman and Pentak, *The Way of the Shepherd*, 100-01.

[448] Hyde, Douglas, *Dedication and Leadership*, 148.

[449] Pope Francis, Homily, 28th March 2013

fisher, someone who daily looks to influence your family, friends, and coworkers. Nothing in your life is by chance. Your mission to lead others awaits you.

An aspect of our leadership includes influencing those with greater responsibility in society. The social nature of humanity naturally leads to some individuals being entrusted with more influence. Each of us should discern who and where we are called to influence in these strata of society. "Whatever its larger influence in the world may be, a culture that is genuinely alternative cannot emerge without faithful presence in all areas of life. This will include networks (and more, communities) of counter-leaders operating within the upper echelons of cultural production and social life generally. These are realms of performance and distinction that may be rare and inaccessible to the average person, but they are still critically important to both the renewal of the church and its engagement with the culture."[450] Trust in the power of your love and desire to serve others. Those entrusted with more power, influence, and popularity need your leadership example. In my experience, these individuals often put on a good front, but inside lack purpose, meaning, an understanding of God's love for them, and deep experience of the transcendent. You can offer them a great deal.

Some of you reading this book already have great influence and power. You find yourself at the center of leading businesses, in political office, having a large following on social media, or fill decision-making roles in the medical, educational, and sports sectors. You are leading scientists and Church leaders. The talents entrusted to you require wisely investing them— God will ask an accounting for this. "To be obedient to Christ's instruction to "go into all the world," then, will inevitably result in some who will exercise varying degrees of leadership in these different spheres of life. Some will even operate in or close to the "center" of institutions of social, cultural, and political life. As such they will have disproportionate privilege, access, and influence that the majority of people simply don't have…To acknowledge and to encourage this is not elitist, as some might say, but rather an obedience to Christ's directive to "go into all the world.""[451] I encourage you to see your role and influence as a stewardship and responsibility. You have the gift to lead. Seek to lead with humility and the other virtues we reviewed in this book. Ask Jesus Christ to give you his shepherd heart to love and serve those you influence.

The vision of leadership explained in this book is challenging. Embracing it requires a deep commitment to formation and personal development. "The task of formation at any time, but not least one that is adequate to a time such as ours, is not an easy task. It requires wisdom, discernment, hard work, and the active guidance of the Holy Spirit in it all."[452] Anyone who has climbed a mountain or ran a marathon knows the effort required to reach such a goal. The

---

[450] Hunter, James, To Change the World, 96.

[451] Ibid, 257.

[452] Ibid, 237.

quest for the source and summit of leadership will not be an easy one for you. I challenge you, I invite you to confidently accept this quest.

Thank you for saying 'yes' to leadership. Thank you for taking up the baton of service and sacrifice for others. Thank you for offering your life for the good of others. Thank you for persevering especially when it seems a thankless road where at best you are ignored and overlooked or at worst persecuted and maligned by the ones you try to help. I leave you with two quotes for the journey. May Christ the Good Shepherd who remains truly present with us in the Eucharist in the tabernacle of every Catholic Church be with you. May he who is the true 'Source and Summit' of leadership strengthen you, guide you and one day reward you with eternal life. God bless you.

When you have succeeded in making men believe that change is necessary and possible and that they are the ones who can achieve it; when you have convinced them that they and the small minority of whom they are a part can transform the world in their lifetime, you have achieved something very considerable indeed. You have put into their lives a dynamic force so powerful that you can bring them to do what would otherwise be impossible. The dull and humdrum becomes meaningful. Life becomes purposeful and immensely more worth living.[453]

You don't need to thank me…what you can do is give me a good return on my investment. Put into practice what you've learned here and pass it on to others along the way.[454]

---

[453] Hyde, Douglas, *Dedication and Leadership*, 31.

[454] Leman and Pentak, *The Way of the Shepherd*, 108.

APPENDIX I – Christian Leadership Model

One Foundational Principle: Jesus Christ the Good Shepherd

4 Behaviors
- Have a Clear Identity and be a Transmitter of Identity
- Dedicated to the Mission
- Embrace Holistic Virtue Development
- Develop the Future Generations

8 Virtues
- Humility: to live in the truth of who God is, who others are and who you are
- Prudence: sound judgment in determining actions
- Self-Mastery: controlling your passions amid personal drive and success
- Perseverance: a strong commitment to overcoming all obstacles
- Prayer: regular communication with God, humbly seeking his will and friendship
- Integrity: Consistency in what one professes to be and how one lives
- Influence: moving others to think and act up rightly through conscientious effort
- Magnanimity: commitment to serve others by putting their needs first

4 Decision-making Principles

- Human Dignity: all people are infinitely valuable, worthy of love and deserving of respect and protection (no matter their age, physical or intellectual ability and contribution to society)
- Common Good: the overall order and stability of society at the service of helping individuals flourish
- Solidarity: you are your brother and sister's keeper. What happens to others must and should matter to you
- Subsidiarity: let the lower level (be it in politics, education, church, business) do for itself what it can without interference and manipulation by a higher level authority (fosters responsibility and maturity at all levels)

Appendix II - Leadership References

Winters, Dick, Beyond Band of Brothers, The Berkeley Publishing Group, New York, NY, 2006

Catechism of the Catholic Church(1992)

The Bible

The Handbook for Teaching Leadership: Knowing, Doing and Being (Snook, Nohria, Khurana)

Leman and Pentak, The Way of the Shepherd

Sea Stories: My Life in Special Operations by Admiral McRaven

Make your Bed by Admiral McRaven

Willink, Jocko, Extreme Ownership: How U.S. Navy SEALs Lead and Win

Hyde, Douglas, Dedication and Leadership

Hunter, James, To Change the World, see Kindle ed., Oxford University Press, 2010

Leivi-Merikakis, Erasmo, Fire of Mercy: Heart of the Word (Volume IV), Ignatius Press, San Francisco, 2021

The Five Dysfunctions of a Team by Patrick Lencioni

Switch by Chip and Dan Heath

Choosing the Future by Stuart Wells

Heroic Leadership by Chris Lowney

Strengths Based Leadership by Rath & Conchie

The Leadership Challenge by Kouzes & Posner

Leading Through Conflict by Mark Gerzon

The Starfish and the Spider by Brafman & Beckstrom

Influence by Robert Cialdini

Never Split the Difference by Chris Voss
Thinking, Fast and Slow by Daniel Kahneman

Emotional Intelligence 2.0 by Travis Bradberry & Jean Greaves

Meeting the Ethical Challenges of Leadership by C.E. Johnson

Leading with Strategic Thinking by Olson & Simerson

Leadership and Performance Beyond Expectations by Bernard Bass

Diffusion of Innovations by E. Rogers

Made to Stick by Chip and Dan Heath

The New Psychology of Leadership by Haslam, Reicher, Platow

Traction by Gino Wickman

The Speed of Trust by Stephen M.R. Covey

Leadership by P.G. Northouse

The Ideal Team Player by Patrick Lencioni

Crucial Conversations by Kerry Patterson

Getting Things Done by David Allen

The Advantage by Patrick Lencioni

The Dichotomy of Leadership by Jocko Willink and Leif Babin

History's Great Military Blunders and the Lessons They Teach by Gregory S. Aldrete

Weaving Complexity and Business: Engaging the Soul at Work by Lewin & Regine

Good to Great by Jim Collins

The 7 Habits of Highly Effective People by Stephen R. Covey

Team of Teams by Gen. Stanley McChrystal

Turn the Ship Around! by L. David Marquet

The Motive: Why So Many Leaders Abdicate Their Most Important Responsibilities by Patrick Lencioni

The Tipping Point by Malcolm Gladwell

The Source and Summit of Leadership

APPENDIX III – Leadership Growth Plan

(* Adapted from the 'Business Plan for the Soul' with the permission of the Lumen Institute)

To get any job done, having the right tool matters. Have you ever tried changing a flat tire without a working car-jack in the trunk? The right tool makes all the difference in the world.

In our personal and spiritual growth, having the right formation tool also makes a big difference in working with God's grace to achieve progress. Self-knowledge, a clear idea of what we want and measurable and manageable goals are all keys for any formation process. The Lumen Institute seeks the progressive transformation of each member into a leader who can shed Christ's light into one's relationships, family, business and community. That light begins shining from within, from a transformed heart and mind. This transformation, however, does not happen on its own.

You need a leadership growth plan. This will be a roadmap to become the leader you are called to be. It will help you maximize the use of your talents building on your strengths and being mindful of your weaknesses. The proposed growth plan focuses on the virtues covered in this book. I recommend you review this growth plan with your spiritual advisor and executive coach. You will follow a 2-step process to create your leadership growth plan:

  A. Assess the PAST (review the last 3 months) – weigh your performance in living virtuously in thought and action by means of a virtue assessment
  B. Pave the way for FUTURE growth – design a concrete plan around the virtues most needed to be the leader you are called to be.

PART ONE – Virtue Assessment

An honest assessment of your PAST performance is the primary means for establishing a leadership growth plan. 'Know yourself' is always sage advice.

I. **Humility**: to live in the truth of who God is, who others are and who you are

- **Objective**: Here you are trying to assess your living in the truth. Humility is the foundation for all leadership, indeed, for living any virtue. You want to grasp if you live in reality. The reality of God. The reality of others' inherent value and worth. The reality of my value and dignity. This is the existential space in which you are invited to live and lead.
- **Analysis**: Do I see myself as the center of the universe (decisions, happenings, what should or should not be)? Is God the reference point for my existence? Do I see God as a loving Father? Or rather as a

disciplinarian, uncaring or even malevolent? Do I recognize my existence as a gift as well as a mission for which I am responsible? Or do I see life as my chance to live as I want and get what I want? Do I refer praise given me to God or take it as my due? Do I think I am better than others? Do I frequently complain about the pains of life? Do I regularly complain about others? Do I use others for what I can get from them? Are people simply tools and instruments to serve my fancy? Or am I like Jesus who has "come not to be served, but to serve and give my life"?

- **Question**: On a scale of 1 (poor performance) to 10 (excellence), how would I assess my performance in being humble? In living in the truth of who God is, who others are and who I am?
- Give an example of **one setback** directly related to humility of heart in family, work and social relationships:
- Give an example of **one success** directly related to humility of heart in family, work and social relationships:

II. **Prudence**: sound judgment in determining actions

- **Objective**: Here you are looking at conscience, evaluating your ability to rightly reason about people, events, and yourself. You will assess your ability to make decisions through conscience effort based on right reason, truth and common good, as compared to those based on 'what feels right' (what might be easier, more pleasant), or on what one has always done, or on what others do.
- **Analysis**: Am I someone who sees things in mostly 'legal vs. illegal' terms, rather than 'right vs. wrong?' Do I weigh pros & cons before making major decisions (family, business and social), disciplining others, engaging in important conversations, et cetera? Do I tend to be hasty and impulsive, allowing my pride to take the lead, resulting in the same mistakes being made over-and-over again? Do I look at what will be easier or most acceptable to my human nature, or what is most honest, just, et cetera? Do I evaluate alternative courses of action, seek the advice of others (ie those closer to or further removed from the situation), and reflect on previous mistakes before making decisions that influence others?
- **Question**: On a scale of 1 (poor performance) to 10 (excellence), how would you assess your performance in using sound judgment when determining my actions?
- Give an example of **one setback** directly related to prudence in your family, work and social relationships:
- Give an example of **one success** directly related to prudence in your family, work and social relationships:

The Source and Summit of Leadership

III. **Self-Mastery**: controlling your passions amid personal drive and success

- **Objective**: Here you are evaluating your ability to temper yourself, to say "No" to yourself, and to defer gratification, or do without it, in favor of a greater good or love. You are assessing your power to harmonize and order your appetites (food, drink, sex, acceptance, et cetera) with your true good, and to cultivate the habit of enjoying good things in moderation.
- **Analysis**: Do I lose my temper easily? Do my personal hobbies or interests dominate or interfere with family duties? Do I wear my emotions on my sleeve? Do I avoid my duties as father, husband or leader out of fear of conflict or of uncomfortable situations? Do I find myself flirting with someone other than my spouse? Do I lower my standards of behavior as a result of excessively consuming food or alcohol? Do I engage in off-color, inappropriate conversation or texting? Do I medicate or flee from tensions using unhealthy isolation in social media, watching television, surfing the Internet, et cetera? Or, to the contrary, do I control my emotions and passions in any given situation?
- **Question**: On a scale of 1 (poor performance) to 10 (excellence), how would you assess my performance in controlling your passions amid personal drive for success, acceptance, or satisfaction?
- Give an example of **one setback** directly related to self-mastery in your family, work and social relationships:
- Give an example of **one success** directly related to self-mastery in your family, work and social relationships:

IV. **Perseverance**: a strong commitment to overcoming all obstacles

- **Objective**: Here you are dealing with fortitude, resilience, the will and ability to overcome or endure problems and avoid escapism. You will assess your power to withstand hardship, even physical discomfort and pain, and your ability to rebound from setbacks and disappointment.
- **Analysis**: Am I unpredictable, quick to drop commitments or change course at the first sign of difficulty? What might be at the root of those changes? Do I humbly and patiently stick to my principles in important relationships and while negotiating tough deals? Am I able to be constant in my responsibilities at home and work in the face of the tedium of every day life? Do I follow through on my spiritual commitments including daily prayer? Am I habitually one who keeps his word and can be counted on? Am I the type of person who is known by others as an anxious worrywart or complainer? Do I turn anxiety into purposeful, honorable action? Do I get things done without bullying, or bowling people over? Do I try to avoid escapism? What might be at the root of my ambivalence or inconsistency? Pride (not wanting to admit I am ring or to change course)? Sensuality (avoiding

the hard work of perseverance, or jumping on passing fads for the fun and novelty of it)?
- **Question**: On a scale of 1 (poor performance) to 10 (excellence), how would you assess your performance in making strong commitments to overcome all obstacles?
- Give an example of **one setback** directly related to perseverance in your family, work and social relationships:
- Give an example of **one success** directly related to perseverance in your family, work and social relationships:

V.   **Prayer**: regular communication with God, humbly seeking his will and friendship

- **Objective**: Here you will assess your willingness and ability to make prayer a natural part of your personal and family life. A healthy prayer life includes daily exchanges with God in order to cultivate a friendship of lasting importance and seeks to involve God in one's personal and professional affairs.
- **Analysis**: Do I approach God in meaningful dialogue everyday (at specific times for specific lengths of time such as in the case with getting up, meals, on going to bed)? Or am I the person who uses prayer as one would use an oxygen mask on a plan that loses cabin pressure…in a desperate last-ditch effort for help and survival? Do I approach God in a spirit of humility, trust and loyalty, and lead my family to do the same? Am I willing to lead others in prayer or to tell others I will pray for them? Do I allow situations and decisions to come and go without the slightest thought of asking God for his insight and counsel? Do I go to prayer to make personal and professional decisions, thanking God in prosperity and turning to him in times of trial? Do I lead those closest to me to do the same? Do I regularly include the use of Scripture in my prayer? Does my lack of prayer indicate pride – I can take care of myself – or laziness – just do not want to put in the work?
- **Question**: On a scale of 1 (poor performance) to 10 (excellence), how would I assess my performance in being a person who seek's God's will and friendship through prayer?
- Give an example of **one setback** directly related to prayer in your family, work and social relationships:
- Give an example of **one success** directly related to prayer in your family, work and social relationships:

VI.   **Integrity:** Consistency in what one professes to be and how one lives

- **Objective**: Here you will assess your moral and personal integrity. Moral integrity in a person attracts others to follow because it exudes goodness and truth. Harmony of life means integrating what one believes and desires with what one

chooses and lives. The integral man enjoys a healthy continuity of thoughts, words and actions.
- **Analysis**: Do I have any unbalanced attractions or addictions that rob my peace and do not allow me to be who I want to be? Have I worked through them to attain that interior freedom I long for? Do I have times of silent prayer and reflection to address the excesses of my character? Am I just too proud to admit my problems or too fearful to face the healthy and helpful consequences that honesty with myself would imply? Do I practice sincerity with myself, and proper accountability with others in order to help me foster moral integrity? Is confession a regular part of my spiritual life? For those closest to me, am I model of this moral solidity and integral life? Do I sometimes pursue a short-term pleasure or gain at the expense of my moral principles? Am I prioritizing time to grow those areas of my character that are weakest? Do I model those behaviors at home and at work which I wish to find in others?
- **Question**: On a scale of 1 (poor performance) to 10 (excellence), how would I assess my progress in moral integrity?
- Give an example of **one setback** directly related to integrity in your moral choices in family, work and social relationships:
- Give an example of **one success** directly related to integrity in your moral choices in family, work and social relationships:

VII. **Influence**: moving others to think and act up rightly through conscientious effort

- **Objective**: Here you will assess your willingness and ability to influence others. All virtues contribute to increasing your capacity for influence, yet our heart needs to be willing and desirous of using that capacity to influence all we can towards that which is true, good and beautiful. You should find that style of influence that is both appropriate to you while also being effective, real and at the service of others.
- **Analysis**: Jesus desired followers who eventually would go and do what he did: influence others for the good with his own witness of love. Do I really desire to be the "salt and light of the world"? Or do I have a live and let live philosophy? Does that align with Jesus' words and example in the Gospel? What is the impact that I am currently having on others? In general, is it positive? How can it improve? Do I let Jesus influence me through prayer and spiritual reading so he can influence others through me? Do I let fear, human respect, or personal comfort, hinder my willingness to witness or influence? Does the real challenges of sharing what I believe just lead me to give up trying? Or do I rather reflect and commit to prudent yet effective witness.
- **Question**: On a scale of 1 (poor performance) to 10 (excellence), how would I assess my performance in moving others to think and act uprightly through conscientious effort?

- Give an example of **one setback** directly related to influence in your family, work and social relationships:
- Give an example of **one success** directly related to influence in your family, work and social relationships:

VIII. **Magnanimity**: commitment to serve others by putting their needs first

- **Objective**: Here you are trying to assess your "greatness" of heart. Magnanimity is the virtue which prompts one to do morally good acts of exceptional quality. Magnanimous persons embrace actions of admirable generosity, kindness, fortitude and charity. Their goal is not to gain fame, glory or recognition, but simply to do what is right, good, just or needed. A true leader has a big heart, and aspires to what God wants to do in and through him.
- **Analysis**: Do I have a heart that is open to be inconvenienced by other's needs? Am I too busy to notice or too focused on "my" important things to have time for others? Do I allow professional concerns or duties to fill my life so much that I am often unavailable for the needs of those closest to me (my wife, my children)? Do I set my heart on the excellence God has set for me? Am I free to say no to unnecessary things in order to say yes to other more important or essential things? Do I let the difficult, or what is outside my comfort zone, keep me from doing or aspiring to those things that are great in God's eyes?
- **Question**: On a scale of 1 (poor performance) to 10 (excellence), how would I assess my performance in exercising a firm commitment to serve by putting others' needs first?
- Give an example of **one setback** directly related to greatness of heart in family, work and social relationships:
- Give an example of **one success** directly related to greatness of heart in family, work and social relationships:

PART TWO – Roll Out

With this analysis completed, you will proceed to roll out a resource plan for action. You will create SMART (specific, measurable, attainable, relevant, trackable) goals related to your area of needed improvement. This is developed by setting positive objectives to enhance your ability to live as a leader, developing specific Key Performance Indicators (KPIs) that will allow you to track your progress.

The Roll Out is SMART:
- **S**PECIFIC: concrete actions, results, commitments
- **M**EASURABLE: quantitative and/or qualitative
- **A**TTAINABLE: realistic, affordable, doable
- **R**ELEVANT: directly pertinent to the goal to be achieved

- **T**RACKABLE: with a time component to measure progress

You have performed an analysis of yourself based on the 8 virtues presented in this book. The next step is to pick which virtue to develop for your leadership growth. Go back over your virtue assessment and choose the one you think is most helpful at this point in your life.

Develop the Roll Out according to the following specifications:
- Goals – general and encompassing
- Objectives – particular, concrete and specific items related to a goal
- Key Performance Indicators (KPIs) – specific action items related to the objectives.

EXAMPLE

Leadership Virtue (needing the most improvement): Prudence

The main reason why I am having difficulty developing is that I have been struggling most particularly with quick, unthoughtful and self-referential decision making.

I propose the following Roll Out Plan:

SMART Goal (Business): Exercise more prudence in my hiring practices
- KPI: Each Friday I will arrange a debriefing with my HR Director before any new interview I conduct
- KPI: Take at least 24 hours before making a decision about a request (including saying a prayer during this time)

SMART Goal (Family): I am going to be a better, more prudent disciplinarian
- KPI: Before punishment, I will consult my spouse to ensure I have the best sense of what actually happened
- KPI: In the heat of the moment, I let my passions crowd my judgment. I will take note of the basic facts so that I will be able to accurately explain why it is that I am making this correction in my child's behavior.
- KPI: I will begin to make a distinction between major and minor offenses by establishing with my wife and older children pre-determined consequences for any misconduct. This will avoid exaggerated punishments and greater buy in by the children.

SMART Goal (Community): Reduce my participation in organizations that have little or no alignment with my values.
- KPI: In the coming months, I will evaluate the organizations I am involved with and eliminate those that do not align.
- KPI: I will pray over this list asking God's blessing on discerning which ones in which he wants me to serve and which ones to stop serving.

The Source and Summit of Leadership

YOUR LEADERSHIP GROWTH PLAN
Goals, Objectives and Key Performance Indicators

Leadership Virtue (needing the most improvement):

The main reason why I am having difficulty developing is that I have been struggling most particularly with:

I propose the following Roll Out Plan:

SMART Goal (Business):
- KPI:
- KPI:

SMART Goal (Family):
- KPI:
- KPI:

SMART Goal (Community):
- KPI:
- KPI:

Made in the USA
Columbia, SC
01 April 2022